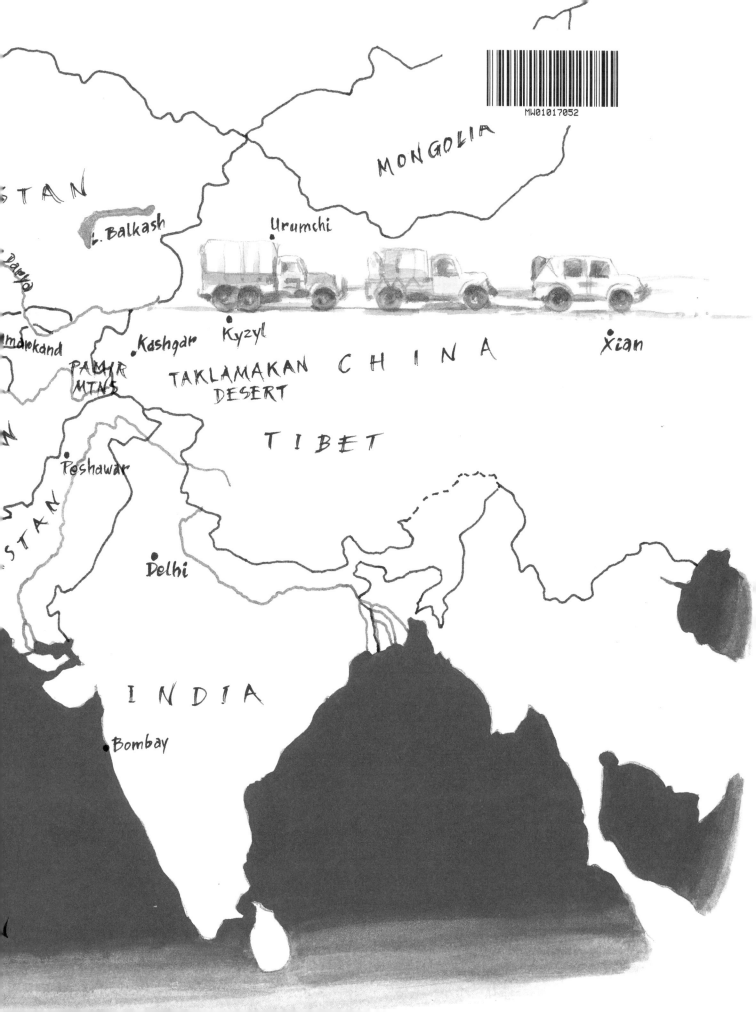

EAST WIND

From Greece to the Great Wall

By Tony Grey

with photographs by Anna-Maryke

For Eric
with warm personal
regards,

Tony

HALSTEAD PRESS

Contents

Inset photos, top to bottom: Turkey, Iran, Central Asia, Xinjiang

Acknowledgement

I would like to thank Penny and Francis Chapman
for their helpful comments on the text in the draft stage

Photographs and Maps

Photographs are by Anna-Maryke except those in Part I and those listed below.
In Part I, photographs on pages 36 and 44 are by Anna-Maryke.

PHOTO SOURCES
Australian Picture Library: pages 14 (lower), 26, 46, 68
Sarah Mannah: pages 160-61
The Photo Library, Sydney: pages 15 (top), 18, 19, 27, 30, 35, 38, 43
Turkish Information Office, Sydney: pages 50, 51, 54, 62, 63 (top left and right),
    64, 65, 84, 86, 88, 89, 102

MAPS by Zbyshek Bilyk

Foreword

OUR ENCOUNTERS with antiquity through the real and tangible worlds of relics from the deep past inevitably arouse in the contemporary viewer the contradictory sentiments of inspiration and humility. Inspiration in a recognition of the relentlessly creative and tenacious spirit of the human imagination and, through such objects that have come down to us, being able to sense and to touch the realities of those ancient worlds. Humility in our appreciation of the sheer majesty and magnitude of those achievements. This is a book that is redolent with those sentiments as it takes us on a journey into the often mysterious but evocative realms of the ancient world. Above all it reveals the author's love and fascination for the lands and peoples and their achievements that have so persuasively shaped the civilised world. It is a journey that invites us through those rich crucibles of creativity, from Greece to Turkey to Iran to China. A journey that reveals moments of sublime beauty, awe-inspiring scale and monumentality, touching sensitivity, extraordinary tenacity and, above all, the stunning resources of the human imagination in conjuring such indelible monuments as Persepolis (p. 144), the Royal Mosque of Isfahan (p. 155), the Registan of Samarkand (p. 182), or the quiet havens of Buddhist cave temples at Kyzyl (p. 253) and Bezeklik (p. 276).

Casting an eye across the impressive wealth and diversity of the cultures of Eastern and Central Asia, certain common instincts and momentums can nonetheless be detected. Perhaps this is a consequence of authorship, but I suspect it hints at the more complex and unending story of the movement and transmissions of peoples and ideas to and fro across the region. Whilst language is without doubt the most deliberate and specific means of communication, the ideas and the instincts borne out of the perpetual and changing communion of peoples have irresistibly propelled existing modes and values of expression and inspired new ones. Thus we see echoes of Persian design in Central Asian Buddhist painting; similarities in porcelain designs as far apart as Turkey and China; and polo players, ultimately from Persia, depicted in Tang dynasty Chinese tomb frescoes.

A profound regard for the truth of the past, one that assumes a reality in the material culture that has come down to us, is a certain means to understanding the world and its sundry divergences that we have inherited. The ancient world may embody values and attitudes that appear quite unfamiliar to us now and yet those encounters that we can enjoy with the ancient world, and which are encountered here, remain powerful and inspiring evocations of the extraordinary domains of human endeavour.

Edmund Capon, Director
Art Gallery of New South Wales

Introduction

People from the West have always been fascinated by lands east of the Hellespont, the classic dividing line between the individualism that characterises 'our' world and the collectivism that governs 'theirs'. Antagonisms and misunderstandings have so riven this fault zone over three millennia that a cloak of mystery has prevented any more than a tantalising glimpse of the East by heirs of the Graeco-Roman inheritance.

In the last decade or so cataclysmic political changes in the Soviet region and China have opened up the vast stretches of the ancient Silk Road in Central Asia and Xinjiang to Western travellers, where formerly they were interdicted to all but the official; and the desire to modernise has encouraged Turkey to become tourist friendly. Iran too, has recently softened the hostility generated under Ayatollah Khomeini. Admittedly Iran was difficult to access for only a few years after the 1979 revolution, but Central Asia and Xinjiang were virtually impenetrable for most of the 20th century and Turkey was considered quite dangerous until recently.

I can not remember when I first became interested in learning about the world of the Orient. Perhaps it was as a boy in high school when a charismatic classics teacher regaled the class with tales of the ancient country the Greeks called Persia. I loved Xenophon's story of how his mercenaries got drunk and disorderly in Cappadocia on local wine imbued with a strength they had never encountered before.

My interest was heightened by the feeling, generated by awareness of the historical antagonisms, that to see the lands of the East, particularly those taken over by Islam, requires a look beyond a forbidden door. The 19th century artists of the Orientalist school appeared to do this when they painted Muslim themes in the Middle East.

It has always seemed to me that our history books' neglect of the East, particularly the Muslim countries, is appalling, even taking into account the natural tendency to write history with a subjective cast of mind. Today the West is almost as frightened of Islam as it was during the Middle Ages. This is, in some respects, understandable, for the clash of cultures is probably irreconcilable. But a committed course of ignorance is always unjustified. Travel can help to dispel this.

I did not start out with a plan to 'discover' Islamic countries, but rather began to visit places in the East that had a particular attraction from a historic point of view. I have always been interested in the rise and decline of civilisations, and particularly by the phenomenon, quite uncommon, of a second and even a third recovery after periods of decadence. By chance I gravitated towards certain Islamic countries which exhibit this capacity for regeneration. It happens that they lie on a geographical line from the Hellespont to China's northwest that seems to form the shape of a crescent.

The idea for this book emerged out of a series of articles I wrote about my travels in the East with my wife, Anna-Maryke, who is a photographer. What I saw there made such an impression on me that I felt driven to put my observations down, not in the form of an exhaustive analysis or scholarly history survey, but rather from the simple perspective of a Western traveller. I happen to be stimulated by the history of things ancient so I have tried to put the places in my journey into historical context.

Time did not permit more extensive travel in the Arabic countries, which, of course, are a fundamental building block of Islam. However, as I was to discover, much can be learned about Islamic revival from the lands that form the Turkic and Iranian crescent.

Travel has always been a feature of human life, either out of necessity as in *The Odyssey* or out of curiosity as in Marco Polo's journey. But until the advent of the democratic age supported by its transportation technology, it was reserved to the privileged minority and the expeditionary military. Attitudes too have evolved. Writing 150 years ago, William Hazlitt hails the pleasures but sees no connection with life back home. "It is too remote from our habitual associations to be a common topic of discourse." For this reason Samuel Johnson dismissed the information brought by travelers as insignificant contributions to conversation, his ultimate test of the civilised person.

These perceptions might have been true at a time when travellers could share their experiences with so few and so little generally was known about foreign lands that knowledge gained abroad was doomed to unarticulated isolation. But today's promotion of demotic tourism, alimented by the hubbub of international news, ensures that talk of travels can stimulate a scintillating conversation at any dinner party.

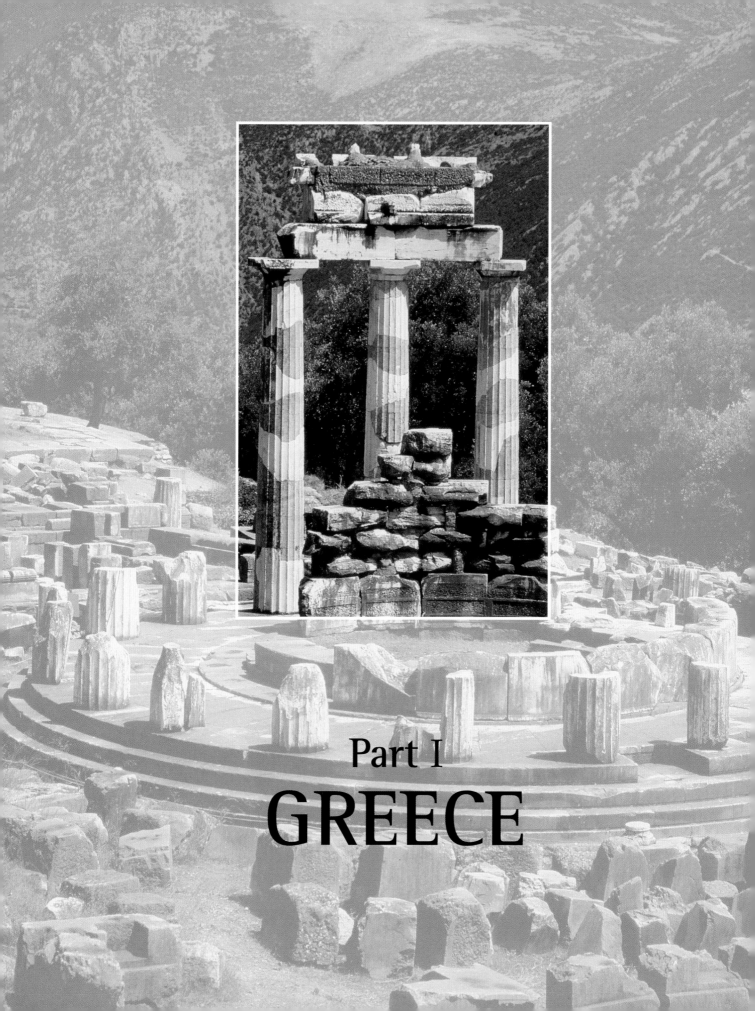

Part I
GREECE

Mycenaean
death mask –
"Agamemnon"

Chapter 1

Western Cultural Compass

In lands east of the Hellespont where the crescent reigns, it seems as if a thousand torches have been lit across the landscape. The flames flicker, bright but unsteady, and many wonder whether they portend a revival of Islamic greatness. Muslims hope so; most in the West hope not. However uncertain the outcome, it is clear that something is happening in that part of the world, known since Chaucer as the Orient, a foreign and mysterious other civilisation against which Europeans, from the ancient Greeks onwards, have defined themselves.

Millions of people there are struggling to lift themselves out of conditions they can no longer tolerate, to regain the pride that enriched their lives in centuries past. It is not only a place where the social manifestations of Islam sharply define its differences with the West, but also an area whose ancient history reveals so many of the influences that nourished the roots of civilisation west of China.

But before venturing into these lands, I wanted to visit the fountainhead of my own civilisation. I needed a reference point from which comparisons could be made. I had to go to Greece.

Although, since the iconoclastic 1960s, many have pronounced our classical heritage irrelevant to contemporary life, no-one in the West can look at a work of art, enter a church, read a serious book, engage in a political discussion or solve a scientific mystery without calling upon the legacy of ancient Greece, whether or not they are aware of the debt. I felt a need to re-examine concepts such as individualism, competition, balance, government, science and universal ideals through visiting the places where these ideas were born. Somehow, I felt, I might then be able to make more sense of what I was to see in the Orient, a region I knew little about. My wife, Anna-Maryke, a professional photographer, accompanied me on the trip.

ATHENS

After our plane had endured an hour-long holding pattern imposed by overwhelmed air-traffic controllers, Anna-Maryke and I finally emerged onto the tarmac at Athens airport in miasmic July heat. The scene inside the terminal was the type of exhilarating, slightly daunting pageant I would normally associate with Asia – crowds of shirted people jostling, gesticulating, and talking at the top of their voices, stirred by a vague but palpable sense of urgency. It made us sweaty before the heat did.

Beyond the airport terminal, city traffic was sulphurous and loud. It frequently ground to a complete halt in front of ugly buildings and at times was so dense that it threatened to spill over the street curbs. The taxi driver expertly manoeuvred us through the swarm, and although our communication was limited to the name of our hotel, he managed to convey a sense of friendliness.

We were looking forward to visiting Olympia, the site where, according to tradition, the ancient Olympic Games were first held, in 776 BC. With the year 2000 Olympics to be held in Sydney, where we live, we wanted to get a sense of where it all began. Competition, after all, is the motivational principle by which Western civilisation drives its progress.

But before setting out for the site, we decided to spend a little time in Athens. It is a horrible city: filthy, fumy and crammed with senescent concrete modern. Yet it is a wonderful city. Enough remains of its glorious past to illuminate for us the passageway into the classical mind, particularly on the aesthetic level. Plato taught that an object of beauty expresses an archetypal essence that is absolute and universal, beyond changing convention or subjective opinion. As such, it exists on a timeless plane and is accessible through the agency of the intellect. Hardly a modern concept, but just as valid now as in Plato's day.

Daylight was fading by the time we reached our hotel on Syntagma Square – from the Greek word for constitution. As the sun went down in a dusty haze over the olive-studded hills surrounding the city, our attention was caught by the changing of the guard across the street, in front of the parliament house. Two soldiers dressed in short tunics and white tights, rifles at the shoulder, stood at attention in front of tiny blue-and-white sentry boxes, built with awnings and placed 50 metres apart on the smooth stone square. Surrealistically, they began to move forward so gradually that it would have been easy to miss the movement, right leg lifted parallel to the ground and toes pointed. It reminded me of break-dancing in Europe. Abruptly the toes turned up, and stayed that way for a few seconds. Then the foot came down, taking a small step forward, all movements slowly synchronised. At every other step, the right arm would snap up in a Nazi salute, a gesture that seemed droll in a country so strongly identified with the democratic tradition. The guards took a few steps towards each other in this manner, then smartly wheeled and headed for the columned house of democracy, alternately marching normally and goose-stepping in slow motion.

In the morning we walked to the National Archaeological Museum for a historical orientation. The asphalt of the streets was at melting point, and the city swarmed with loquacious people and impatient traffic honking and belching. Construction sites along the road tossed up dust, which mixed with the carbon fumes to produce solid air. We arrived at the museum before opening time, but already a queue had formed. In a modern replay of the interrupted building schedules of ancient history, construction of the building had commenced in 1860 but took until 1940 to complete.

After waiting in line for 10 minutes, we spotted a guide desk through the crowd. There was only one guide left by the time we got there, so we hired him immediately without attempting to bargain on the rate. As we were making our arrangements, an English-speaking couple of unidentifiable nationality bustled over to inquire about hiring guides. Our man said they were all busy but promised to find them one if he could. The place was so crowded that Anna-Maryke and I had to stay close to avoid getting lost in the mêlée.

Half an hour into our tour, the couple reappeared and began complaining about the absence of guides, accusing our man of breaking his promise. Brushing aside his excuses, they demanded to use him if no-one else was available. At first the husband did all the talking, but his wife soon added to the pressure. I began to worry that our guide would succumb, leaving us in the lurch, so I joined the skirmish, calmly at first, if a touch abruptly. But after a few aggressive exchanges, I felt a rush of anger. For a few femtiseconds, a madness gripped me and I nearly clocked the fellow. Fortunately, civilised instincts checked the impulse. The guide rallied, informing the couple he could do nothing more for them, and they shuffled off aggrieved.

The contretemps was soon forgotten as we were quickly immersed in antiquity. We started at the chronological beginning of the displays – Neolithic society on the Thessalian plain in northern Greece – but hurried through the sparse collection to the more interesting Cycladic room.

Flourishing between 3200 BC and 2000 BC, the Cycladic is the first Greek civilisation whose archaeological signature is sufficiently detailed for a distinct personality to emerge. Its name refers to the Cyclades islands, so called because of their circular embrace of Delos, birthplace of Apollo and his sister Artemis. Minoan Crete, not far to the south, eventually coalesced with this magical ring, thought to have contained also the lost city of Atlantis. The resultant rich and creative civilisations were generated centuries before Greek mainlanders emerged from primitivism.

Most fascinating of the vestiges of Cycladic genius were the stylised stone figurines, their flattened,

elliptical faces devoid of mouth or eyes but featuring elongated isosceles-triangle noses. I thought them evocative of the abstract quality Western scholars were to observe 3000 years later in African sculpture. Their simplicity of form and innate elegance inspired Picasso in his search for the constructional basis of the human figure.

The next room stored the treasures of Mycenae, city of the warrior king Agamemnon, who led the long-haired Achaeans to the sack of Troy in 1184 BC. Emerging in 1600 BC from the ashes of the Minoan empire sacked by its rampaging invaders, the Mycenaean was the first mainland Greek culture to grasp the torch of civilisation.

The sumptuous wealth of the Mycenaeans, derived as much from the plunder snatched by their marauding armies as from agriculture and seafaring trade, was spoken of in awe by poets and intellectuals along the pathway of time. Sophocles referred to the gold of Mycenae as a defining characteristic, just as we mention the riches of the Incas two millennia later. Excavation at Mycenae has yielded a heritage of more wrought gold than has been discovered at all other Greek sites put together.

The National Museum has a breathtaking collection of treasures from the period. Cabinet after cabinet is filled with superbly crafted gold and silver objects. The solid-gold funeral mask of an ancient monarch that dominates the chamber was wrongly thought by Schliemann, 19th-century discoverer of Mycenae, to be that of Agamemnon himself. It continues to be known as the mask of Agamemnon, even though its true owner remains a mystery.

The museum provides a living link to past events so world-shattering, so inspiring, that they have shaped Western attitudes towards the human condition even to the present day. The bronze daggers decorated in gold with hunting scenes flashing on the verdigris-covered blades are of the same type

Mycenaean dagger

used by Clytemnestra and her lover Aegisthus to do away with the cantankerous husband upon his victorious return to Mycenae. Figure-of-eight shields and long swords hanging heavy on the wall are manifestations of the warlike era. This legendary period of heroes, whose courage and honour were transmitted by the blind poet Homer down the ages, was to provide the Western canon of manly virtue. King Arthur and Charlemagne were the mediaeval inheritors, two millennia later. Only in the last three decades has the West begun to turn away from this definition of masculine standards (though they still reign on the football field).

The Trojan War is said to have lasted 10 years, but was actually part of a surge of Indo-European migration backed by arms and lasting several decades, a tidal wave that inundated the Anatolian Peninsula and crashed up against the venerable New Kingdom of Egypt in a series of catastrophes that shook the unshakeable. This confrontation between East and West marked the beginning of a clash of civilisations that continues to this day. Large-scale migration has occurred several times in history and, once it reaches a critical mass, is unstoppable. The threat of a recurrence creates disquiet today in Germany along its eastern frontier, in the United States at its border with teeming Mexico and in empty Australia when it looks to its populous north.

The Heroic Age ended around 1100 BC, a few decades after the victory at Troy, with the destruction of Mycenae by the Dorians, a barbaric, fair-haired tribe from the north. For three and a half centuries, Greece lay gripped by a dark age of economic depression, population decline and cultural degeneration. Practice of the arts and intellectual pursuits were neglected or spurned. But in the hearts of many, a yearning for the great civilisation of the past continued to burn like an endless love.

In the eighth century BC, helped by a practical Phoenician-derived alphabet which replaced the cumbersome syllabary used by the later Minoans and Mycenaeans, the Greeks relit the torch of civilisation. Homer grasped it in the middle of the century, writing with warmth and humanity about inspirational events that had occurred long before but were etched still on the psyche of the Greeks.

As we examined objects that had been used by real people in those faraway times, people tormented by the same feelings of love and hate as ourselves, the same desire to succeed, the same fears of failure, we appreciated the value of a good museum. Too often, museums are dry storerooms of worthy but boring relics, interesting only to curators indulging themselves in arcane scholarship, far removed from the living world. But the mood in the Athenian museum was nothing short of vivacious. It seemed that sturdy Ajax was in the room, pulling down his spear from the wall, while amidst the distant shouts of battle, Apollo the Deadly Archer goaded the Trojan ranks to sterner effort against the hated Greeks. Athena, champion of the other side, wielded her Medusa-emblazoned shield to deflect the Trojan javelins from her favourite heroes. The spears, the javelins, the swords and the menacing full-face helmets conveyed the ferocity of war. On the walls hung the round, bossed shields of the period, so heavy that it is a marvel men could have wielded them for hours at a time, as they had to do in the desperate Trojan charge that pushed the invaders back to their hollow ships but which then faltered when swift-footed Achilles emerged from sulking in his tent to rejoin the battle.

Gold wine cups, exquisitely embossed with hunting scenes displaying the lions that inhabited the Peloponnesus at the time, echoed the grandiloquent toasts drunk at the palace of Nestor, the boastful old warrior of *The Iliad*. Intricately carved seals in gold and a superb bronze rhyton in the form of a bull's head disclosed the Minoan origin of this rich culture and its love of beautiful craftsmanship.

The products of the Grecian past testified to one of the truisms of history: virtually all great civilisations are launched by superiority in warfare. The energy and discipline that propel them to be conquerors are later channelled into the arts, sciences and higher living standards. The Greeks did it; so did the Egyptian, Persian, Roman and Anglo-Saxon societies.

Seeing the objects of life in forms that varied so little over vast spaces of time demonstrated what one knows but seldom contemplates: the exponential acceleration of change that marks our world today. The

Cycladic statuette

Mycenaean cups

Mycenaean cup

remnants of that ancient civilisation that dominated the Mediterranean for half a millennium revealed how long past societies remained essentially the same. Egypt is, of course, the primary example, but all enjoyed longevity. Psychologically, their perspective on time could afford them a security of soul that comes from stable institutions and accepted patterns of thought, even against a background of near-continuous warfare. The anxiety-ridden modern era of shifting values and blurred moral distinctions seems to be in contrast at a defining level.

The move in the 1960s away from the Platonic absolute to the relative as the fundamental reference point in moral distinctions seems the predominate reason why the contemporary intellectual establishment is inclined to forget the classical past. The clear definitions of right and wrong, the conventions of civility that used to distinguish the civilised from the barbarian, together with the stern measures of enforcement, run counter to the precepts of our age. Paris' breach of personal duty and his assault on the vows of marriage in running off with the wife of his host were understandable casus belli in those times, but today his actions might well be considered only minor antisocial behaviour, warranting at most a mild verbal rebuke. We would allow for the possibility that the attractive Helen was unhappily trapped in a marriage that had irretrievably broken down, accepting the right of the lovers to seek personal happiness as they deemed fit. We might even see their elopement as a dash to freedom.

As we passed through the collection, which included much more than just war memorabilia (the pottery was particularly alluring), I was impressed with the aesthetic majesty that infused the remarkable people who passed to us this legacy. Though form and grace reached their zenith in the Classical period with the construction and decoration of the Parthenon, attention to beauty in everything is evident from the beginning of Greek civilisation, over two millennia before. The aesthetic sense of the Greeks was in the latticework of their philosophy, its symmetry and balance an analogue to their ideals of justice and stability.

It is unwise to stay in a museum to the point of cultural overload; so at the expense of rushing past some important exhibits – though not too many, since this was no Louvre – we said goodbye to our guide.

Outside the building, I approached a taxi driver in the queue and asked him the fare to our hotel. I knew it should not have been more than 600 drachmas. Indifferently, he said 1000. As I tried to bargain him down, an American couple materialised from the dust and suggested that we share the cab, as they were going in the same direction. Again, I asked the price. This time, the driver replied, "2000 drachmas". I demurred theatrically, trying to be good-humoured. It just annoyed him. "See that cab across the street?" he snarled. "I would rather leave my car here all day than accept less than my price. Take one of them if you want."

It was the hidalgo pride that sometimes drives the Greeks to action against their interests despite their inclination at other times to negotiate. With no trouble at all, I was able to hail another taxi, which took us all for 500 drachmas.

As we left the museum, I recalled our voluble guide telling us that 80 per cent of the Western world's art has an ancient Greek origin. I already knew that 12 per cent of English words are derived from the Greek language. Perhaps he exaggerated, but he was probably in the right dimension.

Of Greek works of art, none is more influential than the efflorescence that lives on the Acropolis, the distinctive signature of Athens and our next destination. In the eighth century BC, as Greece began to emerge from the Dark Ages, the upper class of Attica relocated to the small settlement that was Athens at the time. They built a fortress on an easily defended high promontory, touching off one of history's most amazing developments in civilisation. For years, the Acropolis housed the entire population, affording it the protection so vital for prosperity.

The story of Greece is largely the long and symbolic counterpoint between its two most famous city states, Athens and Sparta. Thucydides saw it as much as a clash of ideals as of interests. Athens represented progression from aristocratic rule based on privilege to government whose legitimacy rests on the consent of the governed, the unshakeable belief in the value of the individual, and the importance of ideas, freely expressed, in the shaping of the human condition. Its legacy is the wealth of creation in the arts and sciences signified by the empyrean temples and sculptures on the Acropolis.

In contrast, Sparta, significantly a Dorian city and based on a rigid aristocratic regime, was the most fascist state in the ancient world. Through a military caste system where boys were separated from their families at the age of seven for warrior training and young men forbidden to marry before age 30, Sparta produced the best land armies of the time but little else of import.

After the Lacadaemonian powerhouse defeated Athens in the exhausting Peloponnesian War (431 BC to 404 BC) and established hegemony over the whole of Greece, its high-handed style of rule soon provoked the widespread rebellion that ultimately brought down its regime. Nothing remains today of the once-dreaded power, for monumental buildings and art were considered a costly distraction from the military imperative.

Through its participatory function, albeit operating on a narrow base, the Athenian democracy engaged the true loyalties of a larger segment of the community than was possible under the monarchical alternative. Its propensity to fragment power and diversify its implementation tends to dilute envy and protect against abuse, in contrast with Eastern despotism, which the Greeks saw as a badge of inferiority.

The steep hill that rises out of the colourful and boisterous old section of Athens, past the girdle of souvenir shops selling classical images in takeaway form, was drenched in Mediterranean heat. The winding path bulged with tourists, a mass of human particles slowly moving in the same direction. At the top stood the Parthenon, temple of grey-eyed

Acropolis

Athena and the soul of classical Athens. From the ancient marble terrace, we looked down over the terracotta roofs painted chaotically in dusty colours. Modern Athens was seeping into the valleys and up the surrounding hills in capillary action. At the time of Pericles, 150,000 people inhabited Greece's largest city. Now there are about 3.5 million.

The special Greek light, hard and clear, shone from a cloudless sky. The olive trees planted on the slopes gave off a restless glint, evocative of the insatiable activity of those remarkable people who ran so far with civilisation's torch, then tripped and fell, passing it on to Rome, from whence it came to us.

Riding the tide of confidence flowing from the epic victory over Xerxes and his Persian invaders, Athens rose to its political and cultural zenith during the 30-year reign of Pericles (who died in 429 BC), a paragon of the well-rounded man of the time – soldier, orator and statesman, and the inspiration for the Renaissance Man. The adornment of the Acropolis was the supreme building project of his age. Just before their pivotal defeat in the naval battle of Salamis in 480 BC, the Persians had sacked Athens and devastated the temples, leaving cleared land for Pericles.

With the most gifted artists in the Mediterranean at his disposal, the great archon chose three prodigies to lead the project: Pheidias, the sculptor, and

Parthenon

Erechtheion

architects Ictinus and Callicrates. Pheidias designed the frieze on the Parthenon, a wonder that displays some of the finest sculptures in the history of the art form. To occupy the temple, he created a 40-foot statue of Athena Parthenos (the 'virgin') in wood, with flesh of ivory, draped in garments of gold leaf. In early Byzantine times, the work was carted off to Constantinople as a pagan curiosity, and was later destroyed by fire.

While the brilliant artist was being feted as a national celebrity, the doom of classical Greek tragedy stalked alongside, proceeding towards its baneful climax. Hubris, that infuriator of the gods, had infected him. When the public discovered that a breathtaking temerity had led him to represent himself on the shield of Athena, patroness of Athens, community outrage erupted. For the sacrilege he was tossed into prison, where he ultimately died, a warning to all who believe themselves above the human plane.

The buildings on the Acropolis – the Parthenon, the Propylaea, and the Erechtheion, with its beautiful Caryatids – express the affinity the ancient Greeks had with higher purposes. Their simplicity of form, achieved through infinite pains in the service of the permanent, is the signature of the noble, a state in the domain of the gods. Not too long before, half a world away, Confucius had embodied the same sense in his philosophy.

At the heart of the Greek vision of the universe was the exalted position of the individual human being, free and capable of achieving the highest state of excellence, only marginally below the divine. This view is the Greek legacy to Western civilisation; it drives our attitudes towards saving human life, our ambiguity towards killing, and our concern for human rights. In the time of rediscovering Europe's classical heritage, Shakespeare expressed the concept through Hamlet's words:

What a piece of work is a man, how noble in reason, how infinite in faculties; in form and moving how express and admirable, in action how like an angel, in apprehension how like a god: the beauty of the world, the paragon of animals.

The Greek gods were idealised forms of this image, providing inspirational role models, even though their nobility was pockmarked with all the lust, vanity and spitefulness that bedevils the human species. Perhaps it was because of these flaws that they were so compelling as exemplars. They were also the instruments of punishment for arrogance, which wise heads knew would be a side-effect of the high level of self-worth this anthropocentric view promoted.

In the Acropolis used to stand a bronze sculpture of Marsyas, a brilliant flautist whose fame reached such heights that, no longer content to be feted as merely the greatest talent among mortals, he challenged Apollo, god of the arts, to a musical contest. The prize was to be that the winner could do whatever he wished to the loser. Apollo picked up his lyre and played at a level impossible to match, defeating Marsyas, after which the affronted god had the presumptuous mortal bound to a tree and flayed alive.

Our Greek guide to the Acropolis was awed by the antiquity of the buildings. Walking past the Erechtheion, which was partly obscured by thronging admirers, he pointed and said, "That's 2500 years old". As we looked at the beautifully formed Caryatids, he gushed, "Just think of the skill these people had 2500 years ago". And at the Propylaea, he told us the same thing. But how could you blame him?

His prodigious national pride boiled over into a lengthy dissertation on the ancient antagonism the Greeks feel towards Turkey, a sentiment that is returned but without the visceral passion. Herodotus begins his formidable history with an analysis of the enmity that, even before his time, had been so long perpetuated between the Greeks and the peoples beyond the Hellespont they called barbarians. According to him, the cause was, from the Greek side, the abduction of Helen, and from the other side, the invasion of Troy, a reaction considered excessive even by the patriotic Greek historian. Ottoman hegemony has brought the reciprocal rage into modern times.

As he gave us the facts about the Parthenon – it was built on 19 layers of limestone blocks – he criticised the Classical Age for its prejudices and for its use of propaganda to control public opinion. Half an hour later, while explaining the use of metal pins to join the column sections together in order to provide flexibility in the face of earthquakes, he pitched a diatribe against what he felt were the evils of Muslims, and the threat Turkey would pose to civilisation if allowed to join the European Union. Because Anna-Maryke and I are from the New World, he said that he felt we were his brother and sister, since so many Greeks now live there. As we left, he called out warmly, his voice rising above the crowd of tourists: "Goodbye, fellow Christians."

The country rock that supports Athens sheds a white hue across the landscape, reflecting the metallic light of the Aegean sun. On the Acropolis, the weathered marble columns of the temples stand majestic in the same colour. So perfectly do they seem to fit in with the surroundings that it is difficult to imagine they were originally painted in bright blues and reds. The shining whiteness is so ingrained in people's minds today that while many could accept a reconstruction of the buildings, providing an appropriate proportion of original materials was used, outrage would erupt if someone suggested they be painted.

Walking down from the Acropolis, we caught a glimpse through an olive grove of the strewn blocks of stone that used to be the hospital of Asclepius, patron of medicine. At the bottom of the hill was Gerostou Moriou, which boasts that it is the oldest tavern in Athens. There, under a pergola festooned with pink bougainvillea and ripe grapes, Greeks and tourists mingle to drink chilled retsina, a wine that I think tastes better in Greece than elsewhere.

On the way out of Athens, we battled through crowded, cacophonous streets, harassed by the motorbikes that swarmed around us like hornets. It was hot, dusty and dry. The mobile throng of erratic vehicles of all types (the trucks and buses were the worst) seemed destined for an accident. Greek drivers are aggressive and impatient, particularly in taxis.

The choking smells of poorly combusted carbon exacerbated the 35-degree heat. Noise, ugly shapes and bad smells assaulted us mercilessly. I knew this would continue for at least an hour before we could escape the urban monster's clutch. There was nothing left of the salubrious images of the classical past. They subsided into an entropy of squalid shapes and fetid odours that slapped us around the head like a foul wind. So bad was the smell of organic garbage in the suburbs that I began to feel nostalgia for the carbon fumes of the inner city. What a relief to see the traffic eventually flake off and the clean countryside open out in front of us! We could relax and think about Delphi, our fascinating target for the day.

Chapter 2

Spiritual Vapours

THEBES

Our first stop was Thebes, the Boeotian city-state that rose to hegemony over the whole of Greece after the battle of Leuctra in 371 BC. There, the redoubtable Sparta was eclipsed as a military power for the first time in its history, the great Theban general Epaminondas defeating the Spartans in a brilliantly executed charge of his Sacred Band. We were hungry, but at half past two on a hot, soporific afternoon, nearly all the restaurants were closed for siesta.

We parked the car in the sun, as there was no shade on the treeless streets, and walked into a concrete pedestrian mall that housed a café, its door open. Only one person was inside, a melon-shaped middle-aged man with more hair on his upper lip than on his head. He was sitting in a slouched sleep at a Formica table, a newspaper lying on his lap, mouth at the slack, snoring. The place was newly plastered and tiled, cleanly modern. I went up to the counter and called out, "Anyone home?". No answer, just dry heat and snoring. We walked out and came back a couple of times in indecision. Still nothing.

Anna-Maryke suggested a cool drink at the kiosk we had seen across the street, but by the time we got there, it was closed. We again trudged back to the café, by now irritable with hunger. This time the snorer was up, slowly shuffling behind the counter. I should have shouted louder before. We had just enough time to get a tasteless sausage roll on a greasy doughnut bun, ordered in sign language, before the restaurateur began to close up. Not a word was spoken. It seemed he had overslept and now was late for his siesta. Silently the drowsy owner departed, walked across the street to his car and drove off noisily into the sun, leaving us to finish our Spartan meal outside his restaurant on folding chairs under the awning. We were alone in the street and could easily have walked off with the furniture. For that matter, so could anyone else. But the neighbourhood was like those in the Western world 30 years ago, before the escalation of crime made everyone think like security guards.

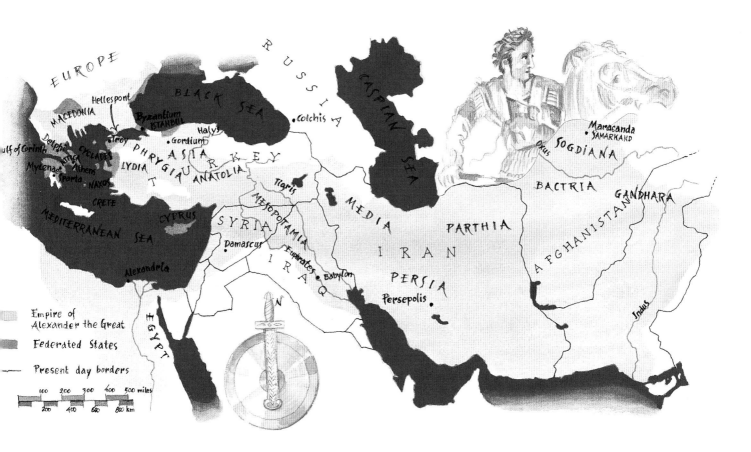

From Thebes, our journey led north to Delphi, spiritual centre of the classical world and one-time rival of Olympia as an oracular seat. We were in habitation-free countryside now, passing through low rolling mountains and scrubby terrain. A sign advertising a ski resort appeared as we approached Mount Parnassos, near Apollo's shrine.

The mighty Parnassos tectonic zone strikes southwest through the heart of Greece and down under the Aegean Sea like a gigantic ridge-backed serpent, its scales thrust in high angle to the sky. The violent creative force of its birth pushed up the two most famous mountains in Greece: Olympus, the dwelling place of the gods, and Parnassos of Delphi, the navel of the world, forever linked as geological twins living a few kilometres apart on its crusty back. Compressive east–west faulting disturbed the

adolescence of the tectonic monster and spread its rocks along the parallel sides of the Gulf of Corinth, which like an Olympian sword slices Greece almost in two.

The country rock shows through in chalky patches under a threadbare carpet of steel-green bushes competing desperately for the scanty rainfall. Its massive limestone has been invaded by exogenous intrusives – granite and its metamorphic state, marble. Formed in primordial times from seabeds layered with crustaceans that have left their mark in fossils, the telltale rock led Xenophanes to conclude that mankind had originated from the sea, an observation made 2500 years before Darwin wrote his *On the Origin of Species*. This had been considered established fact until, in the last few years, scientists have begun to argue that all life originated well beneath the Earth's surface, in primitive bacteria not requiring oxygen.

Greece is a hard country, its chapped terrain prone to erosional impoverishment of the soil. Much of the land is capable of supporting only the hardy olive tree. Plato lamented the tragic environmental degradation of Attica, the territory of Athens. "What remains of her substance is like the skeleton of a body emaciated by disease, as compared with her original relief. All the rich, soft soil has molted away, leaving a country of skin and bones." Arnold Toynbee saw this infelicity of nature as a challenge stimulating a response, the process that generated the vitality of the ancient Greeks. It was sufficient to arouse the spirit but not so daunting as to enervate it.

Mountainous structures split up the habitable terrain of Greece as walls enclose rooms of a house, and this encouraged communities to evolve with a sense of separateness from others. The wide-open landforms of Egypt and Mesopotamia promoted an opposite orientation. It is tempting to think that this phenomenon promoted a concentration on localised identity in ancient times that, aided by the small size of the population, led to an emphasis on the individual as the fundamental societal building block, a tendency so clearly at variance with the collectivist views developed in the East. The grain of sand and the beach both have identities, but dramatically different consequences depend on which one attracts the focus.

DELPHI

Our hotel, on the high outskirts of Delphi, was newly built of limestone blocks, no architectural wonder but commodious. Its feature was a view over the shimmering Aegean past the Delphic mountains, mystically shrouded in a haze that flattened the perspective and created a two-dimensional effect. The sea had cut into the coast below to form a finger and

thumb. Sombre green cypresses stood proud in the valley that spread down to the shore. The surrounding hills were draped in different colours: patches of grey-white, lush textural green, and barren beige. The rich blue water dazzled the eye, reflecting Phoebus Apollo's chariot as he drove it across the bright afternoon sky. The dry assertive sound of cicadas announced the presence of midsummer.

Next morning, the sky was cloudless but brushed with a soft haze. All was tranquil, the background noise almost imperceptible. A dove called unseen from some olive foliage in the distance, linked in myth with Aphrodite, its patron. On a hidden road, the tyres of a car whooshed quietly. In the near-silent heat, butterflies shied chaotically in front of the red and white roses below our balcony, which surveyed the valleyed peace of the Delphic countryside, looking over an abstract sculpture that seemed like a piece of ancient drapery tossed carelessly into the garden. An old man in paint-splotched clothes walked slowly across the lawn, absorbed in his own thoughts. It was a day for contemplation.

We were within walking distance of the spiritual centre of the ancient Greek world, a site whose natural environment is so powerful that every visitor is overwhelmed by a sense of wonder. Vestiges of human habitation there date back to 1400 BC, but Neolithic pottery remains suggest it was visited two and a half millennia before that.

In the lee of snowcapped Mount Parnassos, above the olive plain of the Muses, the Delphic shrine stands ensconced in a jagged mountain forest, guarded by the silent dignity of dark, straight cypresses. Even today, despite the distraction of sloppily dressed tourists, the mystery of the ancient sanctuary hangs in the air. Lonely temple columns stand upright on a natural ledge cut into a huge cliff face of vertically weathered limestone rising steeply 150 metres into the heat haze.

A cleft in the rock that was formed on the boundary of Cretaceous and Tertiary times marks the origin of the shrine, and strange fumes emanate from its mysterious depths. Nearby, the celebrated Kastalian spring offers the purity of mountain water to walk-weary travellers who approach the site along the verdant path said to have been discovered by Apollo in Olympian times. Parts of the polygonal wall that used to encircle the sanctuary remain, the interlocking stone design another reminder of the accomplishments of the classical Greeks. Unruly vegetation grows out of the joints today, but the flexible structure is largely intact, still able to resist the earthquakes it was designed to frustrate.

In a quest for knowledge characteristic of the Greeks, Zeus dispatched two eagles from opposite ends of the Earth in order to find its centre. The sacred birds met at Delphi, which means 'womb' in Greek, identifying it as the navel of the world. From remotest times, a conical stone called an omphalos, or 'navel', marked the exact spot.

According to Homer's *Hymn to Apollo*, the archer god came upon the Kastalian spring while travelling in central Greece. Python, a gigantic female dragon with the gift of prophecy, guarded it with her fearsome presence. He slew the monster after a terrible battle in the dark forest and installed a priestess of his order, establishing a shrine to his worship. Named Pythia, after her predecessor, the priestess was imbued with oracular powers.

From earliest times, the fame of Delphi spread throughout the classical world, drawing even Eastern potentates to make the pilgrimage there to learn the secrets of the future. Sumptuous votive offerings exhibiting the gratitude of satisfied clients enriched the shrine. Midas, the legendary king of Phrygia, donated his own throne. The Lydian monarch Croesus, renowned more for his wealth than for his judgement, sent a lion statue in solid gold, the

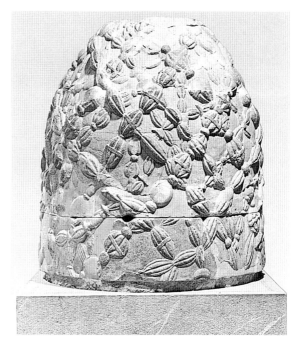

Omphalos

weight of a natural beast. Later, miniature temples of symmetrical proportions, called treasuries, were built to house smaller objects of appreciation, often in gold. The treasury of the Athenians is one, given possibly for the victory at Marathon (in 490 BC), possibly for the start of democracy. It is still standing, partially restored, imposing in its Doric simplicity, placed on the Sacred Way that leads in cobblestone to the temple of Apollo where the oracular pronouncements were made. There, half a dozen headless columns, their drums eroded at the joints, rise from the stone platform of the temple like a clump of primitive totems in supplication to the sky.

The popularity of fortune-telling appears to be again on the rise. It satisfies a human need to explore the supernatural, which seems a controlling force in our lives and to which we can relate with senses not dependent on the intellect. In our own postreligious age, a fissure has opened which many seek to fill as best they can.

At Delphi, most of the methods of foretelling the

Temple of Apollo, Delphi

future known in the ancient world were practised – the art of discovering auguries in the flight of birds, reading entrails, deriving meaning from the flames of sacrificial pyres, and divining by lot with pebbles. In a manner anticipating Freud, Amphyction, founder of the eponymous League, introduced the art of interpreting dreams.

The Pythia, who was chosen from women in their fifties, prepared herself for divination by chewing laurel leaves and by purification in the sacred spring. Dressed in a young girl's style, to signify virginity, she would sit on a tripod placed over the fume-emitting rock cleft, and drift into a trance. Her

Tholos at Delphi

unintelligible utterings could be interpreted only by the attending priest, who would usually articulate the prophecy in dactylic hexameter in order to give it gravitas and to excuse the ambiguity necessary to preserve credibility in the face of the outcome.

The Pythia was the medium through which Apollo, who had the actual prophetic gift, would speak. The question to be posed by the pilgrim was always prepared in advance so that the oracle staff had plenty of time to reflect. Visiting kings and emissaries were entertained in the rotunda at the temple of Athena nearby for seven days, during which time as much information as possible would be deftly pried out of them. They were then led to the inner sanctum where the eternal flame burned, duly imbued with a sense of awe.

There was as much wisdom required in resolving the ambiguity of the prophecies as in composing them. When Croesus asked the oracle to predict the outcome of his intended attack on the Persians, the reply was that if his army crossed the frontier river Halys, a great empire would be destroyed. Delighted by the advice, he attacked across the divide but suffered a catastrophic defeat. In response to the furious complaint that followed the disaster, the oracle pointed out that the pronouncement had not specified which empire would be destroyed.

Later, when Xerxes invaded Greece (in 490 BC), Delphi was overawed by the might of the Persian expeditionary force and foretold doom for Sparta and Athens. The oracle counselled the Athenians to take refuge behind their wooden walls. Some interpreted this to mean the walls around the Acropolis, but Themistocles used the advice to rally support for the Athenian navy. The oracle declared itself vindicated when the wooden ships won the decisive battle of Salamis.

But prophesying was just the more spectacular part of Delphi. Its deeper raison d'être was its exaltation of the spiritual values that underlay Greek civilisation: peace, fraternity and equality. To symbolise the essence of wisdom that expressed these ideals, it was customary to make donations to the sanctuary in the form of a tripod, a configuration that signifies the past, present and future.

Lest we think we live in an age without roots, it should be pointed out that around Delphi, a league of states was established for the promotion of mutual peace and cooperation. Called an amphictiony, it was the precursor of the United Nations. Formed largely for the protection of religious worship, the Amphictionic League gave Delphi an independent

sovereignty, excising it from the surrounding Phocian state.

Like its successor, Vatican City, Delphi and its allies fought wars to maintain its influence. From the hills at Delphi, we could see the coastal town of Krisa in the hazy distance. It reached the history books by provoking the Amphictionic League to destroy it for fleecing the pilgrims who came to pay homage to Apollo.

Sagacious fortune-telling and religion made Delphi famous, but like so much in classical Greece, the city also had a cultural meaning. On visiting the temple of Apollo, intellectual denizen of Mount Olympus, visitors would be confronted by two maxims of classical enlightenment engraved on the pronaos.

The first was "Nothing in excess". Sometimes referred to as the Golden Mean, it has often been misinterpreted as a call for mediocrity, a safe alternative to red-blooded action. The Greeks would have been horrified at the spin. On the contrary, they were lovers of high-risk/high-reward behaviour. However, their propensity toward commitment led to a recognition of the dangers of extremes. The admonition sought to achieve the ideal combination of energy and restraint through which the best outcome in any particular field of human endeavour could be produced. Underlying the notion was the ambivalence that characterised their relationship with the gods. While activated by their example to be like them, they dared not go too far, for that would become emulation, a crime akin to lese majesté. Also, on the psychological plane, in recognition of their highly emotional nature, they preferred to put their faith in the power of the intellect than to trust in the unpredictability of feelings. This orientation led to a supreme faith in a rational approach to knowledge, the intellectual foundation of what they, and we, call science.

The other saying that all visitors would see was

"Know thyself". This call to introspection discloses the supreme value the Greeks placed on the individual human being. The demand for personal knowledge (not the denial of human nature, however flawed its condition may be) implicit in the maxim suggests an active not a passive outlook on the world. It is not a turning away from human desires that ought to engage the seeker of wisdom but, rather, a search for the optimal means of integrating all human properties, including desires, for the purpose of life.

The maxim also links in with the Greeks' approach to literature, which was highly personal in its orientation. Even one of the earliest forms, the epic poem, spoke of human nature in terms that resonate down the ages. In *The Iliad*, Agamemnon's pomposity, and Achilles' grand sulk because he could not get his way, lift the poem from being merely a list of heroic exploits to the realm of great human drama. Later, the Greeks invented tragedy, to deal on the stage with the darker side of human nature in its relation with the gods, and comedy, which satirises human foibles.

The personal dimension is eloquent in the sphinx perched on an Ionic column in the local museum. It is a reconstruction of the demonic creature whose original stood in front of the temple of Apollo. A gift of the prosperous Cycladic island of Naxos in the sixth century BC as a votive offering to the archer god, it represents one of the oldest renditions of the mythical creature that so beguiled the ancients.

The Greek Sphinx expressed a different psychological perspective from its Egyptian progenitor, in a manner that distinguishes the two civilisations and perhaps identifies a general difference between East and West.

Thematically at one with the formal grandeur of the ancient Egyptians, the monumental statue at Giza, which is 140 feet long and 30 feet high, stares haughtily towards the rising sun. Huge and authori-

tative, it smiles serenely in the knowledge of past and future, an eternal symbol of the absolute power of the State.

Far smaller and more intimate, the Greek version – on display at Delphi, though only in reconstruction – expresses the inner world of individual psychology. Instead of bearing a pharaoh's head and symbolising government, the lion's body supports the face of an ordinary woman. Wings, gracefully curving upwards from her shoulders, give the creature a sense of mobility, a property cognate with human emotions. It is a beautiful, mysterious being, a benign form resting peacefully on its column.

However, in the archaic age, the Greek Sphinx appeared as a sinister perversion of the female spirit, her face cruel and menacing. Hera, the patroness of wives, sent her to ravage the lands of seven-gated Thebes in punishment of Laius, its tyrant, who had offended the sanctity of marriage by abducting Chrisippus, a pretty boy, for insalubrious purposes.

The Sphinx's modus operandi was to ambush young Thebans in the woods outside the city or trap them in the citadel. After cornering her terrified prey, she would demand they answer the riddle: "What creature walks on four legs in the morning, on two in the afternoon, and three in the evening?". No-one could divine the solution. As soon as the victim failed to give the right answer, the fearsome monster would swoop down in a screeching rage, grasp him in her predatory claws, and carry him off to be devoured in a carnivorous frenzy.

The depraved appetite of the semihuman monster and its cruelly twisted use of philosophical inquiry symbolised the harrowing consequences of a tyrannical regime, particularly the one that occurred at Thebes during the time of Laius and his successor.

At the head of a popular outcry, Oedipus assassinated Laius, unaware that he was his own father. In the chaotic aftermath, Creon seized power as regent

Treasury of the Athenians,
Delphi

and ruled as oppressively as his predecessor. The Sphinx terrorised the kingdom in a punishing killing spree of even greater atrocity. Desperation gripped
the regent. Unable to do anything more effective, he offered the throne and the
hand of Laius' widow, Jocasta, to whomever could rid the land of the scourge.
Oedipus grasped the challenge, and confronted the Sphinx in her haunt, sub-
jecting himself to the fateful question. The answer he gave to the riddle was
man, who crawls on all fours as a baby, walks on two legs at maturity and leans
on a cane in old age. On hearing the correct answer, the Sphinx hurled herself
to perdition on the rocks below her perch, fulfilling the ancient prophecy.

The ablation of the monster demonstrated the central presumption in Greek
thought – the power of the intellect to overcome evil and pave the way to
human progress. The sense of that faith was revived in Europe by the Renais-

sance, and developed into an articulated premise during the Age of Reason and the Enlightenment, to shape the philosophical attitudes of the Western world throughout the next centuries and down to contemporary times. Its expression through reason and directed intuition underlies our unshakeable commitment to science and technology.

In compliance with his terrible fate, Oedipus married Jocasta, ignorant that she was his mother. Soon after the wedding, a Corinthian shepherd came forward and recounted how he had saved the infant Oedipus when his father, King Laius, attempted to kill him and escape his baneful destiny. In this tale, the horrific truth about the unnatural marriage was revealed. With the knowledge, a frenzy of self-punishment seized the pair; Jocasta hanged herself, while Oedipus put out his eyes with her brooch, spending the rest of his life wandering in exile.

It was the genius of the Greeks to draw everything of importance onto the personal level, engaging the subjective consciousness of the individual, even though the methodology of thought stayed on the objective plane. In walking around the partially standing temples, their intimate symmetry still manifest, the treasuries built by the funds of hopeful potentates, the lore of the Pythian wisdom, all informed by the compelling myths and rituals that touched the human condition, I felt the gravitational personality of this place. It was as if it was a moral duty to be there, to come as a pilgrim to touch the birthstone of our culture.

Although best known today as the site of the most influential oracle in history, Delphi was one of four cities that formed the spiritual and cultural framework of Greece. Epidaurus, the birthplace of Asclepius, symbolised healing through the application of science. Delos was the treasury, or central bank and economic head, Delphi the religious centre. Olympia stood for peace, speaking through

Sphinx of Naxos

competition directed to sport, which was meant, at least for a time each year, to take the place of war.

It was the venue of the most famous sporting event of all time, the Olympic Games. Olympia was where we planned to go next. Since the Greeks pulled into separate focus the many facets of the human character, I felt it would be quite different from the reflective tranquillity of Delphi. Once switched in mind, we were eager to find out what this other place so celebrated in history was like.

Chapter 3

Spirit of Competition

We were off to Olympia, which sits on the western side of the Peloponnesus, the Greek peninsula that was home to the first mainland European civilisation. From the heights of Delphi, we had to wind down a narrow mountain road marked intermittently with little shrines to travellers who had fallen victim to the monster of the curves. The jagged terrain eventually smoothed out into the hot Valley of the Muses, dusted steel-green with olive trees. Dark phallic cypresses stood guard where Apollo led the nine winged art goddesses whose name the valley carries.

A ferry that runs non-stop across the Gulf of Corinth was waiting at the wharf when we arrived at Arisso. I drove cautiously onto the parking deck amidst a loud Greek chaos of several dozen cars; but somehow everyone got packed in as precisely as cobblestones in a road. Lardaceous, unshaven attendants with cigarettes flopping from their lips inched us skilfully into place with imperious gestures.

The ride took only 15 minutes, but it was long enough to stare quietly at the receding coastline and watch it grow hazy over the white turbulence aft the stern that cut into the wine-dark sea like a sculptor's chisel.

In full sunlight, the seacoast on the mainland side was like a colourist's painting. Striated haematite staining and the remnants of a bauxite mine painted the steep white limestone cliffs in rich, variegated colour, evocative of shapes from the Geometric period of Greek art history.

After a short drive on the other side, guided by prominent signs, unusual in Greece, we arrived at the sight of the famous games.

OLYMPIA

The majestic ruins that remind visitors of the birth of the Western sporting tradition form the only excuse for the tacky little town built there. A one-kilometre drive down Kondili Avenue, which is encrusted on both sides with the barnacles of the tourist trade, and you are back in the countryside.

Set in the fertile valley carved open by the sacred river Alphaios, which Heracles diverted to clean out the Augean stables, Olympia was a sanctuary known for its oracle as well as for its games. In a deal with its ally Delphi, it conceded its oracular functions and concentrated on sport, free to pursue a virtual monopoly.

In our uninspiring but adequate hotel, we had a late afternoon retsina on our balcony whose view redeemed the prosaic establishment. Within a few minutes of gazing at the distant hills draped in a tranquillising haze, I began to sense the atmosphere of reconciliation on a grand scale that had led Olympia's founders to select this site for a sanctuary. Its personality was expansive and stately, quite unlike the introspection of Delphi.

The quest for excellence through competition is arguably the most popular concept the Western world has inherited from its cultural ancestors, apart from democracy. To them it was the high path to merit; to us it is so integral to our way of life that legislation is deemed appropriate to underpin its economic manifestation.

The United States was the first modern country to pass antitrust legislation, but Europe soon followed with its own version. The American *Sherman Act* is expressly based on the presumption that freedom of competition is the foundation of a healthy economy. Accordingly, it proscribes any act or arrangement that has an anticompetitive tendency. Penalties can result in triple damages and even jail sentences.

The underlying value contained in antitrust statutes can be expressed as a Greek syllogism: competition provides the highest standard of human performance; the highest standard of human performance provides the best economic result; therefore competition provides the best economic result.

The Greeks, of course, saw war as the ultimate extension of the competitive urge, but sport could be a highly motivating substitute, particularly in those events that were testing grounds for manly virtue. Vicarious war could be enjoyed on the sporting fields. We do it today.

The Greeks perceived competition as being at the heart of human motivation. It was central to all activity above the mediocre. Symbolic of its highest form, the gods competed for the right to become lord and protector of cities. Poseidon made a bid for Athens, offering the city a salt spring that flowed onto the Acropolis. But Athena won it by planting an olive tree, which the citizens judged more useful.

Husbands were often chosen by athletic trial, a gating exercise that would be approved by the author of *The Selfish Gene*, a book that explains Darwinism at the genetic level. The hand of Atalanta, whom no-one had ever beaten in a running race, was offered to the man who could outrun the fleet-footed princess. Even the everyday work of ploughing, reaping and grape-picking was enlivened by contests.

The pursuit of excellence, a concept often used in motivational business management today, is a central part of our inheritance from those fractious but brilliant people. The line Homer gives Peleus to say as he bids farewell to his son Achilles en route to the Trojan War, "Always be the best and excel over others", encapsulates the spirit. Achilles applied the advice.

The spirit of competition was so important to the Greeks that they gave it a personality. *Agon*, from which we derive the word agony, appeared as a statue in the sanctuary at Olympia, along with its reward, *Nike* (victory).

Of such moral importance was a victory at the Olympic Games that the lavish prizes of Mycenaean times were abolished as distractions. The only award at Olympia was the *koitinos*, a crown of wild olives.

The plainness amazed the luxury-loving Persians who invaded Greece in 480 BC. Herodotus reports that one of King Xerxes' officers inquired anxiously of his commanding general, "Mardonius, what kind of men are you leading us against, who compete not for gold but simply for glory?".

Despite an intervening period of opulent prizes, the convention of simplicity has been restored to the Olympic Games. While today we award what we call gold medals, they are really gilt, intrinsically of as little economic value as foliage.

As befits the birthplace of democracy, the Greek ideal of advancement through competition rested on the conviction that real superiority is identified not by birth or material wealth but from contest in which each person can take part on equal terms. The Games were open to youths of all ranks. Often, as it is today, athletic success was a sure path to higher socio-economic status.

One of the least felicitous consequences of the passing of the classical world is the schism between sport and art. Today they are almost in opposition. Few athletes have any interest in art and many artists despise sport as mindless. Art has long deserted its mission to represent sport in search of other realities. It was not so in ancient Greece. Competition in the arts spiced the athletic contests. In the oldest recorded funeral games, Hesiod won the prize for his song. Poets and sculptors competed with each other in depicting and honouring the winning athletes. Throughout the classical period, the subject of most Greek sculpture – the beauty of the human form – was based on the paradigm of the superbly trained body.

From the beginning, the Greeks were conscious that boundless competition could never become the norm for ordering civilised activity, games or anything else. Applying the dictates of Lycurgus, the Spartan legislator, they established elaborate rules for the Games, designed to ensure that, as far as possible, true athletic quality would determine the outcome, uncorrupted by deceit or unfair advantage, which would dull the contest and corrupt the spirit. The best should prevail. But within those limits, competition reigned.

Described by Pindar as the 'laws of Zeus', the rules distinguished the Olympic Games from those that had gone on before, contests looser in their administration. Infractions carried heavy penalties, including fines. Exclusion from the Games was considered the most devastating punishment; less serious was public flogging.

In its halcyon days, Olympia was a noble architectural display of function and symmetry, combining facilities for the athletes and temples for the gods. It is the oldest sanctuary in Greece, linked with Pelops, the eponymous king of the peninsula. The roofs are gone, the walls have crumbled away, and only broken columns remain to struggle hopelessly against wind and rain, but the vestiges still stimulate the traveller's imagination.

Central to the holy place is the sacred grove of the Altis, to which, according to legend, Heracles brought the wild olive tree from the land of the Hyperboreans, a felicitous domain beyond the north wind where no-one fell sick. The Olympic flame bowl rests deep in the verdant sanctum, flanked by two columns in front of a retaining wall of ancient bricks. Every four years, to signify the eternity of the Olympic spirit, the sacred flame is lit there and transported by torch relays to wherever the Games are held. Ironically, this tradition started with the ill-spirited Berlin Games of 1936, the Olympiad which also inaugurated television coverage.

It is no trivial task to keep the torches lit during their peregrination, or to choose the torchbearers. In Australia, newspaper accounts of the relays to the Sydney Games concentrated more on the attempts to

Temple of Zeus, Olympia

relight the recalcitrant flame than on any other aspect, except for the choice of the runners. In an explosion of hubris that would have allowed an ancient Greek to identify with modern times, a member of the Australian Olympic Committee arranged for his daughter to replace one of the chosen runners. The furore in the media charged up a drama that dominated coverage for a week and ended with the humiliation of the culprit.

The Altis holds within its vanished perimeter walls the grand temple of Zeus, patron deity of the Olympic Games. The invading Dorians, northern barbarians who destroyed the cultivated Mycenaean civilisation, brought his

Columns of the
Temple of Zeus

worship to the Peloponnesus. Although not built until the fifth century BC, it was a paragon of the simple yet powerful Doric style.

Inside, Pheidias, the famous sculptor of the Parthenon, installed his 13-metre gold-and-ivory statue of the Olympian father, a work so breathtaking that it came to be regarded as one of the seven wonders of the ancient world. It is gone now, deluged at Constantinople by the Byzantine Cultural Revolution.

The once mighty temple, largest in the Peloponnesus, has declined gracefully into the landscape. Its columns lie in neat rows, their discs lined up on the ground like the whitened vertebrae of a dead giant.

We strolled along dusty cobblestones to the stadium and through the restored stone arch entrance, called the *krypte*, that connects it to the sanctuary. The athletes used to file through the narrow corridor, hemmed in by low, curved ceilings, their nervous tension heightened by the darkness that brooded in the long passage to the field of contest.

They must have been awestruck on emerging into the blinding light of the summer sun to the ecstatic roar of 45,000 fans gathered in an age when the entire population of even the largest cities was measured only in the tens of thousands.

I knew it was corny, but felt I had to jog at least a slow circuit around the sandy, oblong sporting ground, past the shadowy presence of the ancient Panhellenic spectators who used to sit on the grassy embankments. The first Games consisted of one event only, a sprint called the stadion, once around the 190-metre track. I thought of the contrast between the emptiness of the place (Anna-Maryke and I were the only people there) and the noise and air of public importance that must have existed so long ago. I felt a certain sense of privilege, being out there on the track where only the world's top athletes had a right to be.

Many people today are inclined to deride competition as inducing unnecessary discomfort. But so deeply is it engrained in our mentality that even those promoting a softer instinct feel obliged to invent a sublimation – competing with oneself instead of against others. But that is not the stuff of classical advocacy. When offered a choice by the gods, the mother of Achilles, most admired of *The Iliad*'s heroes, opted for a short, arduous life of glory for her son rather than humdrum longevity away from the field of strife.

For more than a millennium, the Games constituted the premier sporting event in the ancient world. However, like so many institutions steeped in pagan belief forms, they failed to survive the metamorphosis of the classical age into Christianity. As the new religion, which began to direct the plot by the end of the fourth century, rang down the curtain on the ancient world, in 391 AD the bigoted Roman emperor Theodosius decreed the closure of all heathen sanctuaries. Olympia, one of the most renowned, succumbed, along with its famous Games.

The world waited until 1896 for the idealistic Baron de Coubertin, living in a time of growing religious tolerance, to reinaugurate the Games, this time in Athens. The Greek capital, which is now bursting with 3·5 million souls, then had a population of only 150,000. The Games have been held continuously in their quadrennial cycle ever since, in cities far from Greece. In 2004, they are due to return to Athens.

No longer connected to religion, polytheistic or other, the modern Games still represent the humanistic ideals of their origins. Among the aims of the International Olympic Committee is "to educate young people through sport in a spirit of better understanding, helping to build a better, more peaceful world".

The origins of organised athletic contests have been drowned in the deep pool of time. The Minoans of Crete, who created the first European civilisation, moulded the games, which they had learned about from Egypt and the East, into a higher standard of performance, with some degree of set rules. A linkage with religious festivals imbued them with a system of ideals.

The sole purpose of earlier games, apart from extolling a strong and healthy body, was to produce a spectacle to entertain the public. It was not until the

Minoans and, later, the Greeks, took them on that they acquired an idealistic dimension. One could be excused for wondering if today's Olympic Games bear a closer resemblance to the former variety. Perhaps this would be a cynical view, for at least the modern Games espouse what the commentators call the 'Olympic spirit'.

After the warlike Mycenaeans conquered Crete, circa 1450 BC, they adopted Minoan athleticism with passionate commitment, developing new techniques and adding events such as foot and chariot races.

Rigorous and disciplined physical exercise and the cultivation of athletic skills were vital in the training of warriors. The contests at the Games provided a demonstration. Running, swimming, jumping and throwing were staples of basic training. Even today, many Olympic events require abilities traceable to a soldier's needs – not all, though; it is hard to see a linkage in synchronised swimming.

The heroes of *The Iliad*, a paean to Mycenaean soldiery, were all superb athletes. Homer's epithet for Achilles was 'fleet-footed', and Odysseus was a champion discus thrower. Diomedes of the blazing shield was a chariot racer par excellence.

In the United Kingdom and the New World, sport is a passion so deep that it defines identity. What child does not worship the school athletic hero? In the rest of the world, however, with few exceptions, it is not so central to the precepts of social organisation. In France, for example, sport is treated more as an optional recreation than a quasi-imperative. Outstanding national athletes are celebrated, but at the ordinary level the activity is not lionised.

The New World derives its attitude to sport from the British in their imperial age, building their empire on the Greek ideals of strength, intelligence and bravery, bending to advantage their military applications. The boast used to be that battles were won on the playing fields of Eton and Harrow. The

Inauguration of the modern Olympic Games (1896) in Athens

British created a focus on athletic games unique in the modern world. Yet the Olympic Games were revived not by them, but by a Frenchman seeking to reinstil vigour in his compatriots, who had ignominiously succumbed to Prussian strength a couple of decades before.

Scholars have argued hotly over the original reasons for holding athletic contests. Some think they are related to the murder of a king or to religious rites. But in the absence of written evidence, proof has been elusive. Possibly the most convincing theory, based on the legends of Homer, is that ancient games were funerary events.

To honour his great friend Patroclus, slain by Hector in the dust outside the walls of Troy, Achilles staged foot and chariot races, boxing and wrestling matches, and archery and spear-throwing contests. Even the discus had a place. The Achaean invaders, glad to have a respite from the war, were egged on with lavish prizes supplied by the distraught hero. More than 500 years later, Alexander the Great carried on the tradition, organising games at Babylon, with 3000 competitors, to pay tribute to his dead friend Hephaestion.

To the classical Greek mind, death and life form an endless rotation that links all who went before with all who will come. The dead fertilise the earth, which brings forth new life. In the games, the young athletes draw inspirational strength from the deceased heroes and manifest the regenerative phase of the cycle. Through the rigour of competition, their life forces are stimulated to exuberance and joy, offering hope for the future. So the negative of death is converted into a positive.

The Olympic Games were held every four years in mid-July, in the strength-sapping heat of the Aegean summer. At least it was more bearable for sport, which was played naked, than for wearing armour in the battles that kept the proud and belli-cose city-states on a constant war footing. For a month around the Olympiads, sometimes up to three, a truce ensured peace throughout Greece, a tradition that was breached only twice. Nowadays, instead of suspending war during the Games, we suspend the Games during war. No Games interrupted the two principal conflagrations of the 20th century.

The ideal of peace, expressed by the sublimation of war into athletic contest, was the emblem of the Olympic Games and is now the foundation stone of the modern Olympic movement.

Some today complain about the cacophony of national rivalry that howls around Olympiads. They insist that the unabashed chauvinism mars the Games, which ought to depend on sport for sport's sake. To the Greeks, who were every bit as jingoistic, perhaps even more so, interstate rivalry was not to be deplored, because it expressed in a harmless way a profound and immutable element of human nature. They watched the belligerent and emulous urges of their countrymen, fans as well as athletes, channelled by the process of sporting competition into a pursuit dramatically less destructive than its cognate alternative. Effort was perceived to be more productively employed working with human nature than trying to change it. Man was acknowledged to be an aggressive, violent creature, whose instincts cannot be altered, except perhaps at the cost of destroying his dynamism, a task extraordinarily difficult and ultimately counterproductive.

The American philosopher William James, an avowed pacifist, implies this perception in his seminal essay *The Moral Equivalent of War*, written in 1910, before the two most devastating bloodbaths in history. He concedes that, "Militarism is the great preserver of our ideals of hardihood, and human life with no use for hardihood would be contemptible", but goes on to offer a prescription that seeks to redirect these ideals towards arduous but peaceful challenge.

From Olympia, we proceeded south along the scalloped coast, through olive groves spiked with cypresses. Lush, overgrown vegetation choked the little rivers that struggled to move their stream through the valley floor on our left. I geared slowly up and down the arabesque road, conscious that we should take the time to enjoy the affluent colours in the fields and the regular slopes of the mountains linked together in the distance like steps. On the other side of the range was Kalamata, production centre of the small pointed olives and our destination for the night. The travel agent had said it was a convenient place to stay en route to Mycenae.

Immediately after checking into our hotel, we went looking for the ancient capital of Agamemnon. The map said Messene, an odd spelling, but it seemed close enough, probably the modern influence. The search was a frustrating one, punctuated by overshoots and undershoots, the result of directions we asked for but didn't really understand. As no-one spoke English, we had to rely on the few Greek words we had learned and the place names on the map. The people were friendly and obliging, willing to devote whatever time it took to help us, though their guidance was useful for only a hundred metres before ambiguity set in. Finally, I saw a sign that indicated the way to "Archaia Messene". I stepped on the accelerator and we soon approached the site. The museum by the side of the weed-choked road seemed very small to support such an icon of history and in any case it turned out to be locked. A workman was the only person around, so we asked him what was going on. "Not open yet", he replied. "Six months."

Notwithstanding, we walked past the little museum – there was no gate to the site – and slid down a scraped hill covered in loose stones to the archaeological workings. Barely anything remained. A few small pillars and some classification heaps of shards were all that indicated a dig. Where was the Lion Gate? As I brushed the sweat from my eyes, I saw two German-looking tourists manoeuvring in the shade. There was no-one else; even the workman had gone by now.

We picked our way up the friable hill towards the tourists. When we got close, I mumbled something banal about the heat and the young man responded with something slightly more intelligent. Abandoning my plan to work knowledgeably around to the point, I blurted out, "Do you know where Mycenae is, Agamemnon's capital? We followed the signs that said 'Messene' but we seem to have come to the wrong place".

With a thick German accent and pointing in the direction of the sun, he smiled, "You are a long way from Mikene – 100 kilometres".

I was hot, frustrated and deeply embarrassed. Our travel agent had mixed up the names and sent us to a minor dig miles out of the way. Although suspicious, I did not tumble to this until we had wasted half a day.

We drove back to Kalamata and checked out of the hotel as quickly as possible, for we hoped to reach the real Mycenae by sundown. The desk clerk was very generous, not charging us for the three hours our luggage had occupied the room. He even made a reservation for us at the Agamemnon Hotel in Mycenae.

I drove the two and a half winding and hilly hours to Mycenae with my foot moving savagely between the pedals. Anna-Maryke tensed in silence as we passed lines of cars on uphill turns and raced trucks down the slopes. It is always more nerve-wracking to be a passenger. Greece is the land of the gearbox: making time on the road relates directly to the speed of the shift.

MYCENAE

When we arrived at the Agamemnon, a hyperbolic naming of a hotel if I ever heard it, a girl of around 14 with braces on her teeth ambled over and asked, "You want to stay here?". Thinking she was the welcoming party, I replied that we did. She demurred. "Better you go to another hotel. Wedding here tonight – 500 people, music till three o'clock in the morning."

This sufficiently motivated us to look around town for an alternative. Unfortunately, all the other hotels were full. So it was back to the Agamemnon and a stuffy room with dilapidated air-conditioning and the prospect of nocturnal racket.

We had a reasonable souvlaki and a retsina at the Menelaus. Memories of Greece's Heroic Age lived on in the names of most of the local establishments. Back at the Agamemnon, the wedding was dull and the guests ran out of interest in the music quite early, so we got a reasonable night's sleep.

The site opened at eight in the morning, and we were among the first to arrive. No museum or guide was there to help us, and in a way, this was refreshing, for we were forced to let the feeling engendered by the place be our escort. After the human crush in Athens, it was a relief that there were hardly any tourists here. Finally, we saw the famous Lion Gate. Its massive, flat stone shape had been hiding in the shade when we arrived, but in a few minutes, it was illuminated by the rising sun, which revealed the detailed relief carving of two lions standing rampant on the lintel. It was transporting, like seeing an admired celebrity, in person, close up. Here was the renowned gate of one of the most important cities in history, through whose portal people carrying our cultural heritage passed for hundreds of years.

The gate was fashioned in the archaic manner, before the arch was invented, known as the corbel vault. To span a distance, architects would set the stone blocks of each course composing the structure so that they projected slightly beyond the one below. As the two sides enclosing the space grew higher, they would progressively converge into a pointed vault. The empty part at the top is called the relieving triangle. That is where the carved relief of the Lion Gate was placed. It consisted of a slab of smooth limestone, which contrasted with the coarse pebble conglomerate of the blocks forming the main structure of the gate. In the limestone was chiselled a scene of two lions standing with their front paws on an altar from which a column rose. It was more than just an ornamental carving, though. Shaped into a stylised composition that symbolised the royal house of Mycenae and its position in society, the stone picture can be described as a coat of arms, the oldest in the history of the Western world.

We walked under the colossal lintel and up the steep cobblestone alley of the citadel, which rises above the battlements and dominates the Argive plain 200 metres below, the grassland where Homer said the Mycenaeans bred their horses. For centuries, the capital of the rich Mycenaean civilisation stood impregnable in its rocky heights, surrounded by thick walls of abrasive conglomerate that the Greeks called Cyclopean (because the blocks were so huge that only giants could have put them into place). It is hard to imagine how, and with what number of lives, the bellicose Dorians from the north subdued the mighty fortress in the late 12th century BC.

Mycenae is steeped in legends that have inspired Western culture from Homer to Eugene O'Neill and Richard Strauss. Perseus, the son of Zeus and slayer of Medusa, is said to be the founder, employing the Cyclops to hew the immense blocks of stone from the craggy mountainside and form them into the fortress walls. His family ruled over the Argive plain for three generations. It was at the court of Mycenae that Atreus committed the horrific crime that exploded into the most famous curse in Western literature.

Atreus discovered that his brother, Thyestes, had seduced his wife. Without letting on that anything was amiss, he arranged a State banquet to which the guilty brother was invited. A dish specially prepared for the occasion was brought in and served to Thyestes, who ate it. It consisted of body parts of his two sons. On discovering the monstrosity, Thyestes leaped up from the table, shaking and vomiting, and let loose a visceral cry that transfixed the guests with terror. Eyes demonic in horror, he pronounced a curse upon the family of Atreus and his descendants so elemental that the gods were moved.

Fate took up the curse and played it out remorselessly for two generations. Upon his return home from victory at Troy, Atreus' son, Agamemnon, was murdered by his wife, Clytemnestra, and her lover Aegisthus. In retribution, her son, Orestes, killed them both. Driven mad by the Furies, primaeval earth spirits who exacted punishment for egregious sins, Orestes spent years seeking release, until finally, at Megalopolis in Anatolia (now part of Turkey), after badgering him to bite off one of his fingers, the Furies left him in peace.

Sophocles, Aeschylus and Euripides all wrote versions of the story in the fifth century BC, weaving it into a dramatic psychoanalysis of sin, guilt and the inner demons they spawn. The drama is heightened by the fact that these were real people – archaeologists have discovered the shaft graves of Aegisthus and Clytemnestra. They lie outside the city walls, unworthy to occupy the royal 'grave circle' still in evidence inside the citadel.

The story's tragic conflict, which exists at the base of human nature, has been expressed in various forms, its essence enduring through the ages. In modern times, Eugene O'Neill rewrote it as *Mourning Becomes Electra*, set in a severe New England town. In this version, the Furies represent the Puritan conscience, which flies into collision with romantic passion.

Historians date the Mycenaean age from circa 1620 BC. The beginnings are placed from the time when the local Greek-speaking Indo-Europeans, who had an established culture in mainland Greece a few hundred years before, came under the influence of the sophisticated Minoan civilisation on Crete, which was, in turn, derived from Egypt. Analphabetic, the Mycenaeans learned to write from the Minoans. The islanders adapted their Linear A, still untranslated, to cope with syllables of the early Greek language. The original motivation was to record economic data, such as State revenues and food inventories. Philologists term it Linear B. Using skills he employed as a World War Two cryptographer in the British intelligence services, Michael Ventris linked up with an expert in ancient languages to decipher the proto Greek script.

Taking advantage of devastating earthquakes and a society softened by affluence, the Mycenaeans invaded Crete, sacked Cnossos, the capital, and incorporated most of the island into their empire. The untutored invaders were amazed at the sophistication of the civilisation they encountered. Asking the locals the name of the intricately corridored palace at Cnossos, they learned that it was called Labyrinthos, meaning 'place of the double axe', the sacred symbol of a nation whose economy had been built on timber. So impressed were they by the maze-like complexity, the Mycenaeans incorporated the word into their language, changing its meaning to cover their perception of what they saw.

Homer described Mycenae as a city of gold. As in other cases, his words were based on fact, albeit distantly remembered, for in the grave circle and nearby, Schliemann and Tsountas discovered shaft graves of ancient kings that contained more gold

Lion Gate at Mycenae

Tomb of Agamemnon at Mycenae

objects than have been discovered in all the rest of Greece throughout its entire history.

The wealth stemmed partly from the plunder seized in Mycenae's conquests across the Hellespont, in the Trojan War fought between the two civilisations on the west coast of Asia. The clash led to the first recorded Western attempt to colonise the East, and was to be the precursor of a series of hostile encounters that seemed to create a tectonic fault line dividing the human world. Centuries rolled by, with most people in the West unaware of the turbulent and fascinating history on the other side. Where that history was told, it was usually belittled or distorted.

At a time when institutional religion and the morality of strength seem to be waning moons in the West, they are waxing in the East, in a revival that inspires dread in some Westerners and nostalgic angst in others. The strictures on freedom, particularly when applied against women, evoke a sense of regression, but the emphasis on core traditional values resonates with a concern that all is not right in our societies. Some people fear that an age of predecadence is

Citadel at Mycenae

engulfing the West, a pathology, like pre-cancer (marked by cancerous cells on the surface that have not yet penetrated the underlying tissue). In such a condition, if the dangerous cells are scraped off, the patient suffers no greater chance of contracting the disease than the normal population; left without treatment, the disease gnaws away at life.

We were ready to go east, but first we had to drive to Athens to catch a flight. We got to the outskirts easily, but then ran into the fiendish Athenian traffic and signless roads. The airport seemed like a secret site, hidden from all but the initiated. The time we had allowed to get there was fast disappearing and frustration was turning to anxiety.

Not knowing what else to do, I stopped at a service station and got out of the car. Two men were standing outside the kiosk. I began asking for directions to the airport, showing them my map. It was not very detailed. One of the men spoke to me in broken English, gesturing the way. I simply could not understand him, even though he repeated himself several times. Just when I had given up hope and was about to go off without a plan, he turned abruptly and barked, "Follow me", getting into his car. I scrambled into ours and drove off, struggling to keep up with him as he made several unpredictable turns. Time was getting very tight now. Still no signs. We followed blindly, clocking up the kilometres in the dense and barely moving traffic. Suddenly we were at the entrance of the airport. He gave us a smile and a wave and turned to go back. He had driven well out of his way.

We caught our flight. As we took off, I thought of the invisible chain that links us to the origins of our culture and the complexity of the civilising force that has shaped the lives of our world and given us our identity. A separateness of process forges identity, but the sense of it is largely defined through observing differences from others. We were going to have an opportunity to do that because we were about to cross the Hellespont to a very different place, Istanbul, the first major city encountered by a traveller heading east from Europe to Asia.

Part II
TURKEY

Hagia Sophia

Chapter 4

Into the Tent of the Stranger

From times before Homer, fabled opulence and marvels have distinguished Anatolia, the rugged peninsula that splits apart the Black and Mediterranean seas like a battle-axe of the gods and claims most of Turkey. It was the birthplace of Croesus and Midas, kings celebrated for their legendary stores of gold, the oldest metal worked by human hands. Hattusas, the capital of the Hittites who lived to the east, means 'silver city'. Two of the seven wonders of the ancient world are on its western coast – the tomb of Mausolus, best known as the Mausoleum, and the temple of Artemis. Only one of the seven wonders was located in Greece, the promoter of the concept. The Ottoman treasure, on display at Topkapi palace in Istanbul, ranks with the Persian and the Romanov as one of the three richest of the modern world.

The land was rumoured to sparkle with gold, an El Dorado of antiquity. The mere thought of it beguiled the adventurous ancient Greeks. Jason, legendary patron of navigation, tongue-lashed his hesitant argonauts through the perilous Hellespont into the fearsome Black Sea in search of Colchis, on the far northeastern coast of Anatolia, where travellers spoke of a fleece magically imbued with the noble metal.

Archaeologists inform us that the ancients mined placer deposits in the land of Medea by attaching fleeces to the bottom of riverbeds. Gold particles washed down from the mountains adhered to the greasy wool. Today, Turkey is no longer a gold-mining region, although a major Western company is currently fighting an environmental battle to bring a promising new deposit to production.

Turkey is a direct inheritor of the technological and cultural genius of Mesopotamia, its deep-south neighbour. The Bronze Age appeared there shortly after the Sumerians observed the hardening properties that result when tin and copper are smelted in the same crucible.

Hittites, Phrygians, Assyrians, Persians, Romans, Greeks and Turks clashed on the great land bridge, and folded themselves into one of the richest, most influential genetic soups in human history. Istanbul has been the power centre of both Christianity and Islam. To the fascination of the traveller, the path back into the past can be seen today, albeit in haphazard states of preservation.

However inextricably linked to their cultural formation, Europeans, beginning with the Greeks, have regarded lands east of the Hellespont as so unmistakably different that they warrant identification with a separate continent. That immiscibility remains today, and Islam expresses its epitome.

As Samuel Huntingdon states in his book *Clash of Civilizations*, it seems the fault lines of human conflict are being redrawn from the boundaries of nation-states to where different civilisations meet. He predicts that the most incendiary hatreds, misunderstandings and clashes of interests in the 21st century are likely to be among six identifiable civilisations of the world. He cites the Sinic, Japanese, Hindu, Islamic, Orthodox (consisting principally of Russia), Western, and Latin American. Two of the most likely antagonists are the West and an ascendant Islam. Turkey is on a major line of cleavage between them. Due to phobic perceptions in the West, spawned in the religious clashes of the Crusades and fomented more recently by films such as *Midnight Express*, Turkey has had difficulty selling its charms to the tourist market. Eruptions of violence from the PKK (Kurdistan Workers' Party), demanding an independent Kurdish State, have coloured the country an even darker shade of fear.

But we were to find that on the other side of the curtain of prejudice lies a safe society, where foreigners are treated with respect and a friendliness derived from ancient nomad roots, where the hotels are modern and roads smooth and wide, and where the cuisine is enticing. It is also among the cheapest places in the Mediterranean to visit.

ISTANBUL

We landed in the modern frenzy of Istanbul, which staples Europe and Asia together. Although fogged with the pollution and traffic of 14 million people – more than half having cascaded in from the countryside over the last seven years – the stately seat of the Ottoman sultans exudes a charm that enters the blood, never to depart.

Maybe it is the throb of the shipping that passes between the Mediterranean and Black seas through the narrow passage where Xerxes invaded Greece and where Alcibiades set up an Athenian customs station. Perhaps it is the hazy, domed landscape of a thousand mosques, or simply the Hittite, Phrygian, Greek and Turkish features on the faces of the people. But unmistakably, Istanbul is a compellingly exotic place.

There is a mystery about the city – it is like a great work of art that has been painted over another masterpiece, which covers still others in a rich and varied palimpsest. Somewhere in there is the image of the lost empire of Byzantium, whose capital, Constantinople, nourished by the rich trade between the two seas of civilisation it linked, was once the most powerful city in the world. It was the gene pool from which modern Christian doctrine was generated, conceived in ferocious debate even as Rome was fading into political obscurity.

The drive through the city to our hotel broke through the thicket of ugly buildings that ranged for much of the way from the airport, opening into a vista of the cerulean-blue Bosphorus sparkling beside the road. Cargo ships, oil tankers, fishing boats, even pleasure craft, of all sizes, moved in slow motion or just stood at anchor in the sun-clad water. They looked clean and painterly in the distance. I wondered where they came from: the Black Sea, only a short distance to the north, or the Mediterranean, down past the Hellespont.

On the other side of the sea road, I was gripped by excitement as we saw the first evidence of Constantinople – the old fortified walls of hewn stone blocks, with coloured brick striations running horizontally in layers, the distinctive feature of the Byzantine architectural style. The daunting bastions of the city used to feel the waters of the Bosphorus lapping at their base, but landfill now keeps them dry. Round, striated turrets jutted out of the wall periodically, as if strapped on with rusty hoops of steel. Gracefully domed mosques, like buttons holding the upholstery of the city together, stood out on the undulating surface, giving it a character unmistakably exotic, wholly different from cities in the West. The pervasive atmosphere of Islam they created was a little intimidating. It seemed exclusive, unwelcoming, to belong to an alien civilisation inimical to the West. I was to learn later, after I visited a few mosques, that my first impression was needlessly apprehensive. But certainly, the rounded domes dotted among the city buildings, needle-like minarets attached to them like pickets, formed an identity unlike anything I had seen before.

The faces in the street, with their variety of structure and complexion, were spellbinding. In them I could see the contemporary signatures of a myriad of origins, more than I had ever observed in one place – proof that Turkey has long been a crossroad of civilisational turbulence. I wandered like a voyeur, staring at features that could indicate so many backgrounds, some indigenous, some of invaders – Hittite, Lydian, Phrygian, Persian, Greek, Roman, Turkic. And the crush of people, who loved to stay outside in the streets until late at night, was like an enveloping hot cloud, something I had never experienced in the West.

People flooding in from the countryside are overwhelming the city's absorptive capacity, provoking policy arguments about whether to limit urban growth or let the population continue swelling to the 20 million mark it could reach in a few years' time. The siren song of jobs in the metropolis, which houses a third of the country's factories and is the region's largest entrepôt, promises relative ease compared with the hard life on the land. The dilemma is common among Asian cities.

Flowing through the streets like a sombre ribbon undulating rhythmically among the Western clothing of the majority are the pious head coverings and lumpy coats of Islamic fundamentalists. Only the women are apparent by dress; their male counterparts are in ordinary clothes, discreetly uncolourful, but not wearing shorts, even in the heat. An estimated 20 per cent of the population have adopted strict obedience to the Sharia (Islamic religious law) as their way of life, a startling rise over recent years that has changed the political complexion and threatened the secular basis of Turkish society.

The origins of Istanbul are told only in legend. In the seventh century BC, Greek seafarers emigrated from Megara in search of a new home. A soothsayer told their leader, Byzas, that he should site his new settlement at a place facing the land of the blind. Byzas led his people eastwards, and came upon a small peninsula formed by what were later named the Golden Horn and the Bosphorus. The beauty, fertility and mild climate of the place impressed the trekkers. Besides, it was a natural harbour. Even better, it was surrounded on three sides by water, so was eminently defensible. Upon arrival, the Greek settlers noticed a colony on the other side of the strait. Byzas declared that any people who failed to recognise the obvious attractions of the peninsula, preferring to live opposite it, must be blind. Excited by their propitious discovery, the immigrants built a settlement, naming it Byzantium, after their leader.

Over the next few centuries, the colony prospered, burgeoning into an affluent trade centre at the

Cistern

strategic junction of East and West. In the fifth century, it was a collector of customs. The Athenian ruler Alcibiades arranged for a toll to be levied on the value of all cargo moving through the Hellespont. The Istanbul skyline rose high on the Roman horizon at the end of the second century AD, rebuilt by Emperor Septimius Severus after he sacked the city for non-compliance with the demands of Rome. The city was the largest in Anatolia (the richest province of the Roman Empire), called Asia in Latin.

As the crisis in the western Roman empire deepened throughout the third and fourth centuries AD, fomented by cultural and economic decline in the Italian peninsula, the relative importance of the East blossomed. New social and religious forces generated from lands east of the Hellespont were coursing through the sclerotic arteries of the Imperium Romanum, creating a fatal aneurysm. Internecine strife decimated the old ruling classes, who had presented, in the past, a broad civic outlook. A new elite of successful military commanders rose to dominate the Senate and provide emperors. Cynicism replaced idealism and price supplanted honour. As fewer and fewer Italians were willing to enter the army, the task of soldiering, which led to power, fell to foreigners – Gauls, Illyrians, Berbers and Syrians. Septimius Severus was a Berber from Libya and spoke Latin with an accent.

The only force that held the empire together was the Latin language. During this period of decadence, the virile spores of Christianity, perceived by Edward Gibbon, in his *Decline and Fall of the Roman Empire*, as a seditious force, began to spread from their main base in Anatolia. Eventually, the Roman State succumbed to the political reality that the new faith had captured the hearts of the majority. After his vision of the cross, silhouetted against the sun above the words *in hoc signo vinces* ("by this sign you will conquer"), Emperor Constantine experienced a personal conversion (in 313 AD), affording the religion of the cross the recognition for which so many had died in martyrdom.

Street scenes in Istanbul

In 330 AD, frightened by the growing barbarian incursions from northern Europe, the Romans moved their capital to the Bosphorus city and renamed it Nea Roma (New Rome). I have sometimes wondered whether New York, New Jersey and all the others were inspired by the example.

Tensions between the eastern and western branches of the Roman Empire mounted over the ensuing decades, until, in 395 AD, it bifurcated for all time. The western sector, terminally decadent, collapsed under the tribal onslaughts from the north, never to rise again. The eastern sector, by now called Constantinople, regained its vigour to last a thousand years as the first Christian civilisation, best known to us as the Byzantine Empire.

Amidst the honking urban noise and hot concrete, we descended stone steps to a place where shadows of the Byzantine Empire are trapped in the ground below: a vast cistern built in the sixth century to hold water for the city, particularly in times of siege. Without such cisterns, enemies would have been able to reduce the city to distress by cutting off the supply.

It is an immense cavern of Roman brickwork, supported by a forest of columns rising eight metres into vaulted curves that disappear into acheronian blackness. I calculated that when full, the huge vessel would hold 8000 cubic metres of water. But now it is almost empty, dank and supernatural. It seemed we had descended into an underworld, a magical dimension where Constantinople still lives. Above was the light of a hot, steamy day, bustling with crowds and cars. Down below it was cool and tenebrous, a peaceful relief from the modern world. Intermittently, coloured lights flared dimly in the Byzantine vaults and sombre music played in counterpoint with sinister pings made by condensed water droplets hitting the shallow, motionless pool, dark but clear. Shadows of visitors appeared furtively, then disappeared as the light went by. No-one spoke.

As we walked through the underground penumbra along wooden scaffolding slippery with stale wetness, we came upon a giant stone head of Medusa in the stygian water, green slime clinging to her pale marble face. The Christian builders, ordered to reuse the material of old temples, had turned her head upside down to eliminate the power of the pagan symbol. Somehow it made her more threatening, staring up through the pellucid, silent water. Throughout the construction, the workmen had pieced together fragments of traditional columns and capitals, giving the place an unmistakable classical appearance, but weird – a pagan structure built by Christians. The Turks rehabilitated the cistern in the late 1980s, removing three metres of earth that had settled on the bottom over the centuries.

The Byzantine Empire, smelted in an alloy of classical Rome and the new religion, is known to the point of stereotype for its pious and uniform devotion to Christian precepts. It was people later to be called Byzantines who hammered out on the anvil of heated ecclesiastical debate those basic doctrines,

dogmas and formalities of the Church that, with modifications, still characterise Christianity today. That the great city facing Anatolia should have been the spiritual workshop seems natural, for it was the overwhelming proselytisation in the Roman province of Asia that ensured the success of Christianity.

In the beginning, however, the youthful church had to steer through turbulence and stresses of tectonic proportions, which very nearly submerged it. While its new status as official religion guaranteed State support, it did not eliminate the belief divisions that had always buffeted the yeasty faith.

Even though all adherents were tied to the concept of Christ as a divine being whose teachings called for a new way of looking at life, passionate differences of views, usually stemming from the diversity of local customs and traditions, meant that there were Syrian Christians, Egyptian (Coptic) Christians, Christians from Asia Minor and other Christians. The first task of the official Church was to unify its rambunctious rabble behind a single creed. To accomplish this, Constantine summoned the leaders to a conclave (in 325 AD) at Nicaea (İznik in what is now Turkey). It was to provide a forum for the two main opposing views on the nature of Christian divinity to conduct a tournament of debate.

The Asia Minor Christians charged forward with their assertion that God the Father and God the Son were equal and of the same substance. The Christian neo-Platonists of Egypt and Syria held that God was unique and that the Son, while given a type of divinity by the Father, was not of the same substance. The proponent of this view was Arius. At Nicaea the Asia Minor Christians triumphed with their view of consubstantiality. Later, the Aryans counterattacked, and the controversy was not settled until 381 AD, at the council of Constantinople, where the Aryans were finally defeated, being condemned as heretics to live outside the canon law.

Another cataclysmic dispute flared up in 431 AD. This time, it was over the divinity of Mary. Nestorius, the patriarch of Constantinople, vigorously opposed the view put forward by others in the Church that Mary was the mother of God as well as of Christ. He believed that she was only mortal. Losing the debate, Nestorius was deposed from his patriarchal see at the Council of Ephesus and the divinity of Mary was proclaimed. A part of the Syrian community refused to accept the verdict and seceded from the Imperial Church. Because of the close bond between Church and State, this amounted to secession from the empire. The rejected Nestorius led his dissidents out of Syria and into exile, setting up a religious community in Persia. The Nestorian diaspora, having several aspects in common with the Jewish, spread further east, along the Silk Road into Central Asia and as far as China. It survives today.

Controversies over dogma in Christianity did not cease with these major rulings, but continued to rock and split the Church, culminating in the Great Schism, which led to the distinctive Roman and Eastern Orthodox rites that have divided it ever since.

Emperor Constantine played the key generative role in the formation of the great city of the Bosphorus and gave his name to it, but it was Justinian, ruling a couple of hundred years later, who guided the transition from late antiquity to the Byzantine civilisation per se. He rode the tsunamic cultural and religious tide that engulfed the old classical world by the end of the fifth century – the sequela of the Roman Empire's collapse. Ever dynamic and unruly, the Christian Church went through a metamorphosis that was to have far-reaching social and political consequences, while fluid tribal migrations and internal moral decay in the Italian peninsula meant that new ideas and different imperatives would challenge the established classical order.

The monastic movement, which began in the Nitrian Desert in Western Egypt and spread into Anatolia, emerged as one of the forces of change, creating institutions within the Church that persist to this day. Individuals of an ascetic temperament, revolted by the ways of the world, retreated to the isolation and tranquillity of the desert to find a vision of God (*visio dei*) through a life of simplicity and self-denial. The monks perceived the Church as worldly and corrupt, because it was in alliance with the State and therefore supportive of the existing social order, which they considered was dominated by materialism.

The monastery founded at Constantinople by St John of Stoudios in the middle of the fifth century grew so powerful that no emperor could ignore its monks, known as the Sleepless Ones because they celebrated the divine liturgy in relays 24 hours a day. Every year the emperor was required to visit the monastery by sea for a feast to commemorate the decapitating of John the Baptist, the head of the saint being the Order's most precious relic. The severity of their asceticism must have struck an icicle into the heart of any politician seeking their counsel. Each day, they would take off their clothes and pile them in a heap. They would then pick garments from the pile at random to wear, whether they fitted or not. The sin committed by a monk in giving his mother a kiss on the cheek was punishable by saying the kyrie 50 times.

While no doubt extremists, these ascetics did have valid criticisms, for the Church was suffering from venal abuses that were sapping its vitality. Fires of scandal enveloped the personal morality of priests. The Church's financial condition was parlous, with clerics obliged to engage in trade to earn a livelihood and debt repayments forcing the sale of property.

Convinced of the need for reform, Justinian encouraged the monastic movement to exert an

Blue Mosque

influence. The official blessing emboldened its members to penetrate the ecclesiastical hierarchy; monks became bishops, patriarchs and even popes. Celibacy, a logical outgrowth of self-denial, was introduced among senior priests and bishops. The monks seized control of education, precipitating the downfall of the great universities of the classical era.

The Church achieved total domination over intellectual thought, completely supplanting the culture of antiquity, which from then on was to hibernate in obscurity until revived in the East by Islamic scholars and in the West by the Italian Renaissance. The purpose of art changed from the free expression of what the artist observed to a controlled manifest-ation of God. The dominant form of painting turned religious, based on the icon, a tradition derived from Egypt. Human figures became rigid and mannered; faces glowed with an inner light. The polyphonic songs of the Church were replaced by hymns sung in unison, their simple melodies varying only slightly within a strict form. Church architecture metamor-phosed, the old linear Roman basilica ceding to the dome brought from Syria, an obeisance to the reli-gion's Eastern origins.

We went for a long walk through the Sultanah-met district, the oldest section of town and a cornu-copia of Istanbul's monuments. It stands high on the proboscis of land called Seraglio Point, overlooking the narrow waterway called the Golden Horn. Byzas sited his colony there – opposite the land of the blind.

The streets were narrow and hilly, crammed with old structures that seemed to be apartments or offices or both. We walked up a road that was contin-uously winding, obscuring unusual buildings until the last moment. As we rounded one of the bends, the mighty Hagia Sophia Cathedral suddenly reared up in front of us. Like a cliff face in the forest, it took us by surprise. We were looking at the low, un-remarkable buildings lining the street, half concen-trating, when the bend abruptly revealed the tall, rounded majesty, clothed in a subtle red, of the famous church built by Justinian as his personal statement to God. Designed in the Syriac style of the day, its noble dome rising 55 metres, well above the tree line, it looked like a giant mosque. Indeed, the conquering Mehmet turned it into one for a while, after he sacked Constantinople, and he and his suc-cessors added minarets.

Then the largest church in the world (still today, only three are larger), the Hagia Sophia was consid-ered the omphalos, the centre of the Earth. Its name is Greek for holy wisdom. The patriarch crowned Byzantine emperors there. Now, the mighty cathe-dral, which housed the solemn rituals and plainsong chanting of the Byzantine hierarchy, is an official museum, but a most unusual one.

It is not just a place where things are collected, stored and displayed. Its objects – the gold tesserae mosaics, the iconic frescoes and other superb exam-ples of Byzantine art – belong to the place in the sense that they were integral to it when it was a functioning church. They were venerated in an ac-tive devotion, the profundity of which we in the modern world can scarcely imagine. We can dimly sense it, though, in the building, whose every design feature was aimed at elevating the spirit from the mortal plane. The vastness of the nave directs the vision upwards. First, the eye encounters the grace-ful tiers of columned arcades rising high on each side, then it enters the intimacy and mystery that inhabit the top of the dome.

In full use, the lofty and sombre spaces would have resonated with the spiritual power of those pioneers of Christianity whose victorious armies and ingenious diplomacy spread the Word outwards from Constantinople, creating what came to be known in the Middle Ages as Christendom (mean-ing 'dominion of Christ'). From the penumbra that hugged the marble floors, I looked up to see a ring of light that seemed to hold the magnificent dome in a floating state, even though it was so heavy that but-tresses had to be added to keep the walls from splay-ing. Arched windows set around the bottom of the dome like torches took fire from the glowing sun. But along with the majesty, we saw the evidence of its fate – large panels of Islamic calligraphy that hung on pillars next to Christian stained-glass iconography.

Chapter 5

Glory of the Crescent

Today, Constantinople belongs to the Turks. This was evident in the mosques, in the restaurants serving mezes and shish kebab, in the high cheekbones of many people we saw on the streets, and in the Islamic garb. The Graeco-Roman influence has receded into history. Contemporary Istanbul owes its character to the East.

In the 11th century AD, a convulsive ethnic tremor shook the Anatolian Peninsula as dramatically as did the Trojan War. The Turks, an eastern people of Mongolid race who can trace their ancestry back to Xinjiang in what is now western China, thundered on horseback out of the Central Asian steppes like a violent duststorm, uprooting all they encountered. They belonged to the Ural-Altaic linguistic group. Although they and Han Chinese have racial links, their languages are completely unrelated.

The first Turks known to history are the Huns, who appear in Chinese annals as early as the third century BC and against whom Qin Shi Huang Di built the Great Wall. In the fifth century AD, they migrated west in a devastating intrusive under their heroic king Attila, pushing over the enfeebled Roman Empire. Such is the subjectivity of history that the name which strikes terror into Western hearts is a favourite for Turkish boys. I have a good friend named Attila.

The mass migration west was unstoppable; it surged over the local communities like a lava flow, changing their culture forever in one of the most apocalyptic clashes of civilisations in history. Out of the process, some curious stories emerged. None is stranger than the case of how one invading tribe acquired a new religion.

In the fifth century, a Turkic tribe called the Khazars migrated into the land between the Black and Caspian seas where the Don River converges with the Volga. Over the next 300 years, they built a rich and powerful empire that stood as a block to Arab expansion into Europe and Byzantine hegemony north of the Caucasus. Legends abound as to how it happened, but the most authoritative theory seems to be that exposure to the two dominant but polarised empires of the day convinced opinion leaders to abandon their simplistic shaman practices and adopt a sophisticated religion. Perhaps this was intended to gain respectability in the world at large, or to give the ruler the heightened legitimacy and authority that comes with a privileged connection to a single, supreme being. For whatever reason, once the policy direction was formulated it became necessary to find an appropriate faith. One account suggests that a high official advised the khan to call for tenders from each of the three sophisticated religions: Islam, Christianity, and Judaeism. He took the advice, despatching emissaries with invitations to bid for the souls of his empire. All institutions responded by sending advocates of their cause to plead before the khan in his palatial tent.

Impressed equally by the spiritual credentials of the three, the wily khan made his decision on the political plane. He chose Judaeism, eliminating the other two faiths on the grounds that the power of their empires would make him a spiritual vassal if he adopted them. Once selected by the sovereign, Judaeism became the official religion of the State, a puissant domain standing on the commercial crossroads between Asia and northern Europe, capable of projecting its influence in both directions. Later, the khanate fell beneath the hooves of the Mongol invasions unleashed by Genghis Khan. The catastrophe pushed the Khazars to step up a migration to the west they had already begun, into the Slavonic lands of Europe. They settled eventually in Russia, Poland and Hungary. For years until the 10th century, the Magyars, who were the dominant tribe in Hungary, were bilingual, speaking Khazarian along with their own language. Controversy and lack of direct evidence cloud what proportion of eastern European Jews, known as the Ashkenazy, owe their ancestry to these Turkish migrants, but history is clear that many do.

In the sixth century, references to the Turks appeared both in Chinese sources in the East and in Byzantine records in the West. They pushed south and west from the region that is now Mongolia, covering a vast fan-like area. They established an empire in the northern part of what was known as Russian Turkestan, now the Central Asian Republics. To the east and south of the Altai River, in the part of Mongolia that was called Chinese Turkestan, the Oğuz federation of Turkic tribes rose to dominance. Until then, Indo-European peoples had inhabited these regions.

As they pushed west, the Turks brought with them their traditional carpet-weaving skills. Today, in Istanbul, Turkish rugs are everywhere. Around the mosques, in the bazaars and on the streets, insistent, ingratiating men sidled up to us constantly, softly whispering: "Where are you from? Would you like to see my carpets? Come into my shop – very good price". They were pests, but polite, and soon desisted when ignored.

Rugs transmit the zest of Turkey. They cover the floors of mosques, set overlapping each other in a profusion of colour and design, protecting shoeless feet from the cold of the stone. The better restaurants are graced with their atmospheric decoration. They adorn homes like floor paintings and are usually the principal article of furniture. Often, they are a store of wealth passed from generation to generation. Their strong and distinctive colours woven in tribal patterns, the eye-wrenching knots tied by women who yield patiently to the demands of the repetitive task, are unmistakably Oriental; there is no linkage with the city's European past. They look east, to the nomadic traditions of vast and empty spaces, where nature's colours are bland and time is as free to use as is the open air.

Exploiting the technique of archery on horseback mastered centuries earlier by the Huns and the

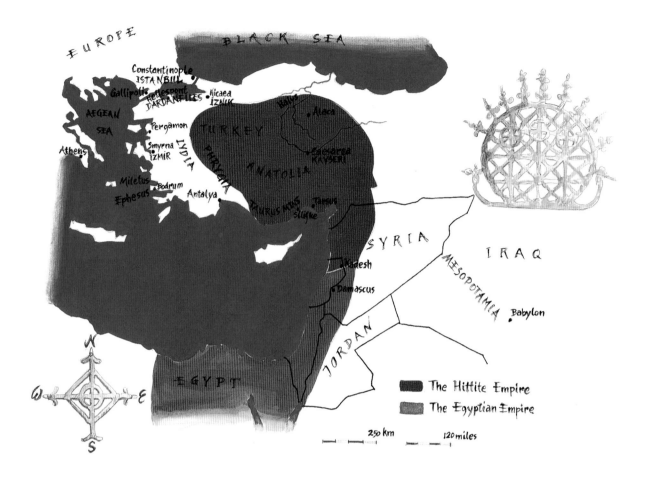

The Hittite Empire
The Egyptian Empire

250 km   120 miles

Chinese, the Turks developed it into the most devastating form of warfare of the times. Their fluid tactical movements, ability to kill at a distance, and capacity to cover vast distances to catch the enemy by surprise enabled them to dominate Asia and Eastern Europe for centuries. The unwieldy Byzantine armies, composed largely of different ethnic groups who distrusted each other and who had little sense of patriotism for the greater cause, were no match for the skilled horsemen of the steppes.

As a result of frontier contact with the Arabs who had formed the great Islamic caliphate to the south, the Turks gradually replaced their traditional shamanism with Islam. The religion of Mohammed was appealing because it facilitated a superior form of political organisation and offered the solace of a community.

In the latter part of the 10th century, an Oguz noble living in what is now Kazakstan (in Central Asia, east of Iran), adopted Islam, and led several campaigns against the pagan Turks of the steppes. This Islamic champion, whose name was Seljuk, and his grandson Ṭughril, went on to found the eponymous empire that dominated part of Iran and half of Anatolia for 300 years.

Ṭughril's nephew Alp Arslan (which means 'strong lion') defeated the Byzantine army in the critical battle of Manzikert in 1071, on the upper reaches of the Euphrates River in eastern Anatolia. The Turks drink a strong liquor named raki, made from anise, which they refer to as arslan sutu ('lion's milk'), because it turns white when water is added, like Pernod. We drank it frequently in Istanbul. Alp Arslan won by employing the traditional Turkish tactic of feigning retreat, allowing the pursuing forces to become disorganised, and then suddenly wheeling around, catching them off-guard. For the first time, a Byzantine emperor was captured. The catastrophe was lamented as an omen throughout a shocked Christendom.

So demoralised were the Byzantines after the disaster that the Seljuk Turks could have taken over their whole empire. Surprisingly, Alp Arslan resisted the temptation. He freed the emperor, Romanus Diogenes, for a ransom, and made an alliance which left Anatolia to the Byzantines. However, few doubted that the Seljuks could enter the territory at will.

During the Middle Ages, the Anatolian people, including the Turks, viewed the peninsula as part of Rome. They proclaimed it 'Rum', even though they knew the term was empty of any political relevance. The name of the city of Erzerum, in eastern Turkey, means 'gateway to Rome'. On the other hand, from the time of Barbarossa's Crusade, near the end of the 12th century, Western writers have called it Turchia, and this has stuck ever since.

The power vacuum that opened up after the annihilation of Byzantine strength at Manzikert sucked Turkic tribes into the peninsula, despite Alp Arslan's refusal to drive home his victory. By the middle of the 12th century, half of Anatolia belonged to the Seljuk sultanate. Two hundred years later, however, the empire fragmented into fractious principalities. The most aggressive of these, in the northwest, was led by a warrior chieftain, Osman, whose clan became known as Ottoman.

Riding out of their capital at Bursa, south of Istanbul, the Ottomans gobbled up neighbouring tribes until they had swallowed all the Turkic peoples in Anatolia. But their expansion was interrupted when Tamerlane burst onto the scene with a series of incandescent victories. Although one of the greatest military commanders of all time, Tamerlane lacked any sort of political capability, passing from the smoke and death of his meteoric career without leaving an imperial establishment.

We took a ferry to Bursa, across the hazy, shallow Sea of Marmara, which connects the narrows of the Hellespont and the Bosphorus. Schools of leaping dolphins breached the calm surface a few metres from the boat. Smaller than the open-ocean species, they shot out of the water in formation, caught the sun in flashes, and slowly re-entered, still visible at depth. There were over 50, and they stayed with the boat a good part of the way, like companions.

As the first capital of the Ottomans, Bursa is revered in Turkey. Its industrial prowess – it is a principal automobile-manufacturing centre – competes with its attraction as a place of history. Nevertheless, some monuments remain. The Green Mosque, its elaborate and intricate carving signifying the Turkish style, is a work of beauty, while the old wooden Ottoman houses in the citadel district are some of the best such examples in Turkey.

After the disastrous defeats by Tamerlane, the Ottomans revived their expansion. Their formidable tribal leader Mehmet II, celebrated as the Conqueror, marched to Constantinople with 100,000 soldiers, 12,000 of whom were the redoubtable and fanatical Janissaries. Formed in 1330, the Janissaries were a praetorian guard composed exclusively of Christian boys forcibly taken from their families at age 10 and brought up as fervent Muslims to serve the sultan as an elite force. They came from what are now Bosnia and Serbia and grew into what many regarded as the toughest fighting men in the world at the time. Absolute obedience was mandatory and all took an oath of celibacy. In return, they were well paid and particularly well fed. So much of the pleasure of life revolved around food that when, in later years, the central government declined, the Janissaries would signal their opposition to the sultan by overturning the cauldrons in which their rice pilaf was cooked, signifying that they would no longer eat his food. It was a chilling tocsin, for it often led to strangulation with a bow string, the traditional means employed by the Turks to assassinate the great.

For a month, the young sultan moved his large and disciplined army towards the Bosphorus. The Muslim troops were fired with religious passion heated to ceramic temperatures by the prospect of subduing the famous Christian centre, the fabled city of the infidel about which they had heard since childhood, a three-sided monster bounded on one side by land and on the other two by sea. The Byzantines had virtually given up hope of saving their capital, leaving only 40,000 terrified people there, including a mercenary army of Venetians and Genoese. The emperor suppressed a local report that the defence rested on an army of merely 7000 men.

Two earth tremors thrashed by torrential rains visited the threatened city that spring – omens foretelling the fall of empire and coming of the anti-Christ prophesied in tradition. But the citizens, sparked by fear and faith, worked without rest to toughen the fortifications and to prepare missiles that would be showered down on attackers from atop the stalwart walls. Engineers built a huge chain boom with massive links that stretched across the opening to the Golden Horn, preventing enemy ships coming in from the Bosphorus – some of the black iron links are on display today at the archaeological museum, macabre relics of war. The city that had withstood so many sieges in the past would not be taken without a sorry cost in enemy lives. Even nuns carried stones to the walls. But all knew that their only real hope was to be allowed to perform the holy rites of their last Easter and to pray for a deliverance that had more chance of being granted in the next world than in this.

The Turks had a daunting superiority in numbers, but how were they to cope with the formidable Byzantine walls that had kept them at bay in the past? The year before, a Hungarian engineer, Urban, had visited Constantinople seeking a commission from the emperor to build a new type of artillery, a gigantic cannon several times larger than anything else that was available. The emperor, deciding he could not afford the fee, turned Urban down. The determined engineer went to the sultan, where he had more success. Thrilled at the prospects for military advantage offered by the technology, Mehmet engaged Urban, paying four times the amount he had originally asked.

Cannons had been in use for well over 100 years. But they were not powerful enough to knock down masonry. To succeed in penetrating the thick walls of Constantinople required an advance in technology. Urban was up to the task. The artillery built for the attack had the largest calibre and range ever devised. One cannon was tested successfully over a one-mile distance and using a ball weighing 1200 pounds. The breakthrough was to change forever the nature of warfare. From the second half of the 15th century, existing fortifications became ineffectual, except against small-scale assaults, and castles were no longer built to withstand sieges.

On Easter Monday, after a seven-week siege,

spurred on by trumpets and pipes so loud that their martial braying could be heard on the other side of the Bosphorus, an apocalyptic death cloud descended upon those Christians left alive after the heavy and sustained fighting. Turkish troops poured through a small gate accidentally left unbarred after a sortie and stormed past the inner wall, delivering the bastion of Christendom forever into the hands of Islam. The Conqueror then proclaimed the customary three days of pillage and rape, the average duration of his troops' stamina.

The earth tremors that presaged the fall of Constantinople were the rumblings of an earthquake zone bedevilling Anatolia that runs parallel to the Black Sea coast and splits under the Sea of Marmara. Violent episodes that can reach 8.1 on the Richter scale erupt at intervals of a few decades. The last occurred recently in the Istanbul region, leaving a tragic aftermath of bodies crushed beneath piles of substandard concrete.

Mehmet immediately set about rebuilding the city, making it his capital. The conquest of Constantinople had been the dream of the Turks for over 100 years, since the collapse of the Seljuk Empire. The feat laid the foundations of an empire that was to last almost 500 more years and leave its footprint on modern times. Like the Romans, the Turks, although a rough, conquering people, quickly learned the arts of civilisation from their subject peoples.

The sumptuous palace Mehmet constructed as his seat of power, against the old Byzantine walls linking the Sea of Marmara with the Golden Horn, remains today, preserved as one of the most alluring museums in the world. Its name, Topkapi (meaning 'Cannon Gate'), is derived from the artillery that protected its portals. We were able to walk there along the winding streets from the Hagia Sophia in a few minutes, a journey out of the Byzantine past into the world of Ottoman potentates.

Everything of importance in the empire emanated from the palace. Poets and writers could not achieve success, no matter what their talent, without its support. The sultan's slaves, whom he could elevate or destroy at his pleasure, were educated there. It is a graceful melange of courtyards, long corridors and domed rooms housing things of beauty and fascination, a virtual city of sensual delight. Flower gardens, pools and fountains cool the fierce outside heat.

We passed through the Imperial Gate and into a wide courtyard that had a discreet passage on the left. It led to the harem, the abode of love that cast a spellbinding web of fascination tinged with prurience over the Western mind, particularly in the 18th century, the high period of Orientalism. Mozart's *Abduction from the Seraglio* was set in an imaginary Topkapi. Every year, the real palace hosts a production of the tuneful opera.

Spread through 259 rooms, the harem – literally, a place forbidden to enter – was partitioned into three distinct sections: one for the black eunuch (who was in charge), one for the women and one for the sultan, all lavishly appointed with brightly coloured tiles on the walls and patterned rugs on the floors. In the most important rooms, gold leaf decorated the domes that rose in sensory splendour out of graceful pillar capitals. The apartments of the women opened onto three marble-paved hidden courtyards surrounded by intricately designed porches.

In the opulent Hall of the Emperor, the sultan and his odalisques spent long evenings graced by music and dancing, performed by specially selected and highly trained women of the harem. The lavishness of the vast room was breathtaking, the colours and shapes of the tiles on the walls so elaborate and complex yet somehow creating restful harmony. Twenty-six windows formed a high circle underneath a vast rococo dome rising high in the air.

Topkapi

The sultan's throne was recessed in an elegant field of blue and white tiles set about with Chinese porcelain vases. In a corner of the room, a mirrored closet disguised the secret door which discreetly enabled him to access other parts of the forbidden place. While usually he had a choice of several hundred concubines, at one time there were over 1000 women living in the harem. Even though it was considered a great honour for a concubine to go to bed with the ruler, particularly if she bore him a child, especially a son, occasions are recorded where women successfully refused.

The darker side of the Ottoman society was the kul (slave) system. Machiavelli observed that the Ottoman Empire was an absolute monarchy utterly dependent on slavery. In the 17th century, Istanbul alone absorbed 20,000 captives a year. They not only replenished the ranks of the Janissaries but performed all roles necessary to operate the State. It was an institution that inculcated a sense of subordination of the individual to the correct ordering of the government, culminating with unconditional obedience and loyalty to the sultan. And even he was subject to regulated codes of behaviour: the monarch was obliged to observe meticulously the elaborate protocol of the many ceremonies through which he was required to relate to others, often constrained even in the words he could use. The role of the vizier and the civil administration further limited his freedom, so that, except for a few powerful personalities, the sultans were mechanical parts of the machine, just like everybody

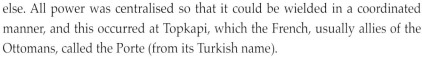

Above: The Spoon-maker's
Diamond

Left: Harem

Below: Dagger

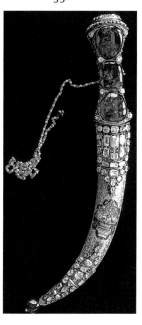

else. All power was centralised so that it could be wielded in a coordinated manner, and this occurred at Topkapi, which the French, usually allies of the Ottomans, called the Porte (from its Turkish name).

As Ottoman power burgeoned, wealth poured into Topkapi out of conquered territories and beyond, from trade along the Silk Road that started in China and from presents given by foreign monarchs to curry influence at the Porte. In the Hall of Gifts, a pear-shaped diamond of 86 carats surrounded by 49 smaller diamonds was one of the gifts – and a reminder of how possible it is to overlook value. For years it was lost, until accidentally rediscovered after being traded to a scrap dealer for three spoons. It is now called the Spoon-maker's Diamond.

When we entered the treasury, the hordes of tourists were so vast that the opulence was viewable only intermittently as we shuffled along with the others, locked together like the vertebrae of a giant snake. Swords, daggers, boxes, clocks and even divans glistened with lavish encrustations of precious gems. Most spectacular was a divan the size of a living-room sofa that was completely covered in diamonds, emeralds, rubies and amethysts. It didn't look very comfortable, but soft cushions would have covered the stones.

On display was the curved Topkapi dagger, made famous by the Peter Ustinov movie. It has appeared in so many publications that it looked familiar, yet it was still enormously impressive. Three huge emeralds dominate the

Istanbul Grand Bazaar

handle, while rows of diamonds cover the sheath with a sparkling crust. An emerald mounted on the hilt conceals a small clock.

Other rooms in Topkapi house possibly the world's best collections of Arabic calligraphy, soaked in lapis lazuli and gold leaf. Ten thousand pieces of Chinese porcelain, much of it the blue and white of the Ming dynasty, are shown in relays, too numerous to display at the same time.

No wonder the West has been fascinated for so long with Topkapi and its objects, more impressive by far than the crown jewels of England. Seeing it all there drove home to me the staggering concentration of riches in the Ottoman Empire and reminded me of how differently great wealth was expressed then than it is today.

The most glorious of the Ottoman monarchs was Süleyman, who became sultan in 1520, the time many historians say modern history begins. It was an epoch when the Ottoman conquests were creating uncountable wealth for Turkey, when silver from the New World was propelling Spain to a pre-eminent status in Europe and when the Elizabethan English were experiencing their own Renaissance. Inevitably, the ambitions of Turkey and Europe clashed again, and exacerbating the imperial competition was the religious divide.

From the beginning of his reign, the new sultan turned to expansion in Europe, taking Belgrade to open up the northern route to Europe. In 1526, he conquered Hungary in a battle on the plain of Mohacs which destroyed 200,000 combatants. By the age of 32, he was ruler of the largest empire on Earth, the culmination of half a millennium of Turkic military prowess.

The Venetian envoy to the royal palace gives an acute description of the man the Europeans called the Magnificent and the Turks referred to as the Lawgiver:

> Deadly pale, slender, with an aquiline nose and long neck; of no apparent strength, but his hand is very strong, as I observed it when I kissed it, and he is said to be able to bend a stiffer bow than anyone else. He is by nature melancholy, much addicted to women, liberal, proud, hasty and yet sometimes very gentle.

The Turks always had wolfish eyes for Europe, a prey whose taking would eliminate for all time the hated rival of Islam. In 1529, Süleyman attacked Vienna at the head of 250,000 men. The odds were pathetically uneven, the defenders of the Christian frontier able to muster only 16,000 troops behind their city walls. It seemed that the disaster of Constantinople was certain to be repeated. For three weeks, the invaders swarmed around the walls.

The Europeans, however, held on, aided providentially by torrential rains that prevented Süleyman from bringing his wall-bashing artillery into play. The Turks ran out of food, unable to live off the land, which the Europeans had scorched as they retreated to their fortifications.

Rebuffed at the gates of Vienna, Süleyman was obliged to lift the siege and return home to Istanbul. This check to Turkish military might signalled the apogee of the Ottoman Empire. From there, it started its long decline through a succession of weak sultans and a disease of the State marked by insidious corruption. By the end of the 18th century, Turkey was called the sick man of Europe, its death-dealing scimitars merely a frightening memory.

Turkish cuisine

At this time, however, the shadow of decay was still over the horizon. The reign of Süleyman the Magnificent was an age of affluence across all aspects of civilised life. Booty poured in from the empire and stimulated economic activity, civic life was elegant and refined, and the arts and sciences flowered. Nothing better expresses the times than the efflorescence of architecture commissioned by the cultivated sultan. His famous architect Sinan was responsible for over 400 mosques, the constructional signature of Islam. Of these, the most renowned is the Süleymaniye in Istanbul, a must see for the visitor.

We walked up a steep, winding street, past traditional Ottoman houses with their distinctive closed balconies of wood slats thrust over the road, towards the imposing domed monument built for Süleyman to honour his faith. Men in long-sleeved shirts, and women, some in Western clothes, others in beige or grey Islamic garb, thronged the street. Everywhere in Istanbul was crowded. Ottoman houses intrigued us; the unpainted wooden balconies that looked over the street with closed eyes seemed to typify the hidden nature of life in the old Orient. Unfortunately few remain, for they were built of wood, susceptible to the numerous life-destroying fires that have plagued Istanbul. We wanted to go inside one, but could not, for they were privately owned.

From its vantage point on top of a hill overlooking the muddy waters of the Golden Horn, the Süleymaniye rises high above the urban brick babble, serene among the insistent throb of small-shop activity and bustling people. What amazed me most on seeing it up close was the architect's reconciliation of a blizzard of complex smaller structures with the main building. It created a harmony whose overall impression was simplicity of form. I think it was accomplished by the skilful use of domes of various sizes throughout the multiplex as a unifying feature. That form has a poignant symbolism for the Turks, its shape reminiscent of the yurt of their ancestral home on the steppe.

Not far away is the better-known Blue Mosque, guarded by its six minarets, an unusual array, four being the common number. Designed by one of Sinan's pupils for a descendant of Süleyman, its name reflects the awe-inspiring blue tiles inside. We took our shoes off and entered through one of the three impressive doors. A massive wall-to-wall carpet covered the stone floors, woven into individual prayer panels. A lustrous glow emanated from rows of arabesque stained-glass windows lining the walls. A soft blue light suffused the air, generated from the faience tiles that clad the walls and the wide-ribbed pillars. It rose like a miasma to the lofty dome, which was held up by a numinous circle of light-emitting windows in the manner we had seen in the Hagia Sophia. When viewed from underneath, the dome formed a delicate and complex geometric pattern. Each mosque in Istanbul has its own dome, unique as a snowflake.

I felt a spiritual calm in the mosque, a sense of wellbeing. It didn't seem to matter that I was in the house of a religion with which I was unfamiliar – the uplifting atmosphere made me feel that the distinctions between religions, the cause of so much conflict over time, are capable of being elided, at least at the basic level.

The several hundred people in the mosque made a sparse crowd in the vastness of the space. We spotted a small group of men praying, facing the white marble mihrab set with precious stones and a piece of black rock from the sacred Ka'ba. The mihrab is the niche built into mosques to point the direction to Mecca. An elderly man was leading a small boy to prayer in an area cordoned off from tourists, the child swinging his arms playfully. Muslims are required to pray five times a day. Mohammed taught the faithful to tick off the prayers on their fingers, but beads are often used to keep track. It seemed somewhat intrusive for visitors to be there, driven by curiosity not faith, next to the devout performing their religious devotion. But access to mosques is open to all, and all can sense the atmosphere.

Istanbul is a city of mosques, over 1600 of them, the lead roofs of the older ones taking on a bluish oxide hue on the misty horizon. It was the domes that seemed to give the city its distinctive character, masses of them hunkering in the distance like giant crabs staked into place by spiky minarets.

We walked through the Sultanahmet park, laid

out as a square next to the Blue Mosque. Wooden slats in a long pergola covered with grapevines lined a flower garden in the middle. Unexpectedly, we came upon a museum of mosaics that exhibited floor and wall panels from the Byzantine era. Scenes of the mortal battle between Bellerophon and the Chimera, the eagle (representing the power of light) killing the snake of darkness, the winged lion displayed the imaginative heritage of the classical age with a fluidity and subtlety that rose above the strictures of the digital art form. It seemed fascinatingly incongruous among the mosques.

As we wound through the cramped and lively streets, a muezzin's nasal voice emerged from the top of a minaret, amplified by loudspeakers, to remind the faithful multitudes that it was time to pray. Within seconds, it was followed by another, then several at once, building into an a capella fugue that turned the entire city into an outdoor concert hall. The haunting, unmistakable calls rising all over the vast metropolis one after another, blending together in strange accidental chords, brought home to me with greater certainty than anything else that we were in the civilisation of Islam.

From the Middle Ages to the end of the First World War, which led to the fall of the Ottoman Empire, the Turks were the dominant military figures in Islam, disciplined and ferocious in battle. Frightening legends and myths sprouted up in the West about the Turkish threat, made more alarming by the religious challenge of Islam. Twice, the thundering Oriental hordes had crashed upon the Christian bastion of Vienna, gateway to Western Europe, filling hearts with apocalyptic terror. Fear-mongers predicted a repeat of the Christian catastrophe at Constantinople.

The second assault on Vienna, launched in 1683, collapsed, as did the first. It marked the last time a non-Western power attacked a society in the West

until Pearl Harbour. After the failure of the Turks at Vienna, the dynamics of world power shifted dramatically in favour of Western nations, leading inexorably to their colonising initiatives in the East during the 19th century and to the economic and military dominance that characterise international relations today.

The outnumbered garrison at Vienna held out against the Turks for two months, often in extremis. At one stage their distraught commander sent a message from the field saying, "The situation is hopeless but not serious".

During the action, a Christian cook baked loaves of bread in the shape of a crescent, as a gesture of defiance against the symbol of Islam on the Turkish flag. Marie Antoinette, an Austrian, later popularised the style in France, as the croissant.

The fundamental law that governed the peoples of the Ottoman Empire was the Sharia, the religious tenet of Islam as revealed by Mohammed. The State had a civil law, under the control of the sultan, which operated where the Sharia was silent, but in the case of any conflict, it was over-ruled by the dictates of the Prophet. The government was a theocracy, the ultimate purpose of the State being the defence and extension of Islam. In this society, which was rigidly hierarchical, the role of civil justice, essentially, was to prevent abuse of authority by the sultan's representatives, the sultan being the judge. His subjective handling of complaints and ability to protect his subjects from oppression by the authorities, particularly in matters of taxation, was the most important element in maintaining power.

In contrast with the West, the Ottomans never embraced the concept of a universal or natural law that applied to all human beings, a philosophical stream that has run deep in Western thought since the times of the ancient Greeks. This distinction is at the base of the difference between the West and Is-

Süleymaniye Mosque

lam, and underlines the opposing views of the world held by the two civilisations. No imperative was felt to develop social unity throughout the empire under a pervasive legal system or social norm. A composite model, not a melting pot, was adopted.

Non-Muslims living within the empire were restricted in their legal rights against the faithful. However, they were allowed to operate within their own legal systems, which derived from their religious affiliations. This led to a high degree of tolerance, except where a threat to the interests of the State was felt. Christians were immeasurably better off in the Turkish empire than were Muslims in Christendom, or even Protestants in France after the Reformation. Tolerance of ethnic and religious differences has longer roots in Islam than in the West. Only very recently, essentially within one generation, have we begun to give it intellectual and social support.

From Topkapi, we took a long walk through the old district, past the spice market, exotic in its fragrance, and over the Galata Bridge, which links ancient Constantinople to the spreading urban stain on the other side, at the mouth of

the Golden Horn. The name of the bridge comes from the Greek word meaning 'milk', from which we derive the term 'galaxy' (an array of stars that looks milky in the distance). The district used to house the milk market. Groups of men, some old, some young, stood in silence on the bridge, fishing rods in hand, lines extending a long way down to reach the warm, flaccid water. Little buckets were at their side; they didn't need to be large, for the only fish they had a chance of catching were virtual minnows (smelts, I think). Talking crowds flowed past them over the bridge in both directions.

On the way back, we browsed through the Grand Bazaar, which was constructed by Mehmet the Conqueror to restore the city's commercial life after its destruction by the conquest. It lays claim to being the largest shopping mall in the world, enclosing 65 city streets. Long corridors of arched ceilings interconnect with each other in a labyrinth that houses thousands of colourful little stalls standing side by side, each seeking to attract prey like sea anemones.

We entered the bazaar where the stalls were grander, closed in with glass windows. It was the gold jewellery section, said to offer the best bargains in the world, the cheapest gold. Chains, bracelets, rings, sometimes in heaps, flashing in the artificial light coming through the windows, formed a vast partitioned treasure trove. The crowds were so thick that it seemed we had lost our individuality; we were subsumed in a process that created a slowly moving mass, a type of gigantic serpent, of which we were merely molecules. It was a bit overwhelming, but intriguing none the less, for it seemed we had changed our identity for a while through a catalyst of noise and bustle and the exotic visual images of Eastern commerce.

The shopkeepers were happy to chat, whether we bought or not. One told us the folk tale of Osman, founder of the Ottoman Empire. He started his career as a tribal chief, not of royal descent but a mighty warrior, insuperable in combat. Disdaining a shield, he preferred to fight with a sword in each hand. While he was teaching his tribesmen the technique, he sat down for a rest under a tree and fell asleep. He had a dream in which the tree grew so large that its canopy spread out over the entire land. After waking, he asked a dervish what his vision meant. The wise man said it foretold his destiny, which was to conquer a vast territory by force of arms. And he did. The tree became the Tree of Life, symbol of the Ottomans, often woven into Turkish carpets.

Unlike their cousins, the Mongols, the Ottoman rulers built an empire of culture as well as power, learned mainly from the Arabs and Persians. Arts and sciences flourished in the realm, none more so than the delectable form of cooking. The tradition is maintained in the food today, and Turkish cuisine is refined and varied.

We enjoyed the custom of choosing the fish in the restaurants at counters full of fresh seafood – crustaceans, oysters, clams and most species of Mediterranean fish, all laid out on flaked ice. Mezes, or hors d'oeuvres, start the meal, with aubergine in different forms, lentil soup, flaked pastries, stuffed vine leaves, olive dishes and a cluster of other delectables so numerous that it is hard to make a choice. My favourite main course is kofte (minced lamb spiced with cumin, and grilled on a kebab), but the pit-roasted lamb with cumin is close to a tie.

The dessert trolley carries baklava in several forms (which can be enhanced by delicious solid buffalo cream called kaymak), a sweet white pudding made from chicken breasts, figs done with a caramel sauce and a tantalisation of other delights. The wine is indifferent however, yielding place to Efes beer, which is quite good.

Chapter 6

Romance of the Ancient

Out of the rich colours and texture of Istanbul, we flew to the nation's capital, not to see the bland governmental centre, but as a stopping-off point en route to Hattusas, ancient capital of the Hittites. The city used to be called Angora, and gave its name to the fine, soft-haired goat cultivated in the environs.

Its wide, quiet streets and modern concrete buildings give the city a nondescript appearance completely devoid of Istanbul's exotic charm. Except for the mosques and some Islamically dressed women, we could have been in a Western city. I felt a little disappointed.

At the hotel, I had a curious experience. When I picked up one of our bags from the taxi, the driver suddenly grabbed it out of my hands and carried it over to the door. His manner was not unfriendly but urgent. Later, a Turkish friend told me that carrying bags is not done if there is a man present whose job it is to do it. A strict social hierarchy exists in Turkey that must be observed. Far from being seen as a cooperative or friendly gesture, what I did was interpreted as self-degrading. One loses respect by it.

ANKARA

Ankara's redemption from mediocrity is its archaeological museum, an imaginative structure comprising two 15th-century Ottoman buildings of long, thin Roman brick that have been integrated into a rectangle. It is the site of an ancient caravanserai, a resting place for caravan travellers. Inside, graceful Ottoman arches form internal entrances. Some are bricked into the walls to create a vestigial decoration. Ceilings fashioned of thin wooden slats give an airy effect. It is one of the architectural successes in combining the old with the new, offering a freshness of style in the presence of past form. The museum contains the best Hittite collection in the world and some of the most important Neolithic and Chalcolithic remains.

Human presence in Anatolia dates back to the Palaeolithic Age, the period

Hattusas

beginning two million years ago and lasting until 8000 BC. Stone tools and bone instruments for hunting and gathering discovered in the Karain, near the south coast, show that a dense and active population lived in Anatolia in these times.

In the Neolithic Age (beginning in 8000 BC), people began to develop agriculture and form towns, compiling surpluses that allowed the specialisation of activity and the amassing of wealth. The most important Neolithic centre discovered in the Middle East is at Çatal Höyük, due south from Ankara, in fertile grasslands. Aided by carbon-14 dating, archaeologists have released 10 distinct construction levels from the dusty detritus, uncovering habitation from 6800 to 5700 BC. The houses are flat-roofed mud-brick rectangles coated in plaster, built around courtyards. Stone Age artists decorated the walls with colourful bulls' heads and hunting scenes. Models of some of these structures are in the museum, complete with imaginary people.

By 6000 BC, the population had grown to 5000 clustered on 32 acres. It formed one of the earliest links between the advent of farming and the agglom-

Bucolic scenes
around Hattusas

erating of habitation in an urban setting.

A stone statuette in the museum is one of the earliest symbols of fertility ever found. It is in the form of a mother goddess giving birth. Also on display are mirrors made from flashing obsidian and materials for cosmetics, demonstrating how ancient is the concept of fashion.

The population of Anatolia increased its density in the Chalcolithic period (5500 BC to 3000 BC), and rubbed up against foreign peoples on its borders. The Balkan and Aegean regions made their presence felt in the west, while Syria and Mesopotamia pressed in from the more advanced east. The geography of the bridge between East and West was beginning to form. Notwithstanding, at first Anatolia was prevented from developing a uniform culture by the mountain spines that segmented its land. But the whole peninsula joined in the exciting advance of civilisation during the copper era, marked by more sophisticated tools and the emergence of complex geometric designs in pottery.

Through Turkish friends, we were introduced to the museum director, who was good enough to show us around. On coming to a case displaying some Phrygian sculptures beautifully fashioned in silver, he told us of the lawsuit over them that Turkey had launched against the Metropolitan Museum of New York a few years ago. Not particularly trying to suppress his pride, he explained that the treasures had been illegally taken out of Turkey in 1965 and later sold to the Met. When this came to light, the resulting dispute as to ownership escalated into litigation. The Met was intransigent, for it did not wish to create a precedent that could apply to other foreign treasures in its possession. The case went before a jury and was fully argued. Just before the verdict was handed down, the Met settled by agreeing to send the objects back to Turkey.

The museum director claimed the Met was afraid a more damaging precedent would have been created had it lost the case in a formal judgement. The action has a widespread relevance – the debate between the British Museum and Greece over the Elgin marbles could be informed by it. The issue of whether cultural treasures belong to the country of origin or whether they are really part of the world heritage and can remain in the care of foreign custodians threatens the very core competency of major Western museums. On the other hand, it touches the sense of identity of countries with ancient roots. As their custodial efficiency increases, which in many cases, such as in Turkey, is occurring now, arguments for repatriation of such items are gaining weight.

From Ankara we drove east, through a late spring green shaggy with young wheat painted over vast rounded hills. The curved lines of the central Anatolian plateau were clean against an immense sky undiminished by the tree cover that once obscured the view. Tamerlane hid his elephants in the forests surrounding Ankara before his victory over the Seljuk Turks. Isolated stands of poplars, testifying to the Central Asian origin of the present culture, are all that remain of the sylvan groves, cleared long ago for agriculture. It is a tradition to give young poplar trees to newlyweds as a dowry. As we drove through the open countryside, we saw a man kneeling in prayer in the green fields by the side of the road. He had parked his car nearby and spread his prayer rug on the ground.

BOGAZKOI

About 200 kilometres east of Ankara sleeps lonely Hattusas, capital of the Hittites, founded around 1700 BC by Hatusilis, their great Moses king. It is a bucolic ruin lying in open hills majestically above Bogazkoi, a little farming village of terracotta and whitewash. Gone are the silver mines that gave the city its name, long mined out by the ancients who built the wealth of their economy on them.

Outside among a cluster of geese, a hundred women were bending down over closely grazed fields, their small curved knives snipping a type of wild spinach. Like most women outside the main cities, they wore the Islamic hejab, which they hiked up over their knees and formed into a sack. In common with all Muslim countries, Turkey keeps its women in traditional roles, which essentially revolve around the home. The women in the field were gathering the groceries for the evening meal. Deep cultural history, reinforced by dictates in the *Koran*, prescribe the appropriate walks of life for men and women. In Turkey, the Western influence in the big cities sometimes allows more freedom to women, but this is not so in the countryside. And the further east one goes, the more traditional are the mores.

Hattusas looms proud among craggy limestone outcrops, whitely dominating a vast fertile plain like a bird of prey. At the height of its glory, it had a population of 25,000, ranking it as a metropolis in ancient times.

The remains of the great Hittite centre rest far away from modern noise. Their signal from the deep past has been enhanced by painstakingly accurate German scholarship, clear enough to stimulate a sense of what once was – imposing temples open to the sun, grand palaces, fortified walls of interlocking stone blocks. It was at Hattusas that I saw the light of discovery in a man's eyes, the same brightness I have observed in exploration geologists who have just found an ore body. Through an introduction, we met the German archaeologist in charge of the dig. He had just opened a tomb of an ancient Hittite king who had lived at a time not previously known. The discovery would change the settled knowledge of his profession. Ecstatic, he could not stop talking about his feat. It is a wonderful thing to see, that fire

in the eyes. It comes not only from excitement; it is informed by a certainty, a knowledge beyond what the individual possesses. The sensation taps into the universal human state at the generative level.

It made me realise why there is such an interest in archaeology today. With greater funding available, more opportunities to get involved in the excitement of discovery are opening up. It is a hard road, though, involving painstaking and detailed effort leading to only small increments of progress. The luck of a major find, as in mineral exploration, is reserved for the precious few. However, the vicarious thrill felt by being even tangentially involved can be stirring.

We were almost alone; only one bus load of tourists intervened, and then when we had been at the site for two hours. Silence joined the sound of the cuckoos.

The warlike Hittites, who appear in the Old Testament, played a principal role in the human formation of Anatolia, building an empire whose expanding tide clashed with the New Kingdom of Egypt. The battle between Rameses II and Muwatallis at Kadesh, in what is now Syria, gave rise to the first recorded peace treaty in history. It still exists, etched in cuneiform and hieroglyphics. Both sides celebrated victory back home – it was before the globalisation of communications.

The mighty lion gate, fashioned from huge stone blocks, still stares towards the ancient road that led to Mesopotamia, staged with resting posts at the end of each day's march. A 70-metre tunnel built with hewn rocks set in a corbelled vault allowed the defending troops to make surprise sorties en masse against besiegers at the foot of the fortified walls. Strong though their city was, the populace was never far from contemplation of the anxious need for armed defence.

In the massive stones of the Lion Gate are

Tunnel at Hattusas

memories of camel caravans, laden with exotic trade goods from cities on the Euphrates and the Tigris, clattering through the portals, their tired merchants relieved at finishing the long and often perilous journey. After a few days of noisy urban chaos, of insistent social pressures, they might have been thankful to return to the empty spaces of the trade routes.

Across the city, half buried in the ground, massive terracotta jars for storing olive oil, wine and water bring a quotidian dimension to the ancient grandeur, linking it to the present day.

ALACA HÖYÜK

At Alaca Höyük, 40 kilometres to the north, lies an even older Bronze Age city, contemporary with the second settlement at Troy and probably built by the Hatti, an indigenous people sometimes confused with the Hittites. The Bronze Age commenced in Anatolia around 3000 BC, very soon after the alloy was invented in Mesopotamia. It was probably by accident that the ancients fell upon the metallurgical discovery that copper alloyed with tin produced a metal harder than both, yet one that flowed more readily into moulds and did not form the recalcitrant oxide gas bubbles that made pure copper difficult to cast. They must have been further impressed by the advantage that copper when in the presence of tin has a lower melting point, about 950 degrees centigrade instead of 1084 degrees.

Writing took longer to migrate from Mesopotamia, not arriving until between 2000 BC and 1800 BC, when Assyrian traders introduced it to Anatolia. The earliest documents were commercial records. The Assyrians who came from northern Mesopotamia had heard about the gold and silver resources in Anatolia and sent their merchant vessels to trade. With them they brought cuneiform to the illiterate Hatti. Their records were kept on clay tablets encased in envelopes of clay, all fired for preservation.

Alaca Höyük reached a high level of civilisation that included use of the cire perdue technique, enabling artisans to cast intricate and complex shapes in bronze. A large-scale rendition of a ceremonial standard found in a tomb, comprising a stag flanked by two bulls, stands prominently in an Ankara boulevard. In the museum of the capital is a meticulously reconstructed royal

Hattusas

tomb from Alaca Höyük. Great care was devoted to the burial of the dead,
worldly possessions accompanying the deceased. The graves were in town,
dug shallow and covered first with a timber roof and then with soil. They could
be reopened when it was time for other members of the family to join.

A stone sphinx gate, covered in a rust-hued lichen, watches over the main
entrance of the city, which boasts a bas relief of a double-headed eagle, a motif
picked up often in Western iconography and later to became the symbol of the
Austro-Hungarian Empire.

The city, so old and collapsed, nevertheless had a recognisable identity. Its
signature was formed from the mighty square-cut capstones near the sphinx
gate, now strewn on the grass, which was alive with daisies, oblong shapes of
royal chambers indicated with stones laid out on the ground, and round
cisterns connected to drainage channels. All existed timelessly in the eternal
elements, a tenuous link to the beginnings of civilisation, but not the actual
beginning, for the city was young when Egypt was old.

Out there in the remote, quiet air laden with sun, I could sense the mortal
beauty of ruins as an art form, expressing the continuum of history and its

endless rhythm of rise and decline. Marcel Proust said, "The past is hidden somewhere outside the realm, beyond the reach of intellect, in some material object".

On that plane the curves and jagged shapes of ruins rise out of the land and decline back into it. Distant sounds of habitation and the pulse of urban life merge into the silence of abandonment. Form slowly changes identity, fading into subtle reminder. A phase change occurs, stimulated by an endless duality of action and passivity, noise and silence, movement and stillness, vitality and decay. But the condition seems not to be death; all is still alive in a certain sense. Some of its essence survives, its energy discernible in virtual form. It is a type of reality, one that has to be informed by imagination, in a mental space where past can be linked with present.

YAZILIKAYA

Not far from Alaca Höyük, a natural rock sanctuary at Yazilikaya reaches back into the essence of Hittite spirituality. It is in a narrow defile where Cyclopean boulders have been lowered onto pillar-like limestone outcrops to form a titanic ceiling.

Inside the solemn chambers, the rock faces are sculpted with large ritualistic figures in relief. The conical headdresses show them to be of the Hittite pantheon. Teshub, the chief god, stands on a mountain formed of his subjects, opposite his consort, the sun goddess Hepatu, who is seated on a panther. Like Zeus, who came after him, he was a weather god feared for his thunderbolts. Twelve scimitar-wielding gods of the underworld indicate the sanctuary's connection with ancient mortuary rites.

In common with the Egyptian religion, the Hittites believed that when a king died, he descended into the underworld and then, with the help of the chief god, rose to heaven, where he was deified.

The Hittites arrived in Anatolia around 2000 BC as part of an unruly migration of Indo-European peoples from the western end of the Black Sea, entering the peninsula across the Bosphorus. Within 300 years, they had subdued their neighbours and extended their sovereign reach over Central Anatolia.

The Old Kingdom of the Hittites lasted from 1700 BC to 1500 BC before declining into a slough of weak rulers, internecine feuding and decadence. But then, around 1400 BC, the society reinvigorated itself to form a glorious imperial period which saw it emerge onto the stage as one of the three great powers of the ancient world west of the Urals, rivals of the other two (Egypt and Babylon). Their armies, equipped with the fearsome chariot, pushed the boundaries of the empire into Syria, forcing the Egyptians, at the battle of Kadesh, to cede much of their rich province.

As their contemporaries, the Minoans, and the Egyptians before them demonstrated, it is possible for a nation to ascend to greatness, slump into decadence and purge itself to rise again. The cycle occurred also in Persia, where the Achaemenid dynasty lifted the squabbling tribes to dominance, then declined under Alexander's phalanxes, only to be replaced several hundred years later by the Sassanids, who rose like the phoenix. China's history, too, has followed the pattern. It is, accordingly, not the destiny of all societies that emerge from barbarism and reach a great height to decline forever into hopelessness. Some do, but history has shown that the first period of decadence need not be terminal.

Since Edward Gibbon published his seminal *Decline and Fall of the Roman Empire*, people have been fascinated by the question why great civilisations slide into decadence. By comparison, little has been written on why they rise in the first place, or why they return to greatness after an intermediary period of decline.

It is beyond the scope of this book to attempt an analysis of the issue. However, it does seem that where a society develops a dream, a sense of grand destiny, it is more likely to generate the spiritual and moral forces necessary for pre-eminence. Through it, the arduous effort, self-sacrifice and deferral of gratification required for achievement are accepted as worthwhile. The Greeks had it through their concept of the Hellenic ideal, so did the later Europeans, who dreamt of bringing the vision of the Enlightenment to the world. And the beginnings of the American nation were bound up in a concept of a New World unsullied by the follies of the old, where all had an equal opportunity to succeed.

Sometimes the dream is no worthier than the urge to conquer, to acquire the riches seemingly flaunted by affluent neighbours. Perhaps that is what motivated the Hittites and the Persians in that part of the world we were visiting. Historical writings are frustratingly unhelpful on the subject.

CAPPADOCIA

South of the ancient Hittite capital, the Anti Taurus range shields the magical province of Cappadocia, particularly beloved of discerning French travellers. When we were there, it seemed that the French outnumbered all other foreigners, and the ones I talked to were impressively knowledgeable on the history of the region.

Serial volcanic eruptions millions of years ago, led by Mount Argaeus, 4000 metres high, spewed up super-heated gas, dust, ash and lava that blanketed the region in volatile material. Gravitational energy later compressed it into tuffaceous rock draped with a layer of tough, dark basalt. Over geologic time, strange shapes emerged from the chisel of differential weathering, some of them looking like crooked cones with black caps. The locals call them fairy chimneys.

The miraculous beds of interlocking beige cones spreading to the horizon in every direction create an otherworldly atmosphere that has attracted people of deep religious conviction since ancient times. It seems possible that the shapes inspired the conical head-dresses of the Hittite gods.

Early Christians felt drawn to the strange and remote place. The trials and privations endured in the formative days of the new religion conditioned the practitioners to a life of struggle, material deprivation and physical hardship. Indeed, it was the conviction of all devotees that one day they would be called upon to sacrifice themselves as martyrs ('witnesses') to the faith. The stark, serene nature of the land of the fairy chimneys resonated with their

Above and top: Alaca Höyük

Left: Lion Gate, Hattusas

ascetic instincts and made it easier to resist the blandishments of this life.

When Emperor Constantine halted the suppression of Christianity and the Nicene consensus became the official religion of the Roman Empire, the noble battle ended. The change left many people with a feeling of emptiness. Some began to sublimate their urge for self-denial into a life of practising asceticism in the service of God.

Breaking out of the Nitrian Desert of Egypt during the fourth century, the ascetic movement, which ultimately created the great European monasteries of the Middle Ages, spilled into Cappadocia. Groups of monks and hermits, mainly from the lower classes, installed themselves in caves chiselled out of the friable rock. Individuals sought to make their mark by engaging in competitive forms of self-denial, sometimes in bizarre ways.

St Simeon the Stylite, after whom the most striking fairy chimney in the Monk's Valley is named, chained himself to a wall so that he could move only a few metres. He lived in such squalid conditions that the skin under his manacles rippled with worms. Later, he moved to even more restrictive quarters, this time on top of a 20-metre column in Syria, where he would prostrate himself 1244 times a day. He had a ladder for special occasions, but usually would communicate in written notes delivered by basket, which he lowered and raised. The word 'stylite', which was the name of his sect, is Greek for 'column'.

Near Göreme, the soft country rock of Cappadocia is easy to carve into dwellings and even churches. The Byzantines fashioned over 1000 from the compliant medium, decorating them with frescoes and carvings. From the outside, they look like ordinary caves pockmarking the rock structure, but on entering, the visitor can see that the space is shaped into the form of churches, with columns included for the appearance of authenticity, though having no bearing function. The Church of the Buckle, one of the largest, is a replica in miniature of the Hagia Sophia.

On the frescoed wall of the Church of the Apple, St George slays the dragon. The patron saint of England was a Cappadocian hero, who saved a princess from the scourge of the land by plunging his sword into the monster as he made the sign of the cross. He is thought to have been a Christian official in Diocletian's army who was martyred in 303 AD.

We came upon a monastery high off the ground. Complete with a separate kitchen, it had a dining room with a long refectory table that rose from the living rock floor, large enough to accommodate 50 monks. Even small storage cupboards were carved into the walls. All was precise and no larger than the minimal, a hall for the disciplined. Stone benches were cut so far from the table that diners were forced to sit upright, prevented by distance from putting their elbows on the table. Each seating place was marked with a shallow groove and placed to economise on space.

Linking up with the caves 20 kilometres away are towns built entirely underground, carved out of the rock beneath the surface. Together, they form a mole metropolis housing a population of 100,000, 20 metres below ground level. We visited one. Narrow corridors, linked by steps and ramps to multiple levels, wander through an immense troglodyte apartment building constructed with bedrooms, kitchens, and ventilation shafts for air and smoke. We struggled to overcome waves of claustrophobia as we shuffled through the cramped passageways, bent over and almost touching the walls. It seemed inconceivable that people would actually live down there, but they did.

The name Göreme comes from the Persian word meaning 'invisible'. Except for small entrance openings, there is no external evidence of habitation; the dwellings are secret structures lying hidden inside the living rock, safe from marauders. Now, they are no longer inhabited. Deeming them unsafe, the Turkish government evicted all dwellers in the 1950s, though not without some angst and opposition.

Göreme turned its back on farming and commerce after the iconoclastic movement (726 to 843 AD) arose, developing as a religious centre. Devout Byzantine Christians had become appalled at the idolatrous excesses of many members of the Church who, over time, transferred the focus of their belief from the holy beings they worshipped to icons that were only supposed to represent them. The icons had taken on a supernatural character and become divine in their own right.

The iconoclasts, or image-smashers, sought to banish the icons in order to prevent what they perceived was an abuse, but extended their zeal into all religious art forms. The movement ran its course and eventually lost force, allowing the return of the controversial objects. After the image-worshippers (iconophiles) regained the ascendancy, monks and priests began anew to build and decorate churches with brightly coloured frescoes and paintings glorifying sacred personalities. Good examples of these can be seen on the rock walls at Göreme, beautifully crafted. Because the artist was constrained by rules of representation (no deviation was permitted in what the subject must look like), the images are generalised and impersonal renditions of what was theologically correct. Adherence to divine purpose blocked any tendency there might have been among artists to develop a tradition of real portraiture, which depends on the particular and personal.

Cappadocia is the carpet centre of Turkey. Carpets are brought there from all over the country for distribution and sale. The best quality comes from Heirike, outside Istanbul, but the next quality is from Kayseri, the old Roman town of Caesarea and largest city in Cappadocia. Prices are quite reasonable compared to Persian rugs but still can climb into the tens of thousands of dollars for a large silk one or for silk on wool. Quality is determined essentially by the number of knots tied to make the fabric, for the fineness of the weave depends on the knot density. The top-of-the-line carpets have 64 double knots per square inch, cheaper ones 46. Young girls generally are the weavers. The work is excruciatingly hard. In the case of silk carpets, the strain on their eyes from tying the tiny knots prevents them working more than three hours a day.

Carpet salesmen in Turkey all seem to have a sense of the dramatic, which they show off in a set performance. First, they get you to sit down in their establishment and offer you sweet apple tea. Then they pull a colourful product off one of the high stacks that crowd the shop and swirl it around in the air like a flying saucer. After it lands, they turn it around so it can be seen from a different angle. Carpets have a grain composed of knots in one direction and tufts in the other. The colour changes to amaze the eye as one looks first with the grain and then against it. After the display, the fulsome explanations begin.

It is really quite pleasant and certainly interesting to see the different styles and hear the pitch, even if you don't buy anything. The men (women rarely sell carpets) are friendly and not overpowering. Their pride of product is forcefully expressed, however, and of course, failure to bargain vigorously will result in paying a fool's price. The claim today is that Turkish carpets are improving markedly in quality and are now on a par with Persian. Many dealers in the West are switching their attention to Turkey as uncertainties cloud the availability of supply in Iran.

Above: Church in Cappadocia

Left: Fairy chimneys

Chapter 7

Double–Headed Eagle

TARSUS

Directly south from Cappadocia on the eastern Mediterranean is Tarsus, the birthplace of St Paul, and called at that time the Athens of Asia Minor because of its yeasty brew of competing ideas and cults. A well in the town, sanctified by visits of the saint and said to have healing properties, still refreshes travellers with cool water pure enough even for queasy Westerners to drink.

Born a Jew in the first century AD, Paul distinguished himself in early life as a Judaeic polemicist and persecutor of Christians. An intensely passionate man, he suddenly converted to Christianity after experiencing a dazzling epiphany on the road to Damascus, which he felt was a personal call from Jesus. Christians later have usually believed that conversion to Christianity must be by way of a personal intervention by Jesus rather than by persuasion or rational argument.

A charismatic, natural leader, Paul launched his ministry in Tarsus, ultimately leading the followers of Jesus to a complete break with the Jewish Christian religion of the time. He differentiated the Church from the Talmudic Law and set Christianity on a course of universality that was crucial to its success. This dynamic was played out in Anatolia, the rich and sophisticated province of the Roman Empire called Asia. From there, it spread west to Rome itself and thence to the whole of Europe.

Near Mersin, a neighbouring town, stands the Gate of Cleopatra, erected to celebrate the attendance of the ravishing queen in answer to the summons of Roman commander Mark Antony. Shakespeare speaks of the fateful arrival:

> The barge she sat in, like a burnished throne,
> Burn'd on the water, the poop was beaten gold,
> Purple the sails, and so perfumed that
> The winds were lovesick with them.

We soon left the little town, more remarkable for its famous visitors than on its own account, and drove west along the Cilician coast, past the ancient town of Soli, where Alexander the Great reviewed his troops before the crucial battle of Issus. Some of the columns along the colonnaded parade still stand. The inhabitants spoke a corrupt Attic dialect, an offence against grammar that gave rise to the word 'solecism'.

Not far away are the Corycian caves mentioned by Strabo. They were called the Vale of Paradise and the Vale of Hell. We descended on steps slippery with mud and soaked with a humidity that increased with depth. Gradually, the oppressive heat from above left us as we moved slowly down, slowly because we were afraid of slipping on the greasy steps. The jagged-walled chasm grew darker and darker as we edged our way carefully down, deeper and deeper.

Suddenly, a low, reverberating roar rolled up from below. It grew stronger as we progressed into the dark, reaching a state of thunder so loud that it drowned out our voices. We could no longer see the scabrous sides of the hollowed-out limestone and were barely keeping ourselves from slipping down the decline. Still, we managed to get to the bottom of the steps, where the cave turned into an underground tunnel formed by dissolving limestone, extending into the bedrock for a few metres, then abruptly ending at a rock-face, the point where the mysterious roar was loudest. It was the voice of the giant Typhon, a pre-Olympian monster whose voracious appetite was the death knell of all who approached. Half-human, half-animal, he was powerful enough to hold even the mighty Zeus captive for a while. The early Christians placed a church halfway down the cave to ward off the evil spirit, and it remains in ruined form today. We discovered later that the spooky sound comes from a large underground aquifer.

During the Cenozoic period, Anatolia rose out of the sea that had covered it since primordial times. In this development, subsurface limestone rock began to dissolve from the action of rainwater and rivers, leaving jagged caves and monstrous caverns, along with underground drainage, in a process called karstification. The limestone rock in Anatolia is so honeycombed by tunnels and openings dissolved out by groundwater that subsurface aquifers can run hundreds of miles, to later emerge in the form of large springs.

Further along the coast, which by now presented top down views of the Mediterranean from the Taurus Mountains, we entered crusader country, through which the chivalry of Europe marched on its way to deliver the holy sepulchre and, in the minds of some idealists, discover the holy grail. Huge castles jutted out of the landscape, their crenellated towers a formidable re-minder of the brutal clash of civilisations that marked the Middle Ages. The largest and best preserved is the castle of Anamur, whose walls and 36 towers

Saracen

are still intact. It was built in the 12th century by the Christian kings of Lesser Armenia, and later used by the crusaders as protection against the Seljuk Turks they called Saracens.

The Seljuks forced the Christian Armenians out of their homes in northwest Anatolia following their resounding victory over the Byzantines at Manzikert. The Armenian civilisation reached heights of brilliance in the Middle Ages in alliance with the Latin culture of the crusaders, but collapsed under the Mongol invasion in the 14th century. After the cataclysm, they retreated to their homelands, east of Turkey.

At nearby Silifke, Barbarossa, who led the Third Crusade, against the great Saracen leader Saladin, drowned in the local river, plunging the Christian armies into a despair from which they never recovered. The grand army gradually disintegrated as it continued its march eastward without its messianic leader. Islam was spared its biggest military challenge and Christendom lost its chance to acquire the Holy Land.

But the passionate toxins generated by Pope Urban II in his sermon promoting the First Crusade to the northern European faithful were so virulent that they have infected the cultural environment, albeit in diluted form, down to the present day. Western prejudice against Muslims is still alive. His theme was as much cultural as religious, an attempt to reduce fratricide among Christians by demonising a foreign society.

"Fight now against the unbelievers, you who are wont to wage private wars against the faithful."

Perhaps it is the Hellenising mission of the ancient Greeks, perhaps it is the origins in oppression of Christianity, the Crusades or the wars of religion, but for whatever reason, the West has always and still is imbued with an idealistic urge to proselytise. No other civilisation has possessed it so consistently

and so fervently, even Islam, notwithstanding its dynamic expansion in the Middle Ages. That was more of a conquering wave propelled by a sense of moral superiority than an attempt to bring enlightenment to others, although undoubtedly there was some of that.

Efforts by Eastern societies are often addressed to controlling the thoughts of people within what they consider their traditional spheres of influence and, at times, marginally beyond, but usually no interest is shown in a reform applying to all human beings, as is the case in the West. For a while, communism might have been seen to play that role but its major proselytisers were Westerners, aided and abetted by the Russians and Chinese more for the purpose of destabilising Western regimes than enlightening them.

The proselytising urge, informed by the concept of universalism, leads the West inexorably into conflict with other civilisations, including Islam, for the message, even when good, cannot be unbundled from the culture that conveys it. Human rights are the contemporary message. It is seen by many people in Islam as worthy in the abstract but fraught with suspicion of self-gain on the part of its proponents. And its universality does not resonate with a civilisation that has its hands full with the struggle to regain the essential features of its own identity.

ANTALYA

Past the rugged coast of Cilicia, the idyllic resort of Antalya nestles in an acrylic-blue harbour set about with whitewashed buildings and a patch of pleasure boats. The hotels and restaurants are worthwhile, and sailing craft for Turkish Aegean cruises can be hired at prices not shocking even to travellers with weak currencies. Turkey consistently wins the blue flag awarded by a Swedish ecological group for the least-polluted section of the Mediterranean. A

Crusader castle, Antalya

consciousness of the need to preserve the environment from the consequences of industrialisation and population increase is a serious factor in Turkey. However, the challenges presented by its industrialising economy are not trivial. Up to now, the tourist industry, so blighting to other Mediterranean countries, has not overwhelmed the environment or spawned tacky resorts. Turkey is still relatively unspoiled. But with its charms so evident and becoming better known, how long can this last?

BODRUM

We flew to Bodrum, a chic holiday resort at the southern end of the Turkish Aegean, where the atmosphere is relatively Western. Very few women there wear Islamic garb. Even though tourists enveloped the town, most were Turkish. The restaurants and shops were not crassly commercial as is so common in the West. The young people who thronged the street late into the night seemed to have an unjaded air.

Bodrum, the old Ionian city of Halicarnassus, is famous for its 15th-century crusader castle built on the harbour by the Knights of Rhodes. The town is near Miletus, one of the 12 Ionian colonies founded by the Achaeans around the time of the Trojan War. Unlike most colonisers, the Greeks considered their

Crusader castle, Bodrum

transplanted brethren not as provincials but as an extension of mainstream culture. They developed as principals of, rather than merely agents for, the original civilisation, contributing astonishing advances in intellectual, artistic and scientific achievement.

Homer was an Ionian. So were Pythagoras and Heraclitus. Thales, known as one of the Seven Sages of Antiquity and regarded as the founder of geometry and physics, was born in Miletus. He was the first thinker to explain nature without calling upon the deities or supernatural powers. His pupil Anaximander, also from Ionia, developed the concept of infinity in cosmology and envisaged a type of evolution of the animal species.

After the collapse of the Hittite civilisation, Anatolia fell into an unsettled period of four centuries where hardly any literature records its events. Huge upheavals erupted that changed forever the dynastic relationships throughout the Middle East. For some unexplained reason, peoples of the region went into motion in waves of hyperactive migration, provoking widespread military conflict. The barbaric Kaska tribe from the Alps of Pontus rushed down from the north into the vacuum left by the Hittites, their traditional enemies. A mysterious and aggressive people from the west, known to the Hittites as Ahhiyawans, exploded into martial aggression at around this time. Historians believe, although the evidence is indirect, that these people are the Achaeans of Homeric fame who fought at Troy. They were a conglomerate of Greek peoples, not a single tribe. Dominant among them were the Mycenaeans, whose king was Agamemnon. Although he was the leader of the host, he did not have autocratic control. He had to maintain his authority by diplomacy, recognising the independence of the various components of the force.

At this time, Egypt was buffeted by waves of warriors invading from the northern sea, whom they called Sea Peoples. These intrusions appear to have been uncoordinated attacks by disparate tribes from Asia Minor and the Greek mainland, including the Achaeans. Little is known of these people, for their deeds were only scantily recorded, except by the blind bard. Correspondence of Hittite kings, however, mentions the rulers of Millawanda, a city on the west coast of Anatolia that was a colony of Ahhiyawa. Circumstantial evidence is overwhelming that Millawanda is Miletus.

Nothing is known of the cause of this prolonged migratory upheaval. Its effect, however, was to place multitudes of Greeks on the western coast of Anatolia and, through the legends memorialising the Trojan War, which was probably just an isolated invasion among many, create a nationalistic impetus that was later to flower into a major civilisation. Among its notable achievements, that civilisation created the Ionic column, a design midpoint between the spare Doric and the elaborate Corinthian.

At one stage, the 12 Ionian cities formed themselves into the Pan-Ionic League, primarily a religious federation based on the cult of Poseidon but which did have some political objectives. Despite their outstanding achievements in civic life, however, the Greeks in the East were never able to forge a unity that would give them the capacity to deal with their Anatolian neighbours from a position of power.

They suffered from the self-centred individuality of their progenitors that produced such irreconcilable rivalries, often unquellable even in the face of invasion. This was sadly demonstrated by the ease with which the Persians later conquered them, rolling them up into their Achaemenid Empire.

Several centuries after the Mycenaean invasions, another group of peoples migrated to Anatolia from eastern Europe. They were the Phrygians, a warlike Indo-European tribe whose circular shields and plumed helmets were quite different from anything else seen in Anatolia. Their headpiece inspired the 'bonnet phrygien' of Marianne, the imaginary mascot of the French, symbolising liberty.

From their capital at Gordium, in the southwest, built on top of a former Hittite settlement, the Phrygians established a kingdom that spread throughout Anatolia to the borders of Cappadocia. According to the Greeks, the Phrygians invented the frieze technique in architecture, giving their name to it.

Gordium grew rich from the regional gold mines, and as a station along the Royal Road of the Persian Empire, linking Anatolia with the Achaemenid capital of Susa, in modern-day Iran. So prosperous did it become that the accumulation of wealth sparked the myth surrounding its last king, Midas, that is remembered today. But Gordium itself is best known for the knot.

In its formative days, the city-state was wracked by civil dissension so poisonous that no-one could garner enough support to rule. A seer prophesied that a natural ruler would come to the people one day riding on a wagon. Some time after, an ambitious figure, Gordius, rode into town on the propitious vehicle. Believing the prophecy had come true, the people welcomed him as their king. Henceforward, the wagon was dedicated to Zeus, and another prophecy emerged – that whoever untied the knot in the wagon's yoke would rule Asia. So cunningly tied was the knot, the ends of the rope artfully concealed, that no matter how many tried, no-one succeeded in untying it.

When Alexander the Great entered Anatolia, he heard about the legend and marched to Gordium to try his hand with the fateful knot before he engaged the Persians. He, too, was stumped. Frustrated by the conventional approach to solving the problem, he unsheathed his sword and slashed the knot in two. Nothing in the terms of the prophecy precluded this method of loosing the knot. The lateral approach typified Alexander's style of leadership.

There is a theory that the Greek alphabet developed as an offshoot of the Phrygian during the eighth century BC. It is established fact that both alphabets are derived from the Phoenician. The early Greek writing was in alternate directions, called boustrophedon (meaning 'as the ox turns with the plough'), as was the Phrygian.

DIDYMA

We travelled towards the Ionian cities through undulating country sometimes reminiscent of Tuscany. Olive groves spread out onto terraces cut into the hillsides and slender Italian cypresses stood guard in rows along boundary lines. From time to time, we caught glimpses of the Aegean Sea. At other points, scattered farmhouses and fields of hay melded in with limestone outcrops on the high lands, displaying the prodigious effort it has taken over the centuries to bring this rugged country into cultivation.

Although Ephesus, Aphrodisias and Pergamon are the most frequently visited classical cities on the Ionian coast, it was Didyma that I found the most moving. Placed close to the real world of Miletus, a thriving commercial town, its temple of Apollo was a sanctuary for the spiritual values of the ancients, derived from the myths, cults and religious figures that had migrated from Mesopotamia across

Medusa, Didyma

Anatolia into the classical world. Spiritual consciousness has played such a pivotal role in the history of Anatolia, and here was one of the most important sites. Still enough remained of the once-mighty temple to get a sense of its awe-inspiring presence and its power over people's minds.

The main body of the temple rises in massive stone platforms, and Ionic columns again reach for the sky – a tribute to modern restoration scholarship. We walked quietly through a 20-metre stone-block tunnel from the front column courtyard to the inner sanctum, where only the high priests could go.

The tunnel was evocative of the earlier Hittite architecture, except it had smooth marble walls, not rough-hewn blocks of field stone. On either side, doves called, their soft notes blending with the hot air.

In a graceful cadence of decline, column discs have fallen like slumped spines and lie among the dark cypresses that partially mask views of the sea. Nearby, a magnificent head of Medusa lies as a fragment on the ground – another reminder of the Greek punishment for hubris. She was an ordinary woman who boasted she could knit faster than anyone, even the gods. Athena took offence and challenged her to

Temple of Apollo, Didyma

a competition. Medusa lost. In retribution, the goddess changed the offending woman's hair to snakes and made her face so terrible it turned to stone all that looked at her.

The importance of the temple of Apollo lies in its expression of the idea of the cult, so vital in the ancient world and particularly in Anatolia. It appealed to people's mystic nature, to their desire to feel the ancient verities without resorting to the rational part of the brain. Understanding is on a different plane; indeed, reason impedes the process, clouding the vision. Often, the practice of a cult was associated with foretelling the future. Didyma was a rival of Delphi, also a sanctuary of Apollo.

The prophecies of the archer god were communicated through a door set high over the floor between two marble blocks that are said to be the heaviest materials in classical architecture. Some claim that the temple might have been added to the list of the seven wonders, had it been finished. As we walked away from the ancient spiritual place, a muezzin's call to prayer broke the air from a loudspeaker nearby.

MILETUS

Archaeologists have uncovered portions of the Sacred Road whose stone blocks led all the way to Miletus, 16 kilometres up the coast. The famous city fattened its treasury with returns from maritime commerce, setting up a network of trading colonies throughout the Mediterranean and as far afield as the Black Sea. Exercising the political influence that often accompanies wealth, it fomented a revolt against Persian rule in the fifth century BC that spread to the other Ionian centres and lasted six years, until quashed after a disastrous defeat at sea.

The Persians followed up their victory by sacking the ringleader, killing all the men and forcing the women to marry their soldiers. The Milesian women swore an oath never to call their new husbands by name or to eat at their dinner table. We still use a refusal to call someone by name as a sign of unwillingness to recognise them.

The glorious history of Miletus lived into the early Christian era, by which time it had to fight a running battle with malaria as its harbour silted up and spawned mosquito-breeding swamps. Shrinking drastically in the Byzantine and Ottoman periods, it was abandoned in the 17th century. The harbour monument, with its elegant triton and dolphin reliefs, indicates how far inland Miletus has migrated. When we were there, its broken columns and plinths reflected their shapes and differential colours in a still pool, but the water was fresh.

Above: Atatürk

Top: Dolphin relief

Driving north along the Ionian coast, we passed within sight of Greek islands, which are part of ancient Anatolian culture yet signals of the fiery historical rivalry with Turkey currently being fuelled by the discovery of petroleum under the sea.

Turkey is a country that faces east and west like the double-headed eagle of the Hittites. Towards the sunrise lies its spiritual heritage. It stems from the nomadic Seljuk and Ottoman Turks who thundered out of the steppes and threw a rug of Turkic culture over a land of disparate peoples chilled into lassitude under the bureaucracy of late-Byzantine rule. To the west lies the promise of higher living standards, carried on the Daedalon wings of modern technology.

I was struck by the observation that the Turkish people I met, some of whom had lived for years in Western countries and were highly educated, knew virtually nothing about the Greek and Roman heritage. The lack seemed to mirror Western ignorance of Oriental history. Some were quite pro-Western, but they were so for reasons of technology and economic wealth and, to some extent, because of the freedoms enjoyed in the West. They had little interest in the culture or its background.

A recent prime minister, Tansu Çiller, argued that Turkey is a bridge between Western democracies and the Middle East. But Samuel Huntingdon speaks of it in *The Clash of Civilisations and the Remaking of World Order* as a torn country, essentially in one civilisation while its leaders want to shift it to another.

After the First World War, Atatürk, hero of the Gallipoli campaign and father of the modern Turkish State, severed ties with the tired Ottoman theocracy and set the nation on a course of secular development patterned on the West.

However, the imperial mentality of the Ottomans has not been entirely eradicated. Its reliance on martial virtues makes it difficult for Turkish society to adapt to the commercialism that underlies the free-market economies of the West. The statist approach among the educated classes isolates much of the natural leadership of the country from the workings of the economy at the entrepreneurial level.

And there is a further problem: while Atatürk's vision is still the theme of mainstream Turkish politicians, the recent rise of Islamic fundamentalist political activity shows that the country is torn, in the Huntingdon sense. A 20 per cent popular vote swept the fundamentalist Erbakan into power a few years ago, in coalition with moderate parties. His policies flared into a threat to the Atatürk legacy, provoking a bloodless coup aided by the army, the self-appointed guardian of secularism. Since Ottoman times, the military profession has held onto the steering wheel of power in Turkey. A continuation of the backlash stung the fundamentalist mayors of Istanbul and Kayseri with jail sentences.

Still, at the level of the ordinary folk, polls indicate that Fazilet, the successor to Erbakan's party, now banned, could count on at least the same proportion of the vote. Since the other parties are split, this could mean a plurality. It is obvious to any visitor who has travelled to Turkey over the last few years that the Islamic consciousness of the Turkish people is stirring. The female dress code is now so much more common in the street, and there is no doubt that women are wearing it willingly. They see it as an expression of their commitment to the Sharia and are proud of it. Mosques are better attended. Sophisticated members of the business community express concern that the rise in religious consciousness, while harmless in itself, could lead to a turning away from the secularism of Atatürk.

But it is important for the Westerner not to confuse what is a growing commitment to Islamic social and spiritual values with the militant political content of fundamentalism promoted by a minority. Sometimes, the definitional net of fundamentalism is cast too wide. Many Turks I talked to feel that fundamentalism is an insulting term used by atheists to put down those with a religious orientation, however moderate. The Sharia does not need to be practised in the extreme. Hands do not have to be lopped off. A modern, tolerant life can work within its essential precepts. But its cultural properties are distinctively different from those of contemporary Western civilisation, notwithstanding convergence on the economic and technological plane and a working alliance with the United States and Israel in foreign affairs.

Pergamon

Basilica of St John

House of Mary

Chapter 8

The Old Informs the New

EPHESUS

North of Miletus, at the mouth of the Meander River (whose name has come into the English language by virtue of its wandering course), stands Ephesus, ranked as one of the most influential religious cities in history. Its vast temple of Artemis, Apollo's brother, is now scarcely recognisable, but in its glory was celebrated as one of the seven wonders of the ancient world.

The city is said by some to have been founded by the Amazons, the matriarchal tribe famous for its spirited female warriors, and was promoted as the cult centre of the mother goddess known as Kubaba by the Hittites, Cybele by their Phrygian successors and Artemis by the Greeks.

So vital to the people of Anatolia was the female deity, symbolising fertility and the feminine virtues, that the early Christians found ready acceptance of the concept's metamorphosis into the Virgin Mary. Indeed, the Blessed Virgin was brought to Ephesus by St John, living there until her death. The basilica constructed near her residence was the venue of the Third Ecumenical Council, in 431 AD, which decided on the dogma of the Divine Motherhood.

We drove up a switchback road threading through a green mass of densely wooded hills to her house, built eight kilometres from Ephesus in the private bliss of nature. Little bird nests hung in the trees outside. The most unusual story of the discovery of the house, in 1892, is told in a notice.

Labarum, Ephesus

> During the 19th century the book 'Life of the Blessed Virgin' was published in Germany. The material for this book come [sic] from the revelations of a stigmatised nun, Anna Catherina Emmerich. She was an invalid and hat [sic] never left Germany. In her visions she described with amazing accuracy the hills of Ephesus and the house where she saw the Blessed Virgin spending her last years.

Ephesus

Accordingly, two scientific expeditions were organised, and they found this place perfectly agreeing with her description.

The first-century stone house was extensively renovated, and now stands as a shrine for Christians. Quite a number of tourists were there as we walked through the small but solidly constructed home that, without its famous owner, would have been unremarkable. Some were carrying their bibles. A sense of reverence hung in the air, awareness that somehow the essence of Christianity, taught to so many people over so many years, was present in a localised and personal form. No-one spoke inside. The only sound we heard was the call of the birds. Outside the house, a sign placed nearby proclaimed in Turkish "How happy is he who says he is Turkish".

The great Ionian city, where the temple of Artemis captured the imagination of the ancients and where St Paul brought the news of his religious discovery, was a pile of rubble in the middle of the 19th century. Not a stone was in place of the grand temple, the amphitheatre or the gigantic Roman baths. Over the last 100 years, much of this heart of classical culture has been painstakingly restored. Columns have been re-erected, discs pieced together, bricks relaid, and fallen stones identified and reassembled, so that the visitor can sense the life of antiquity.

The work is being accomplished with diligent scholarship, a refreshing

Above: Curetes Street

Below: Library of Celsus

contrast with the crass and amateurish desecration that Sir Arthur Evans inflicted on Cnossos. The pace seems to be accelerating; archaeologists erected four pillars of Hadrian's gate in as many months. The city is rising out of the rubble, each year yielding more definition.

Some argue that restoration is a form of destructive human intervention that cuts short the long process of decay, changing irrevocably the nature of ruins. It substitutes the artificial for the natural, degrading what it touches. However, if sensitively done, as at Ephesus in most (not all) instances, it can serve as an illuminating aid to understanding how our ancestors lived. Without it, enjoyment would be limited to those fortunate enough to have experienced the decay before it had completed its work.

With the fame and restoration come the tourists, thronging the ancient streets as if at a fun fair, masses of them, in shorts, in jeans, in baseball caps, in straw hats, lumpy, skinny, old, young, and all loud, clustering around the points of interest and blotting out the line of sight. Groups with flag-holding tour leaders moved through the site like locusts, obscuring everything until they passed. Others would take their place after only a few moments of relief. We found it best to confine our visits to the early morning and late afternoon.

Sufficient has been restored in Ephesus to allow ordinary visitors to imagine ancient life as they walk over the age-worn stones of sacred Curetes Street, lined with columns and spaces for merchants' stalls. Near the bombastic Roman architecture of the Scholastica Baths, used daily by the populace, is the lofty library of Celsus, its information carved in German – a legacy of the city's archaeological custodians.

The two buildings share a secret: a hidden tunnel that leads from the library to the town brothel, next to the baths. Outside, on the way from the harbour, a girl's face had been carved into a paving stone with an invitation in Greek: "Follow me". Signs commenced where the sailors disembarked, and continued at close enough intervals that even drunks could find their way.

At the other end of the moral spectrum, the secret sign of early Christianity appears on the streets, etched in stone. In order to profess their faith and encourage others at a time when the Roman authorities banned their religion and forced them underground, Christians scratched a design (known as the labarum) that was ostensibly a sundial but could also be read as the four arms of a cross. In later years, the shape may well have led to the cross adopted by the Knights of Malta.

The Odeon, which means 'little theatre', is still in use. Sting put on a rock concert there a few years ago, but the limbic sounds and crush of fans overwhelmed the structure's immune system, causing an 18-month shutdown for repairs. Now, philharmonic concerts offer gentler fare.

Wild poppies (related to the tulip, which originated in Turkey) splotched the fields with red while we were there and the haunting scent of coriander spiced the hot air. Fig trees enticed the unwary with their umbrellas of shade, a lethal danger unseen below – the deadly scorpion often lurks in the nooks and crannies of their exposed roots.

A single lonely column rises to tell the story of the temple of Artemis, known as the Artemisium, seven times destroyed and in its prime one of the seven wonders of the ancient world. A few blocks and fluted column discs remain jumbled on the ground, left over from looters. Early Christians flayed the grand building for materials to make their own architectural statements in the Hagia Sophia at Constantinople and St John Basilica nearby, leaving only the useless bits behind.

In its glory, the temple area was larger than a football field and four times the size of the Parthenon, with marble as its stone. According to legend, an arsonist burned the temple, setting its wooden roofs on fire, on the night of the birth of Alexander the Great. When the Hellenistic warrior came by on his campaign against the Persians, he offered to pay for its reconstruction on the condition he be mentioned alongside Artemis in the dedication. This was close to sacrilege for the pious Ephesians. They declined, with the tactful excuse that one god should not build a temple to another.

In Anatolia, Artemis was a fertility goddess, depicted by rows of eggs or, as some writers claim, bulls' testicles, and by far the dominant religious figure throughout the Ionian world. The Ephesians grew rich from votive offerings brought to the deity.

When St Paul's ministry took him to Ephesus, which was the second largest city in the Roman province of Asia, he sought permission to make a major public speech at the theatre, built for the Dionysian festivals and still intact. So popular had the charismatic orator become that the Roman governor at the time had no choice but to grant permission. Strong word of mouth had created such interest that only the 35,000-seat amphitheatre could accommodate the audience.

Caduceus

However, before the apostle could deliver his message of antimaterialist faith, a silversmith named Demetrius rushed onto the stage and shouted that a conversion to Christianity would mean the demise of trade in silver Artemis images. Stung by the awful reality, the crowd erupted into a feverish chant, "Great is Artemis of the Ephesians", drowning any chance of reply. A riot broke out that spilled into the streets, and St Paul was run out of town, his speech undelivered. The sermon the great proselytiser had intended to give was later inscribed in the New Testament book *Letters to the Ephesians.*

Everywhere in the renowned city, legend mingles with history. A marble frieze rises out of the main street disclosing a caduceus, the herald's wand consisting of a serpent entwined around a staff, associated with Asclepius, the demigod of healing. In early times, the incurably sick were banished, for fear they would infect the healthy population. Legend has it

Pamukkale

that one victim was driven to such despair that he provoked a poisonous snake to bite him, in order to seek relief in death. Instead of gaining his wish, he recovered. From that time on, the serpent has been enshrined as the symbol of medicine.

We had a secure feeling there, a sense that we were close to what was important, a seat of human power and achievement, however distant in action. The patina remained. The relevance of the experience of the past to contemporary life can be disputed, and often is. If we view our times as a self-confident break with the perceived evils of the past, like the Byzantine iconoclasts driven by a reforming zeal, it is tempting to reject all but the postmodern experience. But if, on the other hand, we see ourselves as ineffably connected to our heritage, whether we like it or not, an organic outgrowth from it, with perhaps a genetic memory and certainly a cultural one, these tangible reminders are deeply relevant. They help us understand who we are.

KUŞADASI

Wherever one goes in Turkey, the new sits in attendance on the old. Nearby Ephesus, now several kilometres above the silt plain that has pushed the land into the sea, is the contemporary port of Kuşadasi. Its steep and narrow streets are lined with Ottoman houses, their covered wooden balconies protruding almost far enough to allow an outstretched arm to touch another across the road. Around the harbour crammed with white pleasure craft, amidst the shops selling leather, carpets and everything else that can be sold in a holiday atmosphere, crowds of Turks pushed to the edge of the Asian world and the beginning of the West.

The İmbat, which had blown all day, was increasing its pace, driving the Aegean to assault the breakwater near the restaurant where we had chosen our own fish and were watching it cook on an open fire. The sun, wrapped in a diaphanous fabric, was falling fast behind the Greek island of Samos, which lay offshore like a huge whale, its grey-black hills growing darkly menacing as it changed to silhouette. Far above, a Turkish fighter jet inscribed a white pencil line on its side of the contentious sky. It was alone, no doubt tracked by Greek radar. The sea was clamouring now, its blue waters being whipped to a bad-tempered brown by the İmbat.

HIERAPOLIS

In a two-hour drive inland from Kuşadasi, we reached the magical landscape of Hierapolis. Its name Greek for holy city, Hierapolis was built in Hellenistic times on a site famous since the dawn of history for religious devotion. The Hittites and Phrygians always built their shrines around water sources, and here a large thermal spring created a wonder of nature.

The Meander valley slithers along a tectonic fault system that releases a number of thermal springs, their water rich in calcium salts and carbon dioxide. As the calcareous fluid runs down the valley slopes, calcium precipitates onto them and the carbon dioxide escapes. Over time, the deposits have formed white, fluffy-looking travertine bluffs and terraces that look like cotton. The Turks call them Pamukkale, meaning 'cotton castle'. The thermal spring still flows at a 35-degree temperature and forms pools of blue, therapeutic water trapped on the white terraces. It is popularly believed that relaxing in the waters improves circulatory, neurological and kidney ailments. Rheumatism is eased. And, in good news for drinkers, the waters are said to retard liver enlargement.

The water source is in a deep cleft in the rock called Cin Deligi (Devil's Hole). This fissure, which presents like a cave, was known by the ancients as the road to Hades. It contains such a high concentration of carbon dioxide that no animal life can be supported. The priests of the temple built near the source, however, were miraculous exceptions. Asserting supernatural powers bestowed on them by the gods, they would remain inside the cave for long periods of time, a feat that promoted the shrine to celebrity status. The artful priests did not deem it necessary to disclose the technique they had learned of holding their breath while entering the cave, then breathing the pools of oxygen trapped in the pits within.

Alas, the pressure of tourists and indequate maintenance have caused a tarnishing of the Cotton Castle. It is not what it was even a few years ago.

Near the springs, a Greek theatre links the natural surroundings with the classical age, its beautiful friezes commemorating the birth of Apollo and the myth of Marsyas. Athena made a double flute to imitate the lamentations of the Gorgons for their sister Medusa, decapitated by Perseus the hero of the winged sandals. The vain goddess soon discarded it, placing a curse on the instrument for distorting her face when she played it. A Phrygian youth, Marsyas, picked it up, and learned to control its stops so proficiently that, in a rush of bravado, he challenged Apollo, the divine lyre-player. Although slighted that a mortal presumed to compete with a god, Apollo agreed to a contest, with the nine Muses as judges. Both performed equally well until Apollo, not content with a tie, dared Marsyas to play upside down, a feat possible with a lyre but not so easy with a flute. Apollo won, celebrating the victory by flaying his opponent alive. The luckless mortal's blood formed the river Marsyas.

APHRODISIAS

On a high plain cut by the ancient Meander River lie the fragmented remains of the city built to love, Aphrodisias. As we entered the ancient city dedicated to the cult of Aphrodite, red poppies floated before us in a field of weathered marble sarcophagi, carved in high relief. The art of the classical sculptor is the principal attraction for visitors here. Hundreds of broken friezes scattered throughout the site tell the ancient stories – of the battle of Theseus and the Amazons, of Achilles and Penthesilea, of Heracles freeing Prometheus shackled to the rock for stealing Olympian fire for his fellow mortals.

The local museum houses statuary treasures of the Graeco-Roman world that allow the visitor to meet the people of those days, as though they are still alive. The personality in their faces, the sense of movement and the lifelike flesh (slightly uneven, because of the layer of fat underneath) transport them into our world. The fabrics they wear have a sense of weightlessness – light and delicate, sometimes draped gracefully, sometimes scrunched up – all astonishingly realistic. Some of these were the people you might have seen at the Odeon, in the marble seats carved with dolphins, or officiating at the temple of Aphrodite.

İZMIR

From the Meander plateau, we drove our hire car to İzmir, formerly the wealthy Ionian city of Smyrna, on the Aegean coast. When we got to the outskirts, there seemed to be no signs to guide us into the city centre. We had to navigate by guesswork, and asking people on the roadside for directions in sign language, but got hopelessly lost. A service station appeared on one of the streets we blundered into. I drove in, got out of the car and went into the office. A customer with a fierce black moustache and square chin was paying his bill. Another man was behind the cash register. I asked how to get into downtown İzmir and to our hotel, by pointing to a map. The customer understood what I wanted and began to speak in Turkish, presumably giving directions. He soon realised I did not comprehend and asked me if I was driving a car by making the sign of steering. I nodded my head.

Abruptly he motioned for me to come with him outside. I did, not knowing what he had in mind. He then got into his car and indicated that we should follow him. Leading us through a plethora of turns in dense traffic for 20 minutes, he guided us to the hotel, then drove off with a wave and a smile. It was the same generosity we had experienced from the Greek fellow in Athens.

ISTANBUL

We didn't stay long in İzmir, for it is a crowded industrial city that has forsaken its ancient charm. Instead, we returned to Istanbul and spent more time walking around Sultanahmet and the Galata Bridge. The Bosphorus' slack, shiny waters drew a loquacious, thronging human tide to its shores. It was exciting just to drift along, watch the men pull out small fish with their long lines hanging from the bridge, see the fresh-food stalls laden with reds and greens and silvers, and look out over the busy waterway at the boats, some for pleasure but most carrying some kind of produce. Further off sat the rusty freighters and tankers, the city's main commercial lifeline, connecting Istanbul with even more exotic places.

That night we had dinner on the balcony of a restaurant on the European side, overlooking the Bosphorus. Turkish cuisine is among the finest in the world, refined over centuries by Ottoman chefs to a sophisticated collage of flavours. Roast lamb with garlic and cumin, derived from nomadic tradition, was one or our favourites. Sometimes it is cooked and served in a table oven called a tander, cousin of the tandoor used in Indian Moghul cooking.

Across the water's edge, we watched the evening action of the Bosphorus and its populous shores. As darkness rolled into the streets, lights came on serially to illuminate the mosques in the mist that clung to the city like a thick, porous skin. Their domes ruled the horizon, speaking of strength, durability, invincibility. Staked alongside, their slender minarets added a sense of precision and the security of limits. Listless waves lapped up against a white, high-gloss marble terrace below that held back the sea. Cargo ships, black in the gathering night, slowly passed in front of us, some to the Black Sea and some towards the Mediterranean, their presence disclosed only by mast lights high above the water, ghostly, without form. A slender moon rose delicately on the Asian side, and stars peeked out through the mist, which gradually slipped away as the balmy night crept in.

Many of the ships, we knew, came across the Black Sea from Russia, their captains cranky these days from the spaghetti of red tape served up by the Turkish authorities. Still frustrated by its lack of a blue-water port, Russia is seeking to negotiate some sharing of control of the Bosphorus with the Turks. Guaranteed access to the European sea has historically been a centrepiece of Russian foreign policy

and the source of frequent military conflict with Turkey. The only practical way is through the Bosphorus; the straits of Gibraltar are too remote. For years after the Second World War, Britain and the United States were blind to these designs, but when understanding dawned at the US State Department, the negative reaction made the Cold War inevitable.

That factor alone (whose importance transcends the collapse of the Soviet Union and Western investment in the stability of Russia) is enough to ensure the geopolitical importance of Turkey to the West, although there are others. Its role in providing bases on its territory for Western alliance air power is viewed as a vital contribution to the campaign for disciplining the rogue regime of Saddam Hussein in Iraq. Nevertheless, however strategically compelling the need for it, the West does not find understanding its major Balkan ally an easy task.

We are in an age where democracy and human rights, and their affiliate concern for the environment, are the driving paradigms for ordering society. While these ideas, which have a quasi-religious overtone, have preoccupied intellectuals and activists for a few decades in Western countries where the ideas have taken root, in other nations the process has barely begun. Turkey is one of these.

The major political figures in Turkey today are not impassioned by the ideals of democracy. Indeed, while a multiparty system with free elections underlies the government, the traditions of exercising power have stemmed more from an authoritarian than a participatory base. Turks are brought up to be respectful of authority, even to the point of passivity, and to submit to accepted conventions at the expense of individual initiative.

Atatürk, the father of the Turkish State and a figure so revered that it is an offence punishable by imprisonment to insult his name, was a nationalist and secularist, not a democrat. He ruled with an iron hand. His legacy is still the main guide to political thinking in Turkey. The political Islamists, who propose a government based on the principals of the *Koran*, look to the authority of their leaders, not the people, to translate them into policy. The anchorman in Turkish politics is still the army, the force that can be counted on to step in when weak governments fail the State. Indeed, in 1999, Turkey's Chief of General Staff was acting as de facto foreign minister, visiting Turkey's neighbours to deliver messages of State policy. A senior general explained the move in the *Turkish Daily News*:

> None of us are [sic] willing to take control of this country or to become involved in politics. But while some bodies within the Turkish government are in a continuing state of ignorance and negligence, we have no other option. This should not be seen as the Turkish military becoming overly involved in Turkish politics or pressuring politicians. Everybody should understand the Turkish military's sensitivity on Turkey's interests both at home and abroad. Of course we respect the Constitution and the laws by which we receive our responsibility and power. We are always willing to cooperate with governments that are sincerely working. But there are vital issues for us on which we cannot make any concession.

Notwithstanding the differences with the West in style and practice, Turkey is still a democracy and is likely to remain so. Some think that transparency in the political decision-making process, which underlies the Western version of democracy, could increase over time as a result of the breaking of the monopoly on television held by the State-owned Turkish Radio Television Corporation. In 1990, the government privatised television, and Turkey now has about 16 local and national stations, together with a cable network.

Human rights are an issue constantly raised about Turkey, often to the irritation of Turks, who sometimes suspect Western protestations to be the trappings of self-interest. Nevertheless, demons of the massacres of the Armenians in the 1890s and 1920 and of the Slavs in the Balkans need to be exorcised. Liberal opinion in the West is still influenced by William Gladstone's treatise *The Bulgarian Horror and the Question of the East*, an impassioned account of Turkish suppression of a Serbian inspired pan-Slavic revolt that spread to Bulgaria in 1876. The plight of the 12 million Kurds who live in southeastern Turkey burst to international attention with the arrest of Abdullah Ocalan, the charismatic but murderous leader of the PKK, the Marxist-Leninist Kurdistan Workers' Party. And the internal legal framework in Turkey is marred by brutal police practices at times and by malleable judges.

One of the great historical events witnessed by our age is the resurgence of Islam. It is a revival of Islamic precepts that may take different forms throughout Muslim societies, but it is one that resonates with the natural aspirations of over a billion people worldwide. In Turkey, where 99 per cent of the population is Muslim, the State pays the salaries of 60,000 imams. Despite the determined secularism of the Atatürk legacy, a plurality of over 20 per cent lifted Necmettin Erbakan's Welfare Party to government on 28 June 1998. While much of the support for the party came from the peasants, long neglected by the modern economy, and the poorer urban dwellers seduced by food handouts, members of the business community were impressed enough with its programme to join the ranks. Kemalists may brand the Islamic movement reactionary and old-fashioned, but its leadership has taken pains to embrace science and technology within the arms of the faith.

Erbakan's peaceful revolution of Turkish politics did not last long. While a moderate by most definitions, certainly a lot more so than some members of the Islamic movement, his attempts to put more Islamic colour into the government alarmed the Kemalists and their guardian, the army. Erbakan was

Clockwise from top: Dolphin Seat;
statue, Aphrodisias; Artemis

removed from office and his Welfare Party banned. Although the Islamists are out of office, they have regrouped under the banner of the newly formed Virtue Party, and still represent about a fifth of the popular vote.

In the midst of the political confusion swirling around weak governments, nostalgic calls to Atatürk ideals and rising Islamic fundamentalism, Turkish society is changing inexorably. More openness and freedom are casting their allure, the benefits of modern technology are seeping into the economy and a resurgent Islam is refocussing attention onto the moral and social precepts of the *Koran*. But still, the eagle has two heads.

The politicisation of Islam in Turkey has raised fears in the West of a trend towards the fundamentalism seen in Iran, Algeria and Afghanistan. But while a violence-prone extremist brand of fundamentalism does exist in Turkey, most opinion flows along the more peaceful course of reviving Islamic morals and social customs. Even among Islamist politicians, voices speak for a liberal attitude favouring adoption of modern economic management and the separation of religion from the workings of the State.

In the early 1990s, a wave of fundamentalist violence erupted, with the murders of a number of intellectual celebrities who promoted secularism.

The car bombs and shootings aroused the nation to grief and anger amidst apprehension that Turkey could turn radical. After years of failure to solve the crimes, the terrorist responsible was arrested. He admitted that Iranian diplomats were his accomplices, providing him with weapons and arranging for him to be trained in Iran. A new frost descended on relations between the two States, who for centuries have vied for leadership of Islam.

The differences between the nations are vast. Turkey belongs to the Ural-Altaic linguistic group, Iran to the Indo-European. Iranians are Aryans, while Turks, romantically at least, see themselves as part of the Turkic ethnic group. Turkey, while torn, has an eye on the West and even has aspirations to join the European Union. Its involvement in the international revival of Islam is informed by a liberal approach that accommodates modern economic paradigms. On the other hand, Iran is the world leader of a fundamentalist and theocratic interpretation of Mohammed's vision. Our next trip was to that country.

If there is to be a crescendo to the clash between the West and Islam, the conductor will be found in Iran. It is a country that seeks more than any other to define its identity by vilification of what it sees as moral decay in the West. This draws it to a harder sound, yet we had no idea what to expect, nor even how safe it was for Western travellers.

Part III
IRAN

Shrine of Ayatollah Khomeini

PART

III

Chapter 9

The Puritan Phoenix

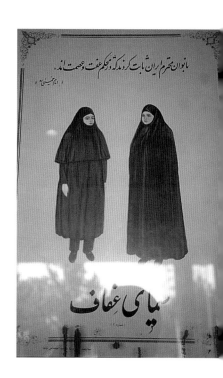

In Iran, all women must wear the hejab, which means 'covering up' in Arabic. In that severe and fundamentalist country, phobic about sexual attraction, the whole female body must be obscured, apart from the face and hands. This is not just a custom; it is the law. There are no exceptions. A busload of sought-after European tourists was turned away at the border because the women on board used scarves to fake the hejab.

On our way to Iran, we stopped at Damascus to buy the sartorial passport for Anna-Maryke. We found a wide choice in the souk and purchased a long black one with a hood. In a gesture of individuality, Anna-Maryke selected a garment with some embroidery, in black thread and discreet enough to pass muster. At first she was amused; it was an adventure to take on an exotic fashion. There was no pretence or awkwardness, as is the case sometimes when Western women wear Eastern clothes such as the sari. It had to be done, whether or not it suited her complexion.

Security police, known as Najas (successors to the infamous Komite), patrol the streets looking for women who are not Islamically dressed. Offenders are thrown into jail overnight. The chador, a formless black shroud, is symbolic of extreme piety, but a long drab coat with bulky shoulder pads, disguising anything recognisably feminine in the figure, is acceptable. So obsessed are the authorities with preventing titillation and salacious thoughts that women must wear the hejab even while swimming or water-skiing. Men, however, are allowed to go into the water in normal bathing suits. Some one told us that, "Iran is the only place in the world where women watch men swim from a hidden place".

The Damascus airport was like most Middle East gathering points – full of relaxed, loquacious people bustling around in a happy chaos, creating a good deal of noise. But it had a distinction. We asked where we were supposed to check in for Teheran and were pointed in the direction of an alcove reserved for

Iranians. The atmosphere there was so different from that of the rest of the airport that the scene almost seemed staged, a pantomime of slightly unnerving characters.

Instead of easygoing Syrians, most dressed in Western clothes, black-clad women were sitting on the floor like heaps of coal, their hand luggage piled untidily around them. Silence, brushed by low whispers, hung in the air. The women kept adjusting their scarves, which seemed to be constantly falling down, threatening to expose their hair. They fussed with their garments nonchalantly, possibly not even aware of the action. No smiles broke their serious comportment. Men were there, but seemed out of place, separate, not part of the community in black. They didn't talk much; when they did, it was in low tones and to each other. Their dress was less unusual than that of the women – shirts and slacks in dark colours, though not always black. Some individuality in style and colour seemed to be allowed, within the bounds of strict propriety – long sleeves and long pants, certainly no shorts.

As we approached the check-in counter, Iranian passengers crowded around, stumbling over the baggage strewn everywhere. There seemed to be more women than men. Perhaps it was because of the uniform clothing they wore. We noticed girls who looked no more than 10 years old in the garb. It seemed incongruous to see children skipping happily across the travertine floor of the airport dressed so sombrely.

All the check-in staff were men. One motioned for us to move four counters to the right. We struggled through the obstacle course, past Islamically dressed women pressing determinedly forward with expressionless faces. Others were covered completely, forced to peer out at the world through the black material hanging over their faces. The staff ordered them back; that held them at bay for a while, but

soon they started again, a sea of black surging towards the check-in counter. I noticed the hands of a particularly aggressive female, the skin mottled with healed-over burns, perhaps from the war with Iraq. I wondered what they were thinking, all these women, so clearly alien.

The men looked hard and tough, some with black moustaches, most with an ominous stubble of beard. None was overweight. They seemed in shape, capable of putting up a determined fight. Like that of the women, their demeanour was serious and alert. They seemed so different from the Syrians, who were lubricous and relaxed and very often portly. Among the Iranians, we saw plenty of mullahs, with beards and white turbans, and imams, distinguished by their black headgear. They looked like they leaned more to the fire and brimstone end of religion than to the compassionate.

I could not help thinking about the press coverage in the West about ruthless hatreds and terrorist atrocities fomented by Iran, and wondered what was in store for us once we had left the relative safety of Damascus.

Half an hour after our Iran Air flight was scheduled to depart, passengers were still alighting from the aircraft – Iranians from Teheran carrying huge amounts of hand baggage, cardboard boxes, picnic baskets, thermos flasks, blankets, plastic bags so heavily laden they had to be dragged along the floor, and carpets. Iranians often bring carpets into Syria, where they sell them in the souk for less than they cost in Teheran. Since citizens are forbidden to take money out of the country, this is a good way to pay for their trip.

We embarked an hour and a half late, ushered on board by female flight attendants wearing black scarves and dressed in baggy black coats with brass buttons and rank rings on the cuffs. They looked fierce, certainly not women to cross. After we were seated, a video came on, a voice intoning: "In the name of Allah, the all-merciful, we welcome you to the airline of the Islamic Republic of Iran". A deep baritone voice recited a poem in Farsi while pictures of flowers marred with static snow flickered on the screen. The lights went out on our side of the cabin. On the other side of the plane, we could see the black shapes of the women sitting quietly in their seats.

Iran is a nation of bewildering contradictions. It governs itself according to the precepts of the *Koran*, an essentially peaceful revelation, yet is notorious as the boiler room of world terrorism. It insists on puritanical social standards, yet tolerates economic corruption. Public comportment rigidly conforms to the strictest interpretation of the Sharia, yet private behaviour often ignores the more inconvenient restrictions. People in Iran say the contradictions are melded into a tolerable modus vivendi through the timeless Asian reagent of compromise. An acceptance of fate also helps them to cope. In Iran, as in all Islamic countries, we constantly heard the phrase 'inshallah' (meaning 'God willing'), which is often said after making a commitment to do something – it removes the anxiety.

If the reason some societies reach the peak of civilisation's mountain only to slide down the other side is an unsolved mystery, what propels them to make another ascent is even more of a conundrum. The feat is rare but not unique. Hamitic Egypt reascended twice after its seminal Old Kingdom fell.

The glorious Sassanid dynasty of Iran, founded by Ardashir in the third century AD, rescaled the heights vacated 500 years before when the celebrated Achaemenid Empire slumped under the phalanxes of Alexander the Great. Can the Iranians do it again? If they do, the whole Middle East will rumble, along with the reservoir that contains half the world's known reserves of oil. Some time ago, the British said Persia had played out its hand – but that was before the 1979 revolution.

Geostrategically placed for expansion, Iran has a population of 70 million (60 per cent teenagers or younger) living on a land mass nearly twice the size of France and Germany combined. A significant oil producer, Iran has recently discovered natural-gas reserves that represent 25 per cent of the world's total, second only to those of the CIS (the remnant of the former Soviet Union).

TEHERAN

When we got off the flight in Teheran, at midnight, the airport was chaotic, like a Tokyo subway station at rush hour. Dark shapes jostled each other in seething confusion as people sought to get ahead of each other at the immigration desk. No effort was made to form a queue. We could not read the signs, which were written in Arabic, language of the Prophet. Atatürk introduced Roman lettering to the Turks in order to reinforce his secular message; Iran adheres to Arabic for the opposite reason. A porter I didn't see elbowed me roughly out of the way, taking charge of our baggage trolley. I didn't like it much but let him guide us though the mêlée to a taxi. It was late and we were tired.

As we emerged into the hot penumbra outside, the crowd suddenly thinned. The porter manoeuvred the trolley towards an unmarked car, which he indicated was a taxi, parked in dark isolation. We were a little apprehensive, but climbed into the back anyway. The front doors burst open, and two huge thugs with three days' black stubble stuck their heads in the car, one from each side. Pointing at me belligerently, the one on the passenger's side roared: "You pay now!".

My objection infuriated him. Clenching his fist, he demanded 50 American dollars for the trip. I refused, fear beginning to pump adrenalin. We were in the car, luggage on board, on our first visit in Iran.

It was well after midnight and we could see no-one around.

I decided the best approach was to claim I had been in Teheran before and knew what the rate was. I offered 10 dollars. He angrily rejected this, but moved to 40. I felt relieved; at least the move to bargaining meant he was not inclined to rob us. We haggled, shouting at each other in the vacant night for five minutes. At the rial equivalent of 18 dollars, and with an expletive of disgust, he grabbed the notes I put on the front seat and slammed the door.

The driver started the car and drove out of the airport without a word. After travelling along an unlit highway for a long time, he took a turn onto a road leading away from the city lights, an alarming direction given our recent treatment. As the wild darkness enveloped our vehicle, lurid thoughts of ransom demands and remote farmhouses ran through my mind. Outside, it was as bleak as a foreign language you don't understand. My palms were sweating.

Just when I was considering whether to grab the steering wheel and force the car into a ditch, the driver turned off the road towards a group of buildings that included the hotel. I relaxed abruptly, realising how conditioned I had been by my Western image of Iran. The driver had merely taken us on a circuitous route to justify charging us more than the normal fare. It can happen anywhere. As it turned out, that was the only occasion on which we experienced any discourtesy or felt ourselves in any danger while visiting Iran.

From the perspective of the West, particularly the United States, the tumultuous Iranian revolution of 1979 cast a chilling shadow across the world. Not since the Cold War had there been such a perception of threat to the inheritors of the Western Enlightenment. It radiated instantly to the deepest level of social consciousness, well below the observation of the events, shocking though they were. Without doubt, the seizure of American hostages in Teheran, by Iranian students retaliating against President Carter's having allowed the hated Shah to escape to the United States for medical treatment, fanned the flames of the drama. The image of innocence abused for alien political objectives played into the culture of television demagoguery launched during the Vietnam War, by then the defining element of public communication in the West. But even more compelling emotions were being stirred in the hearts of the American people, emotions that would outlast memories of the outrageous treatment of their citizens. A successor to the Soviet enemy seemed to be rising out of the struggle with the 'evil empire': an Islam led by Iran. In an implicit reference to Greek perceptions of civilisation, the headline "The New Barbarians are loose in Iran" appeared in an American newspaper at the time.

Many people felt that the assault on the United States embassy in Teheran amounted to an act of war. In a war, the need to strengthen resolve often takes the form of reducing natural sympathy for fellow human beings through demonising the enemy. Images of hate-infused fanatics lusting for the blood of Westerners and absolved from all moral compunction by the jihad are rejected by most Americans as unrealistic but, so powerful is the language often used in the West that the slightest pressure of events can lead to an involuntary acceptance of them, if only for an instant. We were to learn, not surprisingly, that the same process of demonisation occurs in Iran. It is quite eerie to see it from the other side.

Iran is the world's only true theocracy, in the sense that clergy run the government, among the few that have appeared since the ancient world. Savonarola imposed one on Florence, but it didn't last long. Reflecting lower middle-class discontent

with the licentious plutocracy of the Shah, the ascetic
and charismatic Ayatollah Khomeini installed an
Islamic republic after the revolution, austere and
sacerdotal. Until recently, the majority of members of
the majlis (parliament), including the president,
were mullahs. All government policies are correlated
with divine decrees as interpreted by the Supreme
Leader, the successor of Ayatollah Khomeini. Legislation passed by the majlis must be approved by the
Council of the Guardians of the Constitution before
it becomes law.

Najas

Elections are free, giving meaning to the political
process, but only prequalified candidates can run.
Liberals who wish to remove some of the more
extreme restrictions on personal freedom have had
recent electoral success, but their efforts have been
largely contained by the impregnable dam of the
system. Essentially, the principles of the *Koran* as
interpreted through the prism of fundamentalism
form the character of the nation. It is sombre and
puritanical. People turn to Mecca in orison five times
a day. On Fridays, the mosques are full. Over 90 per
cent of the population actively practise their religion.

In Teheran's streets, public demeanour is dour
and restrained. Large crowds are quiet and discreet;
no peals of laughter shatter the composure. Women glide past demurely in the
hejab, eyes modest. The feeling that one has to behave is ever present. Whenever we went out, I felt a certain tightness, as though Anna-Maryke and I were
being observed with a judgmental eye.

On the other hand, family ties are close, meeting emotional needs far more
effectively than could a therapist and providing private control over most
aberrant behaviour. The family is enshrined in the constitution as the fundamental unit of Islamic society. Rape is practically unknown. Women can
walk anywhere, day or night, and feel safe. Standards of civility are far higher
than in the West. More than once, I heard people express the deep satisfaction
that comes from helping others. This benign attitude is in sharp contrast with
the treatment one can expect at the hands of the authorities for conduct
deemed subversive to the State.

As soon as we arrived in Teheran, I sensed that we were witnessing one of

Martyrs

the extraordinary events of history: the rebirth of a nation that had been consumed by the fires of decadence, a renewal akin to the rise of the phoenix, mythical bird of Arabia.

Like all puritanical societies, contemporary Iran pays little regard to the aesthetic dimension. Modern Teheran is no sanctuary of beauty. The morning sun from our lofty hotel window shone wanly on a utilitarian metropolis of medium height, powdery beige and sooty grey, quite Soviet-like. A dark vapour concocted from fumes and dust hung on the horizon like a chador and draped itself over the Alborz Mountains, which ring the city and create temperature inversions. Cranes stooped over unfinished apartment buildings, signalling that the population, at well over 10 million, is proliferating without surcease. Not all was functional drab, however. Leafy patches proclaimed the love Iranians have for green space, so spiritually felt that their ancient progenitors conceived of heaven as a park, their word for it entering English as 'paradise'.

One day we went for a three-hour stroll downtown. Walking is arguably the best way to get the feel of a city, unless it is Los Angeles. The streets of Teheran are imperially wide and clean, but the pollution is insufferable. By afternoon our eyes were smarting. On bad days, radio warnings are broadcast for people with respiratory conditions.

No commercial billboards crowd the urban landscape. The only large signs we saw were inspirational calls to duty. On one, a soldier was praying to Mecca beside an arch of sandbags, against which he had rested his M4 rifle. Shop signs are discreet and devoid of images. The lettering is Arabic, although Farsi, an Indo-European language, is the spoken tongue.

It seemed somewhat clean and wholesome to be devoid of the Western-style outside advertising that can become such visual pollution at times. But even though the messages in Teheran were not commercial, the billboards were actually selling something – the propaganda of the State. In that sense, they were just as bad, perhaps even a little more invasive, for one can ignore a commercial sign without a pang of conscience. But at least there were only a few.

The predominant ethnic group is not Arabic but Aryan, the race that gives its name to the country. However, the language of the Prophet is taught in the schools, and to a much higher level of competence than was the case under the Shah. No food or drink is on sale in public places; it is necessary to go to a proper restaurant or eat at home. Playgrounds and parks are plentiful and well patronised by all ages. People dress within tight conventions: women in the hejab and men in long-sleeved shirts, usually white, and dark slacks, baggy at the knees for teenage boys and young men. We were impressed by how much healthier these teenagers looked than many of their counterparts in the West. So rare are Westerners in Iran that people would come up to us to ask where we were from. A few stared at us with a curiosity informed by a little hostility. Children gathered around Anna-Maryke, noticing in a flash that she looked different even though covered by the hejab.

By the 19th century, European expansion had forced Iran and its fellow Muslim countries into a defensive corner. The balance of power had shifted dramatically to the West from Islam, which had held it during the Middle Ages and for a few centuries thereafter. Europe was on the rise, while Islamic countries, including Iran, were trapped in the mud, unable to find a way forward. The economic and political ambitions of Britain, France and Russia drove the international agenda and constantly threatened the stability of the East. Ascendant technology and its accompanying social ideas undermined traditional culture and its reliance on faith. In the West, religion as the main guiding principle of society had been in a long-term decline since the fateful confrontation between science and Church in the late Renaissance. Now, the Western horse of secularism, technological progress riding on its back, was threatening to trample the sacred fields of Islamic faith.

Even though Iranians retained the power to form and operate their own governments, British and then American hegemony drained the fluids of national pride in an exploitation that lasted for more than a century. Western colonialism was seen by many as a reprise of the Crusades, another assault on

their faith. Indeed, their civilisation's foreign-provoked material crisis was perceived to have a spiritual manifestation: somehow, the community of Islam had strayed from the straight path enjoined by the *Koran*. A malaise of the soul was weakening the people of the Prophet.

The reawakening of Iranian society belongs to a worldwide revival of Islam that is sublimating a chafing discontent with foreign hegemony. Initially, the dissatisfaction was expressed not through religion but in a movement of secular nationalism. The people renamed their country Iran, in order to cleanse the stain of imperialism carried by the name 'Persia', which had been used by the British. Secularism set the stage for technological benefits to flow from the West, but it also paved the way for foreign influences to corrode traditional culture and infect people with a spiritual angst. Delivery of the promised economic benefits, which was to be facilitated by the downplaying of religion, passed most people by, leaving them in bemused confusion. They knew they had lost something that had comforted their hard lives, but sensed that the touted substitute was going not to them but to the powerful instead.

While mobilised largely by Toynbeean challenge and response, the contemporary revival is sourced in the depths of Islamic history. Many times in the past, leaders have emerged out of the Islamic community's realisation of the need to rebuild its strength by setting a course for reform. The trigger was always the same – a diagnosis of extreme political, economic and military weakness within the Islamic world perceived to be caused by an atrophy of moral sinew.

To Muslims, this meant a straying from the straight path, and the remedy was a return to the fundamental principles of the *Koran*. All the movements were aimed at the moral reconstruction of society and were strict and uncompromising. Since, essentially, they were reacting to a laxness informed by hedonism, they could gain success not by incremental degrees based on reasoned argument but only by messianic fervour expressed in some form of moral coercion. In that, they were not dissimilar to the forces that led the Protestant Reformation. Indeed, the uncompromising Iranian teacher Jamal al-Din al-Afgani, who sounded the harsh clarion call for an Islamic revival to counter foreign imperialism in the second half of the 19th century, dreamed of a Martin Luther equivalent for Islam.

Muslims speak of the 'five pillars' of Islam, the fundamental precepts that define the religion, and give it the three dimensions that make it a complete way of life: spiritual, legal and cultural. The first pillar is the creed of the shahada: "There is no God but God and Mohammed is the Prophet of God". Indeed, the word 'Islam' means 'submission to God'. The system of belief extends from that fundamental tenet to cover the other revelations in the *Koran*, some of the more important of which are the role of the prophets and the angels, and the last day, on which all will be judged.

The other pillars are prayer five times a day, the giving of alms to the poor and needy, fasting during the ninth month of the lunar year (Ramadan), and performing the haj (pilgrimage to Mecca) at least once in a lifetime, subject to means. The exhortation to jihad, or holy war, while not a pillar, is only marginally less important. The word 'jihad' means 'struggle' and has the connotation of a worthy purpose. It has come to express, in religious terms, the internal struggle against one's evil instincts. In the historical context of the *Koran*, however, it means armed struggle against unbelievers. Its origins are in the conflicts of the pre-Islamic Arabian tribes whose normal state was war. While all wars between tribes were lawful, a defensive war was placed on a higher moral plane. The *Koran* exhorts believers to use force to defend their faith:

Permission to take up arms is hereby given to those who are attacked because they have been wronged. God has power to grant them victory, those who have been unjustly driven from their homes only because they have said, 'Our Lord is God'.

The early days of Islam bristled with armed battles. Mohammed was a general as well as a religious leader, in the forefront of military defeats and victories, the first practitioner of jihad. The triumphs of the Arab armies in the great expansion of Islam after the Prophet's death were inspired by the doctrine, which was by then interpreted to mean that the entire Islamic community had a duty to expand the territory that was blessed by the newly revealed truth. After the conquests ran their course and Islam settled down to relatively stable borders, legal spokesmen developed the rubric that, in order to maintain the spirit of jihad, the caliph was required to mount a raid into enemy territory at least once a year. The task could be delegated to an individual or a group of individuals appointed by the caliph to carry out the incursion. In other cases, people could assume the duty of jihad merely by taking an oath to fight unbelievers.

Although soft alternatives to the aggressive mode were developed over time, Muslims have always been obliged to join a jihad where Islam is under attack, a duty that places them on the high moral plane reserved for the defensive war.

Opposite a square in downtown Teheran, we saw a banner on top of a long cord strung like a clothesline, from which hung photographs of soldiers. This commemorated the anniversary of the surprise Iraqi attack on oil-rich southern Iran that started the eight-year 'imposed war'. The conflict ended in a stalemate peace, brokered by the United Nations, with no change in territory. Notwithstanding, it is hailed as a patriotic victory in Iran, since the invader was hurled from Iranian land after a bitter struggle. It is ironic that Iraq was once part of Iran, during one of

Martyr

its golden ages. The capital of the Sassanid empire was situated there, in Ctesiphon.

The banner spoke of Iranian casualties, which were enormous:

> Our martyrs are alive and consciously present. They are paradigms for action, witness to right and wrong and to Man's destiny.
> Ramezan Kani, a martyr of the Revolutionary Guards (Place of Martyrdom, Kounin Shar)

We had come to Iran in the middle of Sacred Defence week, a celebration of what was deemed to be an Islamic victory, notwithstanding that it was over fellow Muslims. The photographs were all of 'martyrs' who had fallen as witnesses to Allah's will. Estimates vary, but the number of fatalities mentioned can be up to a million – a chilling number in absolute terms but staggering relative to the 48 million population at the time. Virtually no family escaped bereavement.

Wave after wave of troops, led by yelling mullahs, crashed up against modern Iraqi weaponry, supplied by the West in an attempt to help the regime of Saddam Hussein (suspect though it was) counter a resurgent Iran. Caught unprepared and denied access to sophisticated arms, the Iranians fell back on manpower and motivation.

Troop strength was multiplied by basijis, volunteers who leapt into battle after 15 days' training. The government likes to cite the valour and sacrifice of Hussain Fahmideh, who destroyed an attacking Iraqi tank by diving underneath it, hand grenades strapped around his waist. He was 12 years old.

People we met, some of whom served at the front, told us how officers, lacking appropriate equipment, used teenage boys to blow up the mines with their young bodies. Platoons of hundreds were sent out as minesweepers in front of Iranian attacks. Around their necks hung little army-issue keys, to open the gates of heaven after they had performed their sacred immolation. These were not isolated instances; the slaughter was sanctioned by the high command, mature men in senior positions.

The fervour of self-sacrifice displayed by the Iranians in that war belongs to a state of mind that has disappeared from the West, a religiosity not evident among its people since the Crusades. A pacifist orientation of thought, in the sense of an essential abhorrence of war as a means of resolving human disputes, has been growing in the West, albeit with some notable setbacks, since the Napoleonic Wars, the first occasion where weapons of mass destruction concentrated the mind on the notion of an unacceptable level of casualties. Indeed, Western societies today will not tolerate their governments allowing more than a few hundred fatalities before protests and calls for a negotiated termination of hostilities arise.

In Iran, the traditions of the people and the concept of the jihad propel philosophical orientation in the opposite direction. The fervent belief in an afterworld, a paradise, for the virtuous and the lionisation of 'martyrs' who give their lives for the cause open the way for a glorification of the noble aspects of human nature that can emerge out of armed struggle. In the West, particularly in the last 30 years, literature and the media tend to downplay military heroism, in an attempt to deglorify war. Certainly, the number of antiwar films that have emerged indicates that our concentration is on the folly rather than the benefit of war. Not so in Iran, nor is it likely to be, for Iranians are trying to rebuild their society in what they perceive as a hostile world. To do that, they need military strength at a level higher than they can now muster. Their economic backwardness and their isolation from the main sources of military technology require them to rely more on fighting a war than on managing it with sophisticated weaponry. The success they achieved against the Iraqi invader vindicated such an approach.

It seems to me that part of the antagonism felt towards Iran, especially in the United States, could stem from this different orientation towards war. A revulsion, even a type of derision, is provoked by stories of mass-suicide charges by Iranian troops against superior weapons. The belief in paradise and self-sacrifice is ridiculed. But many people are not comfortable with the dismissive approach, for underneath lurks a fear of the sheer human power of that commitment, an involuntary admiration for the courage, albeit spiritually fuelled, that these men showed. A source of strength lies somewhere on that plane, and not a few wonder whether some of it is dissipating from our comfortable Western societies. Reliance on technology, driven to ever more sophistication by our scientific advances, does provide a protective shield, but is it enough?

Iranians belong to the minority Shi'a sect that

emerged out of civil war within the Muslim community after Mohammed's death, in 632 AD. The followers of 'Ali, the Prophet's cousin and son-in-law, mounted a coup during the reign of the third caliph and installed their man. They believed that the rightful leadership of Islam should go to a descendent of the Prophet, who would be called imam, a leader with special religious status. The majority Sunni sect disagreed, claiming that since Mohammed had not explicitly designated a successor, the choice of leader should not be so restricted. 'Ali was assassinated, plunging the young Islamic community into 30 years of internecine strife. 'Ali's younger son, Ḥusayn, fomented a revolt against the Umayyad caliph, who was part of the Sunni establishment, and fought to the death alongside his 72 loyal revolutionaries on the plains of Karbala, in what is now Iraq. The massacre imbued the Shiites with a passionate devotion to self-sacrifice in the name of martyrdom and to death-defying resistance of unjust authority. An acute sensitivity to persecution is a defining characteristic of Iranians.

In Moharram, the month of mourning, hordes of Iranian men parade through the streets beating their chests rhythmically, chanting, "Karbala, we are coming" in an atavistic solidarity with Ḥusayn and his martyrs. The emotion generated by the thudding blows and shouted mantra goes beyond the words and into the very depths of the soul, into the dark chamber where the instinct to kill lurks. Throughout Iran, both urban and rural, local people put on plays that re-enact the high drama of Ḥusayn's rebellion and martyrdom. Heroes and villains struggle in a passionate metaphor for the eternal battle between good and evil, a duel first formalised in philosophical thought by Zoroastrianism, the ancient religion of the Persians.

To get a feel for weekend public life in Teheran, we took a taxi on a long, rambling jaunt to Ayatollah Khomeini's shrine. So inspiring was the founder of the Iranian revolution that an estimated 10 million people attended his obituaries – said to be the largest funeral in history. Recently built on the outskirts of the city, the shrine sits infelicitously near a natural-gas processing plant flanked by electricity pylons. It is a huge community centre, almost as vast as Tiananmen Square, built in the form of a mosque, with extensive outside spaces delimited by several middle-market hotels that belong to the complex. Four minarets, one built each year since Khomeini's death, stake out the plaza. The unprepossessing style of the shrine derives from the petite bourgeoisie, the dominant element in contemporary Iranian society and the one represented in government. It is still being developed, but the authorities intend to expand this into one of the largest Islamic building complexes of the modern era.

Anna-Maryke and I entered the shrine separately, through the male and female entrances; gender apartheid is standard in Iran, even in airports. At ski resorts, a husband and wife may not even ride in a chairlift together.

Inside, about 2000 people milled around discreetly in a space so wide that even that many people were scattered sparsely. The floor was of white marble, shining as slickly as ice in the artificial light, which splashed down from crystal chandeliers hanging directly overhead. A jumbo dome painted with a huge garish tulip capped the hall in a hue of red. The place looked like a gigantic skating rink, but freely available *Korans* made it clear that we were in a house of God. From a gargantuan picture imperiously high on the wall, the fierce Ayatollah kept a disciplinarian's eye on the host below.

Some visitors chatted quietly in small groups, others walked around in silence. Quite a few were sleeping by the pillars or just resting on their backs. Random clumps of men were hunched over on rugs

Shrine of Ayatollah
Khomeini

oriented towards Mecca, ticking off prayers with their beads. It is not that the
women are less pious; they pray at home. Brightly clothed children ran around,
chasing one another, sliding down the high-gloss marble ramps, shouting and
giggling, their black-garbed mothers content to let them behave as children.
Reverence combined with relaxation. A strong sense of community was obvious; not the slightest incivility jarred the atmosphere. People spoke quietly
and moved slowly, with dignity. The main sound came from the children.
All the while, unarmed soldiers sauntered aimlessly among the hoi polloi, a
reminder that standards of appropriate behaviour could be enforced.

The government controls the media and is determined to block undesirable
outside influences. Foreign films whirr to jerky interruptions as offensive
passages are bleeped out. But the censors are frustrated by Western television
emissions. People find the programmes a relief from the boring, politically
correct State offerings. Watching them is banned, but sinners set up dishes at

Teheran market

night and take them down in the morning. Some people install the forbidden receivers on their balconies and cover them by day with black fabric, so that they look like virtuous women. Travellers abroad smuggle in copies of foreign films taken with their home video cameras in cinemas. Still, access to Western communications is sporadic and limited.

In Teheran, we met Vida and 'Ali, relatives of friends of ours at home. We invited them for dinner at our hotel. Vida wore the hejab and 'Ali the usual dress for men: comfortable shirt and slacks. Ties are rejected as imperialist, linked to plutocracy, an attitude, ironically, similar to that affected by people in the West who consider themselves part of the creative or artistic community. I asked Vida and 'Ali what they would like to drink, to which 'Ali responded, "Some wine, please", and burst into uproarious laughter.

Iran enforces the Islamic ban on alcohol more strictly than do its Middle Eastern neighbours, who generally allow it to be served in hotels that cater to tourists. I ordered Islamic beer, an insipid brew of unfermented barley and hops. At least it was not as cloying as the local cola, called Zam Zam.

Our new friends expressed the same dissatisfaction with the economy that we heard everywhere among the business class. Blamed on government mismanagement and on the devastating eight-year war with Iraq, inflation, estimated at 30 to 40 per cent (no official figures are published to embarrass the powers that be), has drastically eroded living standards. The rial has been devalued so much that carrying the equivalent of 100 dollars makes one feel like a drug-dealer. Foreigners benefit, however: a meal for four in a top restaurant costs what it would for one person in a midrange Western eatery, with no need to pay for wine.

Corruption is systemic, worse apparently than it was under the Shah. Taking bribes is the only way middle- and lower-level bureaucrats can make ends meet. Salaries cover a scant quarter of the rent. At the top end, spectacular sums can be made. The head of the National Foundation, established to nationalise industry after the revolution, was convicted of skimming off 20 million dollars in cheap loans. He got life imprisonment, in an exemplary sentence.

In the aftermath of the revolution, Iran's policy-makers and politicians were at the bottom of the learning curve, and this led to woeful bungling in economic management. Ministers came mostly from the bazaaris (men who work in bazaars), who were skilled traders but had virtually no understanding of economics or industry. The Ayatollah's bodyguard was placed in charge of the National Iranian Oil Company. It is said that at one of his first meetings with the chiefs of production, he asked how long it would take to double the output of crude oil. The reply was that it would take two to three years, but at the cost of straining good engineering practice, which risked damaging the reservoirs. At that, he

pulled out the pistol he habitually carried, placed it on the table and thundered, "Now I want you to tell me how you will do it in six months". It took time and threats of mass resignation to have him shifted to another department.

In the early 1990s, the government expanded the economy too rapidly, building showpiece projects that were bedevilled by waste and inefficiency. Funding came largely from foreign sources (not American), growing into a debt mountain that was not offset by a counterbalancing creation of value. The loans were artfully arranged through letters of credit whose form of capitalised interest circumvented the Koranic anathema of usury.

Balance-of-payments pressures shook Iran's international credit rating, and the government responded by cutting imports and tightening expenditure. Through this disciplined and effective action, Iran achieved a positive trade balance and reduced foreign loans to manageable levels, but domestic standards of living plummeted.

Swept along on the tides of economic doctrine emanating from the West, the government privatised 20 per cent of the nation's industry and set a target of 40 per cent. Foreign investment has been sought for a number of projects. While the State insists on ownership, investors may export product to the value of their capital plus a return.

The measures taken, however, have failed to cure inflation or restore the economy to health. Still lacking adequate investment and technology from the West and relying too much on self-help, Iran seems doomed to parlous economic performance. Even with high world crude-oil prices, petroleum alone cannot ensure prosperity. The United States' sanctions against trading with Iran have not helped the situation, although Iranians point out that most other countries turn a blind eye to evasions of the sanctions by their nationals.

The impact of the economic suffering is most acute among the poor and the lower middle class, the engines of revolution that toppled the Shah. However, though discontent is endemic, the times are not the same as in prerevolutionary Iran. Unlike the Shah, who lost touch with the disaffected, the mullahs are close to the source and read the signs in a flash. They come from the same background as those most capable of effective sedition. Government today reacts swiftly and severely to crush revolt, human-rights considerations no impediment. And the army, which taps into the same roots, is in alliance.

Vida and 'Ali invited us to dinner at their home, a spacious, well-furnished apartment in a new building. Persian rugs created a cultivated atmosphere. When I saw Vida, I did a double take. This demure Islamic lady, whom I had seen only when she was covered by the lumpy potato sack, appeared wearing a see-through miniskirt and make-up. She looked ravishing. Fortunately, the Najas do not usually invade the home, so women wear what they wish in private.

'Ali offered me a whisky, real Scotch – a double. People buy liquor on the black market, smuggled in, or distilled by covert artisans. It is claimed that more alcohol is consumed now than under the Shah. A dinner party is not considered worth attending unless the host serves the illegal potion.

Discretion is prudent, even behind closed doors. Cases exist where diligent neighbours have phoned up the Najas to report noisy parties and arrests have followed. However, the prescribed jail sentence can be commuted into a warning with a few rials. Money, here as elsewhere, can be a great compromiser.

As in other Middle Eastern countries, Iranian laws, even under the puritanical regime, are infused with an elasticity that acts as a shock absorber to mitigate the harshness their strict application would entail. Minor infractions are tolerated, as long as they stay out of the public eye and do not force the authorities into either enforcement or an admission that the standard is unrealistic. The hypocrisy makes life bearable. 'Ali observed that Iranians could not accept a Germanic strictness.

After dinner, one of the guests, an Islamic art dealer who lived in Los Angeles and had dual Iranian–US citizenship, showed us a beautiful 17th-century miniature painting of the rose and nightingale, sign of romantic love. Traditionally, the rose represented the body, symbolising woman, and the nightingale represented the spirit, indicating man. The painting would have been worth a tidy sum in the West, and I asked the dealer how he planned to get it out of the country, for any work of art over 100 years old is a prohibited export. Nonchalantly, he replied, "With connections, it is possible". Smuggling, I recalled, is a time-honoured Iranian tradition.

The dichotomy between private and public comportment was astonishing. The dinner guests were laughing uproariously and cracking jokes, usually at the expense of the regime. It was a spirited and witty gathering of people who showed great warmth to each other. The next day, out in the street, the same people would be dour and phlegmatic, the women silent and dowdy.

We saw plenty of that as we walked in the street towards the bazaar, the focal point of commercial activity and the hive of the politically active bazaaris. Inside the emporium, the narrow lanes were crowded with shoppers, 90 per cent of them men. In some sections, no women could be seen. Almost all the products for sale were utilitarian – fabrics, household goods, clothes – grouped in sections, as in a department store. There was some jewellery, but it was tawdry.

Anna-Maryke brought out her camera, but as soon as she raised it to her eye, a man nearby sternly

Above and opposite: Teheran bazaar

said, "No, no", in English, and then, "Tch-tch", wagging his finger. She quickly snapped off a few shots, kneeling down for one, and then stopped. I felt the mood change as suddenly as if someone had flicked a switch. Looking back, I realised that although not overtly hostile, the men had seemed to resent Anna-Maryke being there, even though she was Islamically dressed. They particularly didn't like it when she kneeled down with her camera. When we went into the jewellery section of the bazaar, which was devoid of women, the mood darkened further. No-one said anything, but men began to brush up against Anna-Maryke before moving on into the crowd. I don't know how much the camera contributed, but it was clear that she had transgressed convention somehow. Out in the main street, the atmosphere abruptly returned to normal – restrained but not unfriendly.

Notwithstanding the egalitarian message that accompanied the revolution, a wide gap still separates the rich from the rest. It is just that different people are rich now. The mullahs, who generally come from the lower middle class, are amassing wealth. Some can be seen driving Mercedes and living in big houses. But generally, discretion has eliminated the flaunting of wealth that so alienated the society under the Shah. We saw some Mercedes and BMWs, but not many. The rich go abroad as often as they can but tell their children not to talk about it. For most people, life is hard. The cost of living is too high for shopping to consist of buying more than the bare essentials. Still, Iran is not a poor country in comparison with its neighbours to the east.

A lot of this was corroborated by an urbane civil engineer whom we met through our contacts. At a lunch of Caspian sturgeon grilled with lime, he gave us a competent rundown on the economy, but what impressed me most was his highly developed courtesy, natural and effortless, neither flowery nor theatrical. His manner was geared not to impress but, rather, to make other people feel relaxed and comfortable. Time was no impediment. In the West, we cut short the role of courtesy, take things for granted, get to the point of the matter. Substance dominates form. We do not place a high value on the process of making another person feel unthreatened. If anything, we are impatient or even suspicious of the circumlocutions required to accomplish the task.

While we ate, we discussed the Iranian economy,

which our lunch partner said was stagnant and wanting in proper management techniques, due to its isolation from the West. Administrative inefficiency and lack of coordination between government departments add to the misery. The economy suffers from the fear on the part of the conservatives in government that economic growth would tempt people to be less pious. They see the issue as a struggle between religion, representing the higher values in life, and materialism. Liberal parliamentarians are less daunted by the consequences of economic activity. However, while some measures have been taken to liberalise, Iran is still dominated by the hard-line clerics, with economically parlous results. Our companion compared the Iranian economy with others: "The First World is going like a rocket, Turkey like an automobile, Pakistan like a bicycle, and Iran follows on a donkey".

The strictures on behaviour at the personal level are chafing for many, provoking calls for some relaxation of the codes, but no suggestion that the Sharia be abandoned is in the air. Iran is in an age of faith. This seemed to me to be the country's salient difference with the West, where one of the most profound social trends is the gradual loss of faith. It has been largely lost in religion, as the established Church forfeited the respect of the intellectual classes, and later in philosophy, which has degenerated into semantics and categorisation. And now it is seeping out of science, as fear of its uncontrollable capacity to drive fundamental change infects belief in its social usefulness. In the process, perhaps, human beings are losing faith in themselves, weighed down by a world weary with cynicism and sophistication. Possibilities are more realistically assessed, but goals are lowered to below what might be achievable with the power of faith. Many people sense an alienation creeping over them, since nothing they are empowered to do seems to have any significance. Because

there is no meaning, standards can be allowed to slip without apparent cost or consequence. This is the malaise against which a resurgent Islam seeks to develop a vaccine for its community. Iranians feel that their country is the laboratory.

Current fundamentalist mores have thrown a dark cloak over the rich and colourful Persian culture that in the past has influenced the world from India to Europe. But underneath the cover, it survives in the social consciousness – particularly in the traditional teahouses. Vida and 'Ali took us to the Azari Tea House, which was built 50 years ago in the form of a caravanserai, with a tent atop raw brick walls. Multiknotted rugs in traditional designs covered the floors, and low tables forced us to sit cross-legged in the traditional way, something I have never been able to do for very long. I was forever twisting and turning to get comfortable. It was so crowded that we had to sit around the edge of the room. I could see that Anna-Maryke and I were the only Westerners in the place.

Most of the customers were young and animated, the women modest in the hejab but laughing and relaxed. The men sported the fashionable moustache and three-day stubble that gives them their 'tough hombre' look, as if they had just come from a stint behind a machine gun. The differences between the sexes are emphasised in Iran, the reverse of the mode in the West.

Paintings on the walls illustrated epics from the early Islamic and Seljuk periods, which coincided with the Middle Ages in Europe. Among them hung a photograph of famous Iranian wrestlers, including the Olympic gold medallist in the Shah's time. In the doorway sat a dervish fortune-teller with a long white beard who looked like Merlin. He was foretelling the future using stick dice. Waiters passed around large hookahs (water pipes) for the cross-legged guests. Tobacco was put in the bowl, then wood chips were added to keep the fire alight. The smoke cooled as it was drawn through the water. There was no evidence of stronger drugs.

From a small stage came music in nasal tones, with runaway rhythms that sounded similar to those from Morocco to Bangladesh. A tambourine and a bongo-like drum accompanied a large flute and a stringed instrument resembling a mandolin. The tambourine man sang. It was the prelude to a story-teller, who recited old poems in the ancient manner, in a song-like voice. There was no particular melody, but he delivered the words musically, as in a recitative.

A steaming pot of chick peas, potato, tomato and lamb chunks appeared. We were meant to spoon the contents into a bowl and mash them with a pestle. It was tasty and went well with sangak, a dark-brown unleavened bread, slightly chewy. To drink, we had yoghurt mixed with salt and water – very refreshing – and of course, we drank tea. After dinner, a man came round with a clutch of incense in a swinging bowl. If you gave him a little money, he would spread a sweet-smelling cloud nearby, said to ward off the harmful jealousies of other people.

Suddenly, a patriarchal actor strode onto the stage to recite the stirring epic of the *Shahnameh*, written by the 10th-century poet Firdausi, consid-ered one of Persia's finest. Through 60,000 drum-beat couplets, Firdausi welded together the ancient legends of Iran into a canon of idealised courage and nobility of spirit. Memory of the sufferings and tri-umphs of the *Shahnameh*, which means 'the Book of Kings', has resonated in the hearts of Iranians down to the present day, helping to hold the nation togeth-er in times when regionalism has threatened the centrist theme. Its broad sweep through titanic vicis-situdes and glory is a tribal reminder that a return to past national unity and greatness can be claimed as the destiny of Iran.

The actor's enthusiasm for his craft reminded me of the old thespian in Hamlet's play scene – passion-ate, strenuous, huge with gesture. We have lost dec-lamatory art in the West, probably through the influence of film, which requires a more intimate style. His wide, white moustache flared and his wiry stature stretched large as he declaimed the monster-slaying feats of Rustan the archetypal hero, his voice booming from the diaphragm, cane flailing the air like a sword. All of a sudden his body contracted and his voice melted into lyrical tones as he recounted how the champion wooed and married a beautiful girl, who bore him a son he never saw until he met him on the field of battle and, in ignorance, killed him. It was the tragic story retold to us by Matthew Arnold in *Sohrab and Rustum*. Around the room, I saw several young Iranians mouthing the words.

Chapter 10

Instruction from an Ayatollah

SHIRAZ

The next day, we took an internal flight to the southern city of Shiraz, a centre of two million people and the origin of the eponymous grape that migrated to the vineyards of Europe and the New World. In France, it is called 'syrah'.

Regimes based on puritanical mores require a devil which, by comparison, demonstrates their moral superiority. In Iran's case, it is the West, led by the Great Satan, the United States of America. Hanging over the lobby of our hotel in Shiraz, a huge sign exhorted, "Down with the USA". Visas to Iran are not easily obtained by Americans. The authorities don't like the British much, either, and Israel, of course, viewed as a Middle Eastern outpost of the West, is an arch enemy.

On the mezzanine floor of our hotel, a television set placed in a large public area was playing an old propaganda video: Ayatollah Khomeini returning to Teheran in the presence of ecstatic crowds, who were using ropes to pull down a statue of the Shah in the main city square. The revolutionary scene dissolved into a close-up of President Jimmy Carter making a speech, but the film had been manipulated so that his head jerked up and down in the manner of a puppet. Every time his head jolted, his eyes would close. The technicians had completely dehumanised him. The screen then showed images of the Iran–Iraq war, bombs exploding on Teheran, missiles fired from helicopters, bazookas firing surface-to-air missiles, and newsreel shots of combat in the field. The Ayatollah was amidst the action, talking to the troops and consulting with bearded generals, against a background of loud martial music.

We met several people who could be described as coming from the lower middle class. Certainly, they were not wealthy. The views they expressed were considerably less critical of the regime than those we had heard in Teheran. While admitting that life was hard, the emphasis was on the positive fact that the revolution had reinstilled in ordinary people a sense of national pride. The humiliation of sensing that foreign powers controlled the workings of their State had been like a choking wreath around their throats; now, it had been removed. They seemed to feel that the rich had been more attracted to foreign interests than to life at home, adding with some satisfaction that the reason wealthy people didn't like the regime was that they now found it more difficult to go abroad to spend their money. The control over social behaviour that chafes the upper socioeconomic class was seen as a strengthening elixir, a means of returning to a life more in keeping with the guidance of the *Koran*.

Since Iranian society is based on moral authority, and especially because it is sourced in revelation, people feel superior to the West, which is seen to have taken the low path to materialism, an essentially inferior destination. This is a widespread feeling, not just one confined to a few fanatics. It is profoundly held and touches something deep in the soul. To get a better understanding of the reorientation process that is going on in the country, we looked for a religious leader who would be willing to talk to us. In Shiraz, which means, incidentally, 'place of secrets' in old Persian, we arranged a meeting with an ayatollah at a medresa (religious school).

Ayatollah, meaning 'sign of God', is the rank given to a Shiite mullah who has achieved a high level of religious learning, usually requiring 20 years of study. Mullahs, from the Arabic word for 'master', form the basic stratum of the clergy and collectively form the ulema ('men of religious learning'). In Iran, mullahs appear in the parliament, teach in the universities, act as judges and court advisers, form part of government ministries and even function as wel-fare officers. Islam is a religion of the law and, as such, is passed on to each generation by teaching. It is less hierarchical than is Christianity, and its mullahs and ayatollahs do not stand in the place of priests and bishops. The gradations of the clergy are related more to study and teaching than to political leadership.

One of the salient distinctions between the two major sects of Islam is where religious authority lies. Sunnis consider that it emerges out of a community consensus that underlies the Sharia, whereas the Shiites believe it arises from the infallible imams, who rank third in importance after God and the Prophet.

We arrived at the Khan Theological School, founded in the 17th century during the Safavid dynasty, and walked into a small courtyard through large carved wooden doors open to the street. A white-turbaned mullah met us in a calm, friendly manner, saying that we had to wait a few minutes, as the ayatollah was praying. It was a hot, bright day, so we were relieved to sit for a while in the shade. The mullah came back in 15 minutes and asked us to follow him. He led us through a cloister around a long rectangular courtyard of laid stone, cooled with a fountain in the centre and planted with old trees in full leaf, filtering the sun. Beds of bright flowers surrounded the pathways. At intervals, large niches appeared in the brick-built cloisters. The ayatollah was installed in one of these, holding court, with about 10 students sitting on a patterned carpet, some of whom were mullahs. In Iran, ordinary people, not just those who have entered the clergy, go to the medresas for religious education.

He was seated on a stack of large brightly coloured pillows, a long piece of brown fabric scrunched up at his side. As we approached, he got up slowly, straightened out the fabric, and wrapped it slowly around himself as a garment in a fluid, easy movement that seemed natural and comfortable,

Above: Ayatollah

Left: Ayatollah and mullahs

almost ritualistic. It took a full minute before he was ready to greet us. All we could do was to stand there and wait awkwardly in silence.

He looked like Ayatollah Khomeini but not as merciless. As he moved towards us, I saw that his eyes were warm, signalling a courteousness that seemed to come from a deep self-confidence to which threat is unknown. He exuded authority without harshness. After we shook hands, he went back to his pillows and sat down cross-legged, back straight, like a sculpture. Thumb-soiled books were strewn around his feet. I said we were honoured to be able to come here to the medresa, and he graciously welcomed us to Iran. To start the interview, I asked a question about how Islam accommodated science within its religious precepts, a challenge that many think is too much for Christianity. He didn't speak a word of English, but spoke slowly enough, at least at first, for the interpreter we had brought along to translate. He appeared to be address-ing the people assembled around rather than speaking to us. I noticed a dignified young imam on my left who seemed to be copying the master's demeanour.

"One big problem in the West is the battle between science and religion. We don't believe in the Pope and his priests, because they have changed the Christian religion. They have mixed it with something that is not true or correct. For example, in the Middle Ages, they had a conflict with Galileo. They killed him because he said the Earth was round. They were wrong and he was right." I did not mention that he was wrong about Galileo. He was not killed, because he recanted. But that detail did not affect the point the ayatollah was making.

"Islam supports the advancement of science," he continued. "It encourages greater scientific knowledge. There is no conflict between our religion and science. Islam wants science to improve, medicine and all other branches. The chemistry and physics that are practised in Western countries are based on the discoveries of Islamic scientists – for example, Jabir ibn Hayyan, the great chemist who was a student of one of the most famous imams. The inventor of distillation of alcohol was Zakariaye Razi of Iran, around the 10th century.

Before the Crusades, Europeans like Germans, Austrians and English were empty of science. But after the Crusades, after they had come into contact with the sophisticated Islamic world and when they started to have good relations with Muslims, they learned science."

I told him I was interested in the fact that Iran had the only government in the world based on religious principles and asked him to comment on this. That really wound him up. I could see him accelerate to full speed in seconds. He spoke in a steady stream that washed like torrential rain over the interpreter, who only had time to scribble down notes in Farsi for later translation. The learned man extended both arms to emphasise his points, then pushed his black skullcap back and forth on his head. He rocked on the pillows and pointed frequently to the little stack of *Korans* on a nearby table. His passion was couched in great dignity and ease of speech. While he was holding forth, people from the medresa began to drift into the courtyard to listen.

Back at the hotel, the interpreter told me, as accurately as his memory would allow, what the ayatollah had said. The essence was:

"From an Islamic point of view, politics and religion are not separated. Religion carries with it the requirement for praying to God but also the need to deal with the political problems of civilisation. In particular, it is the source for defining the correct relationships between people in society.

"Our religion is based on orders from God as revealed in the *Koran*. Iran has the fortune of being the only country that is ruled according to religion. Everything in Iran is decided by religion – the religion offered by Mohammed."

At that, the students and mullahs surrounding the teacher muttered, "Sala-lah" ('Peace be upon him and his family'). Throughout his homily, the ayatollah mentioned the Prophet repeatedly, and each time he did so, the audience muttered the same respectful words.

The ayatollah continued, "Mohammed provided us with the best ordering for society. It is based on discipline, following the revealed thoughts of God. He battled with the bad elements of society at the time, who did not believe in God the Great. Part of his mission was to support the weak and disadvantaged. His words teach us in today's world to do that.

"The teachings of Mohammed compel Islamic countries to resist and eliminate foreign domination. Here, we take inspiration from the founder of this medresa, Khan Allahverdy, who was a leading Safavid figure in the 17th century. The Portuguese had conquered and colonised southern Iran, to the shame of the nation. Following the words of Mohammed being revealed to him, the khan defeated the invaders and expelled them from our land.

"Before the revolution, we owed everything to the West: way of dress, technology, economy. We were shamed. The Shah would do whatever the colonial powers wanted. They kept us down, did not let us learn, so we fell behind. But since the Shah was overthrown, we are independent. Now, each of us tries to be Iranian, not influenced by foreigners. We have an internal spiritual strength much greater than before. Some leaders in the West are worried about the moral problems in their societies. Guided by the principles of Islam, we do not have them here.

"Islamic countries that have good relations with colonising powers, especially the USA, are not really Islamic. You cannot see the discipline that you can observe here in Iran. They are not built on Islamic orders. A true Islamic country is only where the politics are based on the thoughts of the *Koran*."

There were now about 20 acolytes gathered around the teacher, respectfully listening to every word and nodding in agreement at the salient points. Every time the Prophet was mentioned, a low rumble of reverence would emerge from the group. The ayatollah would play with his hat, pushing it onto his forehead and then to the back of his head. It gave him an air of self-confident distraction that emphasised his assuredness.

The constant movement compelled attention, drawing the gaze of the audience to his face. His hot, intelligent eyes seemed to take in everything; you felt you had nothing left to hide. He had the passion of a man convinced he was on God's journey. He continued:

"Some countries have religion but are blocked by their governments from allowing it to be fully a way of life for the people. If all governments in Islamic countries were the same, Muslims everywhere would be united, and permitted and encouraged to practise their religion.

"Activities in Libya, Palestine, Bosnia and Saudi Arabia demonstrate that people want to copy Iran – Turkey and Central Asia, too. Those who oppose their governments show that they are for Iran in their religion. We are a model for all Muslims.

"An Islamic country is only truly Islamic where the politics are based on the thoughts of the *Koran*. Iran's system of theocracy is the right path for the whole of the Middle East. We know the right way and are trying to persuade others to follow. We have the faith and discipline to convert the rest of the Islamic countries."

Somewhere on the perimeter of the medresa, a muezzin started up a call to prayer, and the ayatollah quickly brought his sermon to a close. Still expressing his concluding thoughts, he took off his hat and began to wind the black turban of his rank around his head. He was bald! Somehow, the revelation was shocking.

The interpreter told us that it was time for prayer and that, accordingly, the interview was over. Thanking the ayatollah and the others, I offered to donate some money to the medresa. The ayatollah loftily suggested that I give it to the poor. All the people at the medresa were friendly and cordial but very self-assured, almost haughty. They seemed completely satisfied with their approach to life. It was clear to us that they belonged to a world so different from ours that only a bridge of courtesy could link the two. One should not underestimate the piousness in Iran, a level not reached en masse by Christians since the Crusades.

For a long time, from around 1500 AD, the West has been reordering its societies along principles that are generally considered by successive generations to be modern. This process has coincided with the decline of Christianity as the sole governing precept for society. It started in the Renaissance with the discovery of Europe's classical past and rose on the tide of humanism bequeathed by the ancient Greeks. The classics taught that virtue could arise in parallel with religion, from philosophies and codes of behaviour with a secular base. Religion could play an important role but not necessarily the dominant one.

The vicious sectarian wars of the 16th and 17th centuries in Europe, one of the outcomes of which was the founding of the 13 colonies that were to form the United States of America, caused the modernising West to dread the atavistic passions that can be generated by religious fervour. Indeed, it was the fear of religious oppression that led the founding fathers to enshrine in the American constitution the separation of Church and State described by a subsequent president, John Tyler, as "a great and noble experiment".

In the West, we sense that these religious passions are again stirring in Islam, and in a particularly potent form in Iran, out of its special brand of revival. We know them, and fear their potential force, for they can be arrayed against us. The ayatollah's sermon was a little chilling, because it made clear the fact that he and others of the cloth in Iran are deeply xenophobic, implacably hostile to the Western powers. Their influence will be directed towards rebuilding their society along fundamentalist lines and expanding the paradigm throughout Islamic countries by any means possible, including, I would judge, military.

Ayatollah Khomeini and his successors are trying to restore the moral strength of their nation by the 'cold turkey' application of what we might, in the West, call puritanism: an extreme code of personal discipline backed up by religious faith. In that, Iranians seem to have taken the same course as that charted by Mao Zedong for the Chinese people, who had declined during the 19th century into such a supine condition that they were unable to defend themselves against even the few gunboats and clutch of troops sent by the European powers. It has been estimated that 10 per cent of China's population at that time were opium addicts. Today, after half a century

of reconstituting its moral strength through methods modern Western politicians could not contemplate applying to their own societies, China is on the rise again. During the early rebuilding days, Mao's brand of communism acted as a virtual religion.

The whole system in Iran is built around discipline and control. The people are pious; 90 per cent consider themselves submissive to the dictates of the *Koran*. The mullahs are secure in their power. A theocracy is in place whose purpose is to steer the people back to the true path as shown by the Prophet. The ulema are so certain of their mission that zeal is as natural as breathing. An Islamic militia of basijis, 400,000 strong, train mind and body to the rigours of conflict in preparation for the supreme sacrifice they expect to make for their faith. The commitment is reminiscent of the early Christians, in the days before Constantine saw the sign of Christ.

Islam, especially in Iran, is in a fundamentally different phase of human development from the West. A critical point of distinction is the attitude towards freedom, the predominant value of the modern age in the West, claiming shining lineage from Locke and the revolutions of France and America. It justifies attacks on the established order, colours the 'information age' and shapes personal morality. The immense achievements riding on its back – in wealth creation, science and technology, and the permeation of education throughout society – justify its place in the firmament of values. The mullahs in Iran would argue that their people are free, but it would soon become apparent that the bundle of rights making up their concept of freedom is much smaller than ours. Even the value is positioned differently; while important, it is junior to others. But then, they are trying to rebuild their society, to regenerate. It wasn't so long ago that the West's bundle would seem undersized by today's standards.

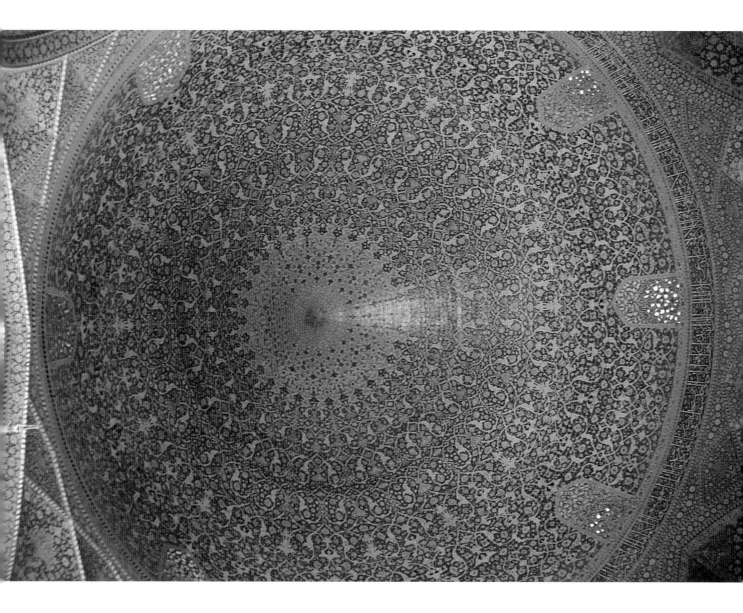

Above: Dome of mosque, Shiraz

Left: Small tea house, Shiraz

Tea house, Shiraz

We left the leafy place of contemplation inhabited by the passionate ayatollah and walked out into the hot streets of Shiraz. As I looked at the old cars and trucks belching particulates from incomplete combustion, I couldn't help wondering how his vision of converting the rest of the Islamic world to theocracy could be realised without an economic advance that would tear apart the stiff social fabric. Many of the cars were Chevrolets and Oldsmobiles, chariots of their Satan.

After a long walk, we entered a park of gardens dedicated to two great Persian poets who lived in Shiraz. Writing in the 13th century, at the time of the Mongol devastations, Sa'di perfected in graceful language the central moral tale of ancient Iranian literature. His *Gulistan*, which means 'flower garden', adumbrated the virtues of magnanimity, repentance and tolerance in an abstract and contemplative style. A hundred years later, Hafiz moved the poetic tradition into lyrical mode.

I thought it informative of the Persian mentality that poets would merit the naming of a park after them. This is not a Western practice; we don't do it even for Shakespeare. The commemorative salute to the poets rested serene among the orange trees and flowers set around a reflecting pool, cool hosts to butterflies and small birds.

Shiraz has another quality: it is within driving distance of what remains of the glorious Achaemenid empire, the ultimate source of Iranian cultural pride and the host of the dualist religion that still influences Iranian Islam.

Chapter 11

Heritage of Glory

PASSARGADAE

We set out in the early morning for Passargadae, the first capital of the Achaemenid empire, founded by Cyrus the Great during his 20-year reign of conquest in the middle of the sixth century BC. It is in the province of Fars, ancient homeland of the Persians, who derive their name from that of the province, the 'F' becoming a 'P'. The vista was grand, wide mountainous terrain ranging like a vast, scrunched-up garment tossed carelessly across the land. Quiet valleys with flat floors, verdant with cultivation, nestled in the folds. We looked up to see the bedding of the country rock twisting and turning on the valley walls, vestigial reminders of the trauma the land had endured in its geologic past. In the distance, dust clouds rose like smoke to obscure the faraway hills and then moved on to expose them. The patches of green testified to the effort irrigation was making to pump life into the thirsty dust. It is tough country; blasted by a harsh, cold wind that blows snow across the land in winter. When Cyrus the Great was advised to move his capital from Passargadae to more clement terrain, he snorted, "Soft lands breed soft men".

As early as 2000 BC, nomadic Aryan tribes began a centuries-long migration from the Eurasian plains of southern Russia. Some swooped down into the Indian subcontinent and established themselves as the dominant ethnic group in the north. Others veered west and passed through Iran to penetrate as far as Mesopotamia and Syria. A third group trekked into Iran from the northeast and settled in the Iranian plateau of Fars, surrounded by high, bleak mountains that scrape the sky at 4000 metres. This group consisted of Persians and their cousins the Medes, who became first their masters and then their subordinates.

By the seventh century BC, the Median cavalry-based armies had grown strong enough to challenge the sagging Assyrian empire that the Old Testament vilified as the scourge of the region. In alliance with Babylon, the

Top: Tomb of Cyrus,
Passargadae

Above: Persepolis

Medes sacked the Assyrian capital, Nineveh, ringing down the curtain on Assyrian dominance. To institutionalise the coalition, a Median princess was given in marriage to the Babylonian king, Nebuchadnezzar, who thoughtfully built the celebrated Hanging Gardens of Babylon for his bride, to cure her homesickness for the green hills of Media. The ancient Middle East was stabilised, but not for long.

Around 575 BC, a son was born to the wife of a minor Persian king, a vassal of the Medes. Mystery surrounds his birth, but it is generally accepted that he belonged to the line of Achaemenes, a Persian ruler in the seventh century. The Greek historian of the Persian wars, Herodotus, wrote that he was the grandson of the Median king Astyages, who had given his daughter, Mundane, in marriage to one of his Persian vassals, a step down in status for the young girl. At the time, the Medes were the ruling tribe. Discord coloured the relationship between father and daughter. Astyages had a dream one night in which Mundane urinated over his entire kingdom. The Magi, whom he consulted for an interpretation, said it meant that his daughter loathed him and despised his kingdom. In fear of the dream's significance, Astyages forced Mundane into the low-key union. Later, while his daughter was pregnant, the king had another dream. In it, a vine grew out of Mundane's womb and spread all over Asia. The Magi interpreted the dream as meaning a grandson would grow up to usurp the throne.

The king's reaction to the threat was to order the murder of the infant. He commanded his kinsman Harpagus, his chief civil servant, to carry out his wishes. But Harpagus took pity on the child and hid him in the mountains, where he was raised by shepherds. The boy was Cyrus, destined to create by force of arms and diplomacy an empire greater than the world had ever seen before.

Astyages eventually discovered his kinsman's disobedience and flew into a rage. In revenge, he served the head of Harpagus' son to him at a banquet, an outrage remarkably similar to the origin of the Atrean curse in Greece. That deed of horror festered deep in Harpagus' soul for years, waiting for the perfect retaliation. The opportunity came when Cyrus reached manhood. Relations between the Persians and their overlords, the Medes, had deteriorated as Astyages became increasingly tyrannical. Harpagus encouraged the young man, who had shown charismatic military talent from the earliest age, to lead the Persians in revolt. In a battle at the Persian settlement of Passargadae, Cyrus won a crushing victory, not by arms but through a mass defection of Astyages' army. The Median king was delivered to Cyrus in chains.

All evidence points to the exceptional qualities of the young leader who was able to unite the Persian and Median tribes under his banner. The Greek historian Xenophon, writing in the fourth century BC, speaks of Cyrus' indomitable spirit, wisdom and physical attractiveness.

The battle at Passargadae produced one of the largest mergers in history, the Medes and the Persians joining together in one empire, interchangeable in occupying the most important government and military posts. The common ethnic roots and background in the steppes facilitated a pathway to equality. Invigorated by the dynamic leadership of Cyrus, the merged nation went on to expand its empire to the west, clashing with the major power in Anatolia, Lydia. The Lydians, under their king Croesus, amasser of legendary wealth, harboured their own aspirations, and tested them against the Medes in a series of battles that resulted in the Halys River, in what is now Turkey, becoming the agreed boundary.

In preparation for an expansionary push, Croesus decided to consult an oracle. He sent out invitations to all the major oracles in the ancient Middle East, including Delphi. To determine the winner, each was to answer a wisdom-testing question: what was Croesus doing on the 100th day after his messengers left Sardis, the Lydian capital? Delphi won by accurately stating that Croesus was boiling a lamb and a tortoise in a brass cauldron. The king was rhapsodical in his admiration of the oracle, showering it with expensive gifts. The Pythia at Delphi was then asked the crucial question – whether Croesus should expand east against the Persians. On hearing the answer that if he crossed the Halys, a great empire would be destroyed, he was delighted and sent even more presents: two gold coins for every man in the city of Delphi.

Failing to notice the ambiguity in the prophesy, Croesus crossed the Halys River, and without even waiting for his allies to arrive, joined battle with Cyrus in Cappadocia, the lances of the Lydians against the arrows and short swords of the Medes and Persians. It was a bloody, day-long stalemate, but Croesus vacated the field, his army intact, to return to Sardis, where he set about preparing for another campaign next summer (it was against convention to fight in the bitterness of the Asia Minor winter). Seizing the opportunity for surprise, Cyrus marched to Sardis so quickly that, as Herodotus put it, "he was his own messenger". Caught off guard,

Croesus had to reassemble his army in a scramble for the troops had been paid off and demobilised. During the battle, Cyrus brought his baggage camels to the front line, facing the Lydian cavalry of lancers. The unfamiliar smell of the camels unnerved the horses, throwing the Lydians into confusion and dismay. Cyrus won the battle, but Croesus managed to retreat into his fortress capital, built on a rock promontory and widely considered impregnable. After a 13-day siege, one of the Persian soldiers observed a Lydian at a part of the wall so steep that it was lightly guarded accidentally let his helmet roll down. Astonished, the Persian saw the Lydian climb down the wall to retrieve the helmet and easily climb back up. The next day, the Persians mounted an attack up the hidden pathway, over-running the city. It was a total victory.

After incorporating the Lydian Empire, Cyrus turned east and annexed lands across Central Asia as far as the Jaxartes River (today called the Syr Darya), before marching south to Babylon, venerable seat of the ancient Mesopotamian civilisation. The approaching doom of the luxury-loving city was foretold to the king's son, Prince Belshazzar, who saw, according to the Old Testament, the fingers of a man's hand write "mene, mene, tekel, parsin" on the wall of his palace. Daniel was summoned to interpret the writing, after the Chaldean wise men had failed. He was told it signified that the days of the kingdom were numbered, that the regime had been weighed and found wanting, and that the kingdom would be delived to the Medes and Persians.

King of Kings, Persepolis

Cyrus was not just a great military commander; he had uncommon diplomatic skills. His policy of treating conquered people with magnanimity gained him widespread support, lessening the need for punitive campaigns. In this regard, the Jewish people remember him fondly. Within a year of subduing Babylon, he allowed its Jewish population, who had been held captive there for almost 50 years, to return home. Gold and silver treasures looted from their temple in Jerusalem were restored. By this gesture, he secured an ally who controlled the vital land route to Egypt, a destination to which he aspired but which he never achieved.

The merging of Egypt into the grand empire had to await Cyrus' son Cambyses. Unlike his restrained and sensible father, Cambyses was subject to violent temper tantrums, particularly after drinking bouts, which sometimes led to precipitate executions of unlucky companions who had offended the monarch, often by failing to show sufficient adulation. Herodotus, who thought Cambyses completely mad, tells of one courtier who found a way of combining flattery with the essence of truth, a matter of critical cultural importance to the ancient Persians. As Herodotus reports, Persian boys were taught three things only: to ride a horse, to use the bow and to speak the truth. He said to the king, "I do not think you are equal to your father, for you have not yet a son like the son he left behind him in yourself".

Little is left of Cyrus' capital, Passargadae, to share with the sheep grazing on the sparse valley floor. Not even a tourist was there as we visited the site. It was once a fortified city, but not a trace of wall remains. A few broken columns stand as relics in the ground outlining the royal palace, but the tomb of Cyrus still demands a visit, impressive not for its grandeur but for its compelling simplicity. Six courses of megalithic block platforms diminishing upwards to form steps rise to hold the burial chamber that sits on top, an oblong of stone with a pitched roof. It rests 10 metres high in the constant wind, beige, and small for a great king's mausoleum. The architectural form is reminiscent of the ziggurat of Babylon and Djoser's step pyramid of Egypt, though much less grand. With the laconic economy of language typical of the warrior personality, Cyrus tells us in the only inscription on the tomb who built it: "I Cyrus, the king, the Achaemenid".

The tomb at Passargadae expressed the unusual restraint of the world's most powerful man. Often, we extol the merits of simplicity, but indulge in pomp when we have the chance. He didn't. His successors did, however, in grand style, as we were to see. Perhaps his achievements and fame satisfied his needs. He stitched together a host of disparate nations into an imperial tapestry that stretched over more land than any monarch had ruled before and set the scene for an even greater empire to come. Informed by a generosity of spirit, attested to by the historians of antiquity, he identified and harnessed the mutuality of interests among his conquered peoples, winning their respect.

We drove out of the Passargadae valley, which had only one exit, through the colours of Asia – light beige patched with brown ploughed fields, then steel-green scrub topped by dark shadows, as one hill was moulded into the next. The road wound through a defile of sheered-off cliffs that bounded a riverbed in planes of rock cut clean by the recent flaking off of pieces. The formations looked like a forest of cathedral spires. Past them, the vertical rock bedding toppled over in uneven folds. Just one narrow river, flanked by herds of goats and sheep, irrigates the entire valley from Passargadae to Shiraz. We continued past the barren, parched hills, whose heights could support no vegetation at all, their faces wrinkled with erosion channels. Dust-coloured tents of nomads dotted the fields, some round, some oblong. Blankets of lush grapevines clogged the valley floor as we got close to Shiraz. We were not ready to go back to Shiraz, however, for we were on our way to another destination, one that lay 60 kilometres northeast of that city and about 50 kilometres from Passargadae.

Cyrus' distant cousin Darius, who assumed the throne under dubious circumstances in 522 BC, extended the boundaries of the empire he inherited and developed its economy to a wealth engine such as the world had never seen. In order to facilitate trade, Darius introduced coins, the new unit being called the 'daric'. Actually, the Persians did not invent coinage; it was their old enemies the Lydians,

Left: Sphinx, at Gateway to All Nations, Persepolis

Right: Bull's head capital, Apadama Hall, Persepolis

under Croesus, who first introduced it to the world. By the time Darius died, his empire extended from North Africa to Pakistan and from Nubia to the southern steppes of Russia, from which his ancestral Aryan tribes had burst on horseback over a millennium before.

PERSEPOLIS

As a sign of the Achaemenids' glory, Darius planned a new capital, grander by far than the frugal Passargadae. He situated it on a wide, fertile plain backed up against a rugged peak called the Mountain of Mercy. His famous son Xerxes extended his father's dream to realise an urban creation ranking with the greatest in history. The city is known by the name, cognate with Persia, given to it by the Greeks: Persepolis. Its remains constitute one of the most exciting archaeological sites in the world. It is proof of the power of the two illustrious builders of the metropolis that both could sustain disastrous defeats in their ill-fated invasions of Greece without inciting revolt at home.

As we approached Persepolis, vultures circled low in the sky, their cape-like black wings allowing them to float on the air currents sucked up from the hot land. Some birds even landed on the road and stalked haughtily along the shoulders, disdaining our car. As we turned off the main road, a huge shallow-domed structure of folded sedimentary bedding came into view, rising like a monument. Past it, a platoon of tall pillars stood on the horizon, taller than the columns of the Greeks. We drove closer, parking the car a few metres from the ancient city of temples and palaces, which inhabited a high terrace cut out of the mountainside above us, overlooking the vast plain where we stood. When we arrived, not a tourist could be seen; some service personnel were the only other people there. Yet much remains of this, the architectural signature of the greatest world power of its day, so rich that when Alexander the Great sacked it, he needed 10,000 mules and 5000 camels to cart away the gold and silver of its treasury. In the harem were installed beautiful women, gathered from a bewildering ethnic diversity, so numerous that Persian monarchs could have the choice of a different odalisque for each night of the year, a selection they made by throwing a golden ball into the air to be caught by the lucky one.

Some believed that Persepolis was conceived as a ritual city whose existence was kept secret from the world at large. However, it appears to have been more a gigantic monument to the power and the glory of Persian imperial achievement, remotely sited so as to be far away from common humanity and safe for the storage of its treasure. Its distance added to the mystique of royalty and the dignity of religious observations. Other cities were used, too, for public purposes: Babylon and Susa for government administration and Ecbatana for the summer residence. The Achaemenid kings were crowned at Passargadae, donning the robes of Cyrus the Great, their revered progenitor, and consuming figs and sour milk, the traditional sustenance of their nomadic forefathers. Persepolis, the centre of the greatest Persian palaces, came into its own every March, New Year in the Zoroastrian calendar. At this time, high-level delegations from the 28 nations that made up the Persian Empire were required to attend and pay homage to the King of Kings.

Lion savaging bull, staircase at Persepolis

The weather was savagely hot, and out in the open, we got no respite from the merciless sun that flailed us from an open sky. Anna-Maryke was suffering in her black hejab. It had been fun, she said, to joke about never having to decide what to wear or worry about sartorial competition, but now it was just sheer discomfort. Nevertheless, Persepolis was so fascinating that she was prepared to bear the heat.

In the seventh century BC, Zarathustra (whose Greek name was 'Zoroaster') reformed the traditional beliefs of the Iranians into a new religion based on the belief in a supreme god, Ahuramazda, who created man and the world. The act of genesis also produced two forces – the truth, represented by light, and the lie, whose domain was darkness – destined to be in eternal conflict. The morality of human beings was determined by the behaviour that arose out of a free choice between these two. Perhaps this was why the ancient Persians put such stock in speaking the truth. Ahuramazda, whose name is a combination of the words 'ahura' and 'mazda', meaning 'god' and 'wise', respectively, would judge a person's life in accordance with the basic moral choices made. An eternity of ease and pleasure would reward those who led their lives according to the truth, but an infinity of torment awaited those who chose the other path.

The duality of good and evil, with its system of reward and punishment following on an exercise of free will, was a revolutionary departure from the haphazard collection of beliefs that had preceded it. Indeed, its basic message was later to inform Judaeism, Christianity and Islam. Daniel, who had served as a high and respected official in the administration of Darius the Great in Babylon and could well have been influenced by the society there, is the first Jewish prophet to speak of souls going to an afterlife that could consist of a state other than the darkness the

Jews had believed in before. He says: "And many of them that sleep in the dust of the earth shall awake, some to everlasting life, and some to shame and everlasting contempt".

The Zoroastrian priests, known as Magi, were renowned among the Greeks and Romans for their knowledge of astrology and sorcery. Our word 'magic' comes from them. While the religion has been almost completely superseded by Islam in Iran, a thriving pocket of Zoroastrianism exists in Bombay among the Parsees, whose name comes from the Persians who fled there to escape persecution. They still adopt the old practice of not burying or cremating the dead, wishing to avoid defiling the sacred elements of earth and fire. The corpses are exposed on high structures, called towers of silence, to be disposed of by vultures.

We mounted steps that rose 14 metres from the plain to the terrace. The staircase, which was double reversing, was built to the right and to the left in risers wide and shallow enough for the horses of the nobility to climb. At the top stood the official entrance to the terrace of royal buildings, flanked by limestone bull-like figures standing five and half metres tall. Xerxes named it the Gate of All Nations, in reference to the passage through it each New Year of the kings of 28 subject nations. A fanfare of trumpeters standing on either side of the portal would announce the official arrival of each delegation.

The noble procession would move to the audience hall, or Apadana, a few metres inside the Gate of All Nations. Only 13 of the 72 limestone columns that supported the huge building remain, but their stone capitals of hanging date-palm leaves standing high in the open air, far higher than Greek-built columns, give a sense of mysterious grandeur from far in the past. The column, which comes from Egypt, originated as a clutch of palm trunks tied together, used as a bearing member for roofs. Later, when

Staircase,
Persepolis

engineers learned to work with stone, the vertical spaces in the clutch were
stylised into fluting.

The nobles would be ushered up a staircase that remains intact. Its sides are
carved in relief, showing figures of the emissaries who made the journey of
homage from all over the Persian Empire. Each is represented in a vignette
separated by a stylised tree of life, the whole like a long film strip showing the
parade in motion. It was led off by the Imperial Guard known as the Immortal
Ten Thousand, for its number was never allowed to fall below that figure. It
constituted the elite corps of the army and corresponds to the Republican
Guards of today. The royal courtiers came next, followed by nobles – Persians
in feather head-dresses and Medes in round caps. In the southern section of the
staircase, the representatives of subject nations have their place. They are
shown with their own distinctive dress, hairstyle, ornaments, weapons, and
products of their economy. There are Egyptians leading a bull; Ethiopians with
closely curled hair, carrying an elephant tusk; Libyans accompanied by a kudu;
Arabians with a dromedary; Syrians bringing a small war chariot drawn by
two horses; Scythians from southern Russia wearing their pointed hats; Cappa-
docians with cloaks pinned at the shoulders; and Sogdians from Central Asia,
with short swords, squiring a horse. Bactrians from Afghanistan escorting their
double-humped camel and Indians wearing dhotis and carrying vases full of
gold dust showed how far to the East the empire stretched.

After passing through the Apadana, large enough to hold 10,000 people, the
dignitaries would enter the palace of the 100 columns. All the columns have

Gateway to All Nations,
Persepolis

been broken off at their base, but structures on the periphery give the vast dimensions of the hall. The great king would sit on the western portico on his elevated portable throne of gold, crowned in the noble metal and holding a long golden sceptre, to review the New Year's procession and to receive his loyal subjects. A red tasselled canopy embroidered with lions, bulls and the winged emblem of the supreme God, Ahuramazda, shielded him from the sun. A courtier would stand behind the monarch with a towel and a fly-whisk made from a bull's tail.

There we were introduced to the fire temple, the principle ritual centre of Zoroastrianism. The temple was in the form of an open square courtyard sunk a metre and a half below the surface, a platform at each corner. Fires were placed on the platforms and the people prayed below. A symbol of purity and the banishment of darkness, fire was at the heart of the ritualistic expression of the religion. Priests who performed the ceremonies wore face masks, to prevent their breath from sullying the sacred flame. They had another curious custom: in preparation for the animal sacrifice, usually of a bull, that accom-

Gateway to All Nations,
Persepolis

panied the ritual, an intoxicating drink was concocted from ephedra, a medicinal herb that grows in the mountains of Iran and Afghanistan. The officiating priests would consume the drink while intoning prayers to Ahuramazda, entering further and further into an otherworldly state of euphoria and divine intimacy.

Inspired by the 20-metre columns, with their exotic caps, near the processional staircases, portals with images of the winged Ahuramazda, and friezes of lions savaging unicorns, our imaginations beamed us into the soaring majesty of this fallen city on its windy platform hewn from the mountain rock. We sensed that we were in touch with the continuum of history. Perhaps the unfortunate Shah felt it, too, as he reviewed a full-scale son-et-lumière re-enactment of the New Year's pageant in 1971, two and a half millennia after the founding of the Persian Empire.

We walked around the ancient monuments, alone on the vast platform, until the sun settled behind the columns into the dusty hills, turning them into dark formless shapes like the women in Iran. The lines formed a shadowy silhouette, unround, like the hejab when it rides on the lumpy shoulder pads, especially when its wearer stoops in customary modesty.

Eventually, the power and majesty of the great Achaemenid Empire declined under a series of weak kings and a lifestyle condemned by Greek historians as hedonistic and rendering the Persians unfit to fight or govern. The sponginess at the centre allowed a regional fragmentation to occur, which was exacerbated by harsh and autocratic attempts at control. By the time Alexander the Great arrived to avenge the Persian defilement of Greek soil, the empire was drained of energy to offer determined resistance. With the fall of Persia, the influence of the East began to wane. The Hellenistic age ushered in by the conqueror reversed the winds of science and ideas, which for 3000 years had blown from East to West. For centuries to come, prevailing intellectual and cultural influences would travel eastwards from Mediterranean lands deep into Asia.

But Persia had sunk only for a time. It rose to glory again under the great Sassanid dynasty founded by Ardashir in the third century AD, five centuries after Alexander burned Persepolis. Centred again in Fars, the Iranian heartland, a reinvigorated people led by Ardashir threw out the Parthian rulers and established a new State that, under Ardashir's successors, was to rival the old Achaemenid Empire in expanse and stability. In the rock carvings at Naqsh-i Rustam, near Persepolis, the story is told how Shapur, Ardashir's son, defeated the Roman

Emperor Valerian and took him prisoner in a battle that destabilised the eastern borders of the Roman Empire. The relief is right under the mammoth tombs of Darius I and Darius II, which are carved high out of the living rock.

The dynasty revived Zoroastrianism, placing it high in the social order. The Sassanid kings promoted the concept that they derived authority directly from Ahuramazda, and ruled as an autocratic theocracy. The clergy gained significant power, the high priest collaborating closely with the monarch, who revived the old Achaemenid title 'King of Kings'. Fire temples combined religious observance with loyalty to the State. The Magi acted as religious judges throughout the provinces and imposed a strict adherence to the faith. The tolerance of the previous regime was reversed; piety was in. Nevertheless, the dynasty was given to implementing government actions in the traditional soft way of the Persians.

Under the famous Chosroes, the Sassanid Empire patrolled the crossroads of Asia, pushing its maritime trade as far as Indonesia and controlling the silk routes of Central Asia. Chosroes' court attracted people of brilliance from all over the world. Medical works of Galen were translated from the Greek, and philosophers from Athens, persecuted as pagans by Constantinople, were welcome. But, like their predecessors, the Sassanids declined, and for similar reasons, so that when the fervent Arab armies came through the East in the seventh century, they had easy pickings.

Chapter 12

Lure of the Straight Path

It was a nightmare checking out of our Shiraz hotel. The establishment would not take credit cards or travellers' cheques, only rials. To change money, I had to go to the bank, and wait in line for what seemed an interminable vigil. The exchange procedure itself was cumbersome and repetitious, expressing the official obsession with control, but there was no alternative. I had heard vaguely about a black market in currency but didn't think it was worth the risk. The strictness that we felt in the air everywhere was a powerful deterrent. If the banks had been closed at the time, we would have had to wait until they opened, perhaps at the cost of missing our flight, even overnight if necessary.

Check-in at the airport was also frustratingly slow, crowds around the counter clogging the system. Black moving shapes hemmed us in. They seemed to put sections of my peripheral vision into shadow, breaking up what I would normally see into changing forms of light and shade. All was silent; at times I could feel a shape pushing past me. I sensed the heat and energy inside it, no words, no sound. It was like the dance of the shapes in *The Tempest*. Certainly, the language barrier and the religion made the place seem foreign, but what set it apart, giving it an alien feeling touched with menace, were the black female forms that looked so inhuman.

ISFAHAN

On the Iran Air flight, we heard a flight attendant announce in heavily accented English: "In the name of God and the Islamic Republic of Iran, we welcome you aboard our flight to Isfahan". The flight was late, since the staff checked everybody's ticket, then came back once we were seated to collect our boarding passes. Most administrative systems in Iran are cumbersome, with copious redundant activity. One gets the feeling there is tight control over everything. It is like being inside a giant fishing net: your freedom is restricted, though you are allowed to breathe – just. However, on the roads there are no rules. All is

pandemonium. Cars manoeuvre past each other in a high-speed game of chicken. Drivers completely ignore white-lined pedestrian crossings. Perhaps it is a type of release from the behavioural strictures in other areas, those that control morality. Driving aggressively and without rules is a licentiousness outside a moral context, where the mullahs don't look.

We flew over flat, desiccated terrain cut by wrinkly hill lines and the tracks of dried rivers or, perhaps, ancient caravan routes. Wherever possible, little villages hugged the green of oases that sprang up at random. Suddenly, a huge mountain range loomed, its sharp peaks showing the clarity of youth. Little valleys of green and snow-patched heights relieved the monotony of the Asian beige. As we landed at Isfahan, we could see what seemed like another mountain chain, its peaks more mellow, framing the city on one side. It was the Zagros, a retreat for thinkers and poets.

The drive into town was elegant. Wide, tree-lined boulevards with median strips of grass, and gardens everywhere, reminded me of Seville, which rose to greatness around the time of Isfahan's golden age. This was a place of charm and aesthetic grandeur, unique among Iranian cities. We saw graceful mosques and tiled palaces of cerulean blue, often the subject of lyrical poetry. They linked the present to the romantic Persian age, the era of the Safavid dynasty founded in the early 16th century by Shah Isma'l.

Isfahan

Shah Isma'l restored internal order in Iran and established the Shiite sect as the State religion. Shah 'Abbas, one of his successors, crafted the society to an order of brilliance still revered by Iranians, moving his capital to Isfahan and building it into one of the most magnificent architectural centres in the world. In military exploits as impressive as his civil, he rolled back the expanding Ottoman Turks and tossed the Portuguese out of the colonies they had established on the Persian Gulf. The ayatollah we visited in Shiraz used the Portuguese affair as an inspirational example of Islam eliminating foreign domination.

This was a period of empire-building throughout the world. Charles V of Spain was expanding the Hapsburg Empire from the New World, while the

Maidan Square

Ottomans were pushing against the frontiers of Europe with the heavy artillery of Süleyman the Magnificent. Indeed, Shah Isma'l exchanged correspondence with Charles V about forming an alliance against the Ottomans, but to no avail. Blocked in the West, Russia was extending its power into Central Asia, left exhausted by the ravages of Tamerlane in the previous century. Shah 'Abbas was a contemporary of Elizabeth I, who ruled over an outward-looking England, confident in its newly founded naval expertise.

The Safavids, descendants of a Sufi leader, or 'shaikh', claimed to be part of the bloodline stemming from 'Ali's wife and one of the 12 Shi'a imams. In the early days of Islam, the belief emerged among Shiites that underneath the ostensible interpretation of the *Koran* lay concealed a secret truth, one that had been privately transmitted by Mohammed to 'Ali and thence to his heir. This led to the doctrine that the most authoritative spokesmen for Islam were the successors of 'Ali, to whom the confidential perceptions had been communicated. Imbued with this mystique, the privileged clerics became imams, or religious leaders of the community. Over time, they rose to superhuman status and acquired the characteristic of infallibility. The most important Shiite sect recognised 12 imams, the last of whom was prophesied to return, hence the name of the sect, Twelver, the one in power in Iran today.

Isma'l grew up on the run from Turcoman enemies, kept alive by the loyal Sufi followers of his father, who was a shaikh claiming descent from Shaikh Safi of the 14th century. Safi had founded an order of dervishes in Azerbaijan, a mountainous land bordering Iran's north. A gifted leader and fanatical in his devotion to the Shiite sect, Isma'l was able to attract a number of Turcoman tribes to his ambition, welding them into a force strong enough to rid his part of the Middle East of the Mongol yoke. After he was crowned Shah of Azerbaijan in Tabriz, a minor part of Persia at the time, he began to attract the jealous attention of the powerful Ottoman Turks, who were Sunnis. Fearing a rise of the rival sect, they began to persecute the Shiites, an act that created sympathy in Persia for Isma'l's cause. Religion, and specifically the Shiite sect, became a powerful unifying force that, along with the external threat of the expanding Ottomans, forged the Iranians into a nation once again, with Isma'l as their shah.

Shiism, informed by the mystical, ascetic ideas of Sufism and driven by the vivid images of guilt, repentance and self-sacrifice of its origins, was ideally suited to reinvigorate a society that had sunk into weakness and disunity. Shah Isma'l built the State into a powerful theocracy based on Twelver Shiism and on acceptance of him as the incarnation of the Twelfth Imam. Some people in modern times claim that Ayatollah Khomeini, too, was the resurrected leader.

Shah Isma'l led his religion-inspired peasant soldiers, called up with virtually no military training, against the Ottoman army of Sultan Selim the Grim at the battle of Chaldiran. Despite exceptional valour and chilling casualty rates, they lost, their raw courage unable to prevail against the modern artillery and well-trained Janissaries of the Turks. The conditions seem similar to the war waged against Iraq nearly half a millennium later by their successors in

the faith, although the outcome was different. Ultimately, the Turks were checked by Shah 'Abbas. Notwithstanding 28 years of war, the Sunni Turks failed to eradicate Shiism, so deeply had it penetrated the soul of Iranians. It still animates them today.

Some aspects of Sufism, it would seem, not only influenced the Iranians at the formation of the Safavid dynasty but still inform the Iranian character today. Ayatollah Khomeini often used his dreams to give a mystical foundation of authority to his political decisions. I felt that the otherworldly cult could not be far from the consciousness of Isfahan, direct inheritor of the Safavids, at least on one level.

The call to mysticism in the Islamic world is similar to that heard by Christian monks, taking its roots from some of the followers of Mohammed in the early days. It spread as the Arabs fanned the flames of their religious fervour into other parts of the world. The belief form stemmed from an ardent commitment to commune with God in a pure and concentrated form, the signal clear of all earthly noise. Pleasures of the flesh and all worldly considerations were seen as distracting the soul from its longing for union with God. Asceticism leaned towards the natural orientation of the introspective personality, the one that felt most comfortable in the personal psychological dimension. While the movement was inhabited by a wide scope of adherents, ranging from fairly simple souls to the intellectually gifted, it was marked by a common renouncing of the material world and a delving into the depths of internal space. Indeed, it was sometimes referred to as the 'inner science'. Franz Kafka explored the same region in his novels.

In the 11th century, a group of ascetics formed themselves into a cult known as Sufiyya, a name which seems to have been derived from the word 'suf', meaning 'wool'. Members wore woollen shirts, the garment traditionally associated with penitence, discomfort from the sharp fibres a constant punishment. It was also the sign of commitment to piety through a life of poverty, for rough wool was cheap. The Persian word for pauper is 'darwesh', leading to 'dervish', the term for a Sufi practitioner. Westerners are most familiar with the sect that started in the Turkish city of Konya, known as the whirling dervishes. As a means of intensifying their feeling of religious love, Sufis have traditionally listened to mystic poetry and music, often transcending the normal state into a realm of ecstasy that places them in direct contact with God.

By the end of the 11th century, Sufism moved into a stage of encouraging visionary and occult experiences that purported to demonstrate progress in the understanding of the soul. Dreams and visions were seen as important manifestations of recondite truth, and were interpreted on the psychic level by Sufi masters, in a manner that presaged Freud.

In 1598, at a time when Shakespeare was writing his plays, Shah 'Abbas moved his court to Isfahan, where he began an architectural programme that transformed the city into one of the most beautiful in the world. At one million people, it was also one of the most populous. We went to its heart – Maidan Square, now renamed Imam Khomeini, one of the largest in the world. Measuring 500 metres long and 165 metres wide, it was used as a polo field. The goal posts are still standing. Grass surrounds a massive fountain pool in the centre and trees line the inside perimeter. Shah 'Abbas used to march his regiment of royal guards in the square, ordering his men to change their uniforms twice during the parade in order to triple the apparent numbers. Mussolini did the same.

At one end of the majestic square stands the Royal Mosque, its flashing dome glazed in pale blue saluting the dusty Zagreb Mountains surrounding the city. The colour of its tiles slips into different hues in sympathy with the sun as it passes across the sky, altering the identity of the building. At the grand entrance, rising 30 metres, on guard with two graceful minarets, a cascade of stalactites acts as a transition from the square base to the circular dome, typical of Islamic architecture. They dazzle the eye with their highly fired tiles set like encrusted jewellery. Various patterns, so intricately repeated that to follow them in detail is a brainteaser, decorate the walls and ceilings in different colours. Graceful Kufic script, acknowledging the presence of God and announcing the achievements of Shah 'Abbas, frames the picture. Inside the mosque are vaulted sanctuaries tiled in a profusion of coloured geometry. From the centre of one, under a gold-leaf dome representing heaven, sound reverberates in eight echoes throughout the entire building.

Shah 'Abbas spent 26 years realising the grand project, suffering many frustrations, sometimes exacerbated by his own impetuousness. He ordered his main architect, 'Ali Akbar Isfahani, to install tiles on the building before it had time to settle. Unable to convince the impatient monarch of the need to wait, the architect fled Isfahan, and cringed in hiding for three years. Before he disappeared, however, the cunning 'Ali Akbar measured with chains the height of those columns already erected, then hid the chains. An enraged shah ordered his arrest, offering a reward, but to no avail. After three years, 'Ali Akbar returned, bringing out the chains to demonstrate that the building had indeed sunk as he had predicted. He was able to prove that had the tiles been installed, they would have slipped off. The shah forgave him, but ordered him to cover the façade with mosaics, a task the embattled architect said would take 100 years to complete. He got away with a compromise, using larger tiles, which he placed in skilful combinations to produce a gradual shading from blue to yellow.

Bazaar, Isfahan

We strolled beside the line of shade trees inside the square, past a myriad of artisanal shops busy with trade. We came to the six-storey 'Ali Qapu palace, built in the 17th century and said to be Iran's first skyscraper. It served as an administrative centre for government, a reception area for dignitaries and a vantage point for monitoring city life in the square. The luxurious furniture of the halcyon days has gone, but the porch of 18 elegantly shaped wooden columns retains the grandeur of the bygone age. Curtains of rich fabric used to hang between them. From there, Shah 'Abbas enjoyed polo games and archery contests in the square below. Somewhere outside, we could hear a flute play-ing. It sounded like a dull whistle, its tri-note melody repetitive and hypnotic, a reminder that we were in the grasp of the East. Isfahan is as far from Istanbul as Istanbul is from Paris. Relations with Afghanistan and India are much more immediate than concerns with Western politics.

In the receiving hall, where delegations from all over the world paid their respects to the wealthy Shah, peacock frescoes adorned the walls. A music hall,

Royal Mosque, Maidan Square

Isfahan

with niches to absorb the sound, echoed the cultivated luxury enjoyed during the period. The musicians would be installed on the second floor, behind curtains, so that the sound seemed to come in a supernatural flow out of the walls.

At the end opposite the Royal Mosque, the grand square metamorphoses into a brick-domed bazaar that stretches two and a half kilometres in a sinuous line across the city to the Friday Mosque, built in Seljuk times. The central corridor of the mercantile serpent was encrusted with a profusion of caravanserais, medresas, baths, factories and shops like the growth form of rock crystal. Shafts of light intruded into the space through openings in the domes. The high, vaulted ceilings that form a series of graceful Persian arches over the long curvaceous spine brought an atmosphere of nobility to the world of commerce.

Isfahan grew rich from its business activities, encouraged by a benign policy framework under Shah 'Abbas. Its textile industry employed 25,000 people in the city, producing fabrics in colours, weaves and patterns that were sold at the top end of the market across the world. The Shah imported Chinese ceramicists to teach his artisans the technique of making the blue-and-white porcelain of the Ming period, in high demand in Europe. Safavid metalwork reached a standard admired everywhere. The bazaar was the centre of trade and industry.

Today, the bazaar seems to have lost none of the verve that distinguished it under the Safavids. It is bustling and full, the sounds of commerce prosperously cacophonous. New products have emerged, such as the motorcycles that crowd the sides of the main thoroughfare, but much of the traditional is still traded. We were enthralled by the miniature paintings, the size of a page in an ordinary book. Indeed, most of them had been painted on a blank page, the other side of which contained old poems in Arabic script. Demand for them was large enough to warrant a section of shops devoted exclusively to their sale. Works by national masters can be bought at reasonable prices.

By the 14th century, Persian artists were illustrating their classical manuscripts in support of the narrative. In time, the illustrations developed into intricate paintings that could stand apart from the text on the pages facing them. Gradually, they developed into single-page paintings and drawings, but the size remained diminutive, small enough to be kept in albums. The scale creates an atmosphere of intimacy that pulls the viewer into a tight focus on the precision of the brush strokes. It has appeal to the perfectionist. Under the Safavids, Persian miniatures blossomed into one of the highest art forms of the age, their beauty and compositional harmony a non pareil. Portraits of courtiers, hunting scenes and paintings of ordinary people in various poses give an aesthetic insight into the times, the ideas and what was important. They show life in an idealised form – how it should be, not how it is. Persian artists resisted European advances into the realm of perspective, with its greater realism, staying with the two-dimensional design and its more stylised approach.

In the West, we see a major distinction between the artisan who can faithfully repeat an existing product with skill and the artist who brings originality to his work. In Iranian art history, such a distinction is meaningless; it is never made. The result is that existing subjects and art forms do not need to disappear under the pressing need to demonstrate a clearly observable originality. While scope exists for innovation within bounds and, accordingly, for progression over time, artists are content to rework the traditional forms. A similar view towards artistic creativity informs the Chinese tradition – indeed, the Persian style was influenced by Chinese painting.

Persian miniature on camel bone

Persian miniatures on paper

Persian miniatures on paper

sian miniature on camel bone

Sheik Lutfollah Mosque,
Maidan Square

Hence, today, it is possible to see superbly crafted miniatures painted by contemporary artists famous in the land, even though they are using themes that have their origins deep in the past. The execution is part of the creative process in the same manner that a pianist brings something special to the musical composition. In the West, we equate creativity in art with uniqueness, an abrupt break with earlier works. Even though a particular style may have currency for a while, we require the artist to produce variations that, while suffused with influence, are sufficiently unique to avoid the sin of derivation. Soon, the scope for variation is exhausted and a paradigm shift becomes necessary. That is not so in the East.

To my mind, it is, above all, colour that sets the Persian miniature apart as an art form. The brilliance and placing of the blues, the yellows, the reds and whites on the small page bring a sensuous stimulation to the eye that lingers long after seeing it. The arrangement of the colours is so skilful that a sense of dynamic harmony emerges, adding an extra dimension to the forms in the scene. In cases where expense was not a constraint, the artists used gold, silver and lapis lazuli, with red extracted from cinnabar and green from malachite, an oxide of copper. According to a 16th-century writer, the favoured brush was made from squirrels' tails, but some artists used the long hairs of Persian cats.

While the *Koran* does not explicitly prohibit the representation of living things, from the eighth century a strong policy emerged within Islam against it. It was feared that drawing or sculpting images of human beings and animals could lead to idolatry and, possibly, to a sharing of divine power with God, errors that were indeed anathema. The *Koran* states: "God does not pardon setting up partners to God but pardons anything else". Perhaps leaders of Islamic thought reacted against the excesses of Byzantine icon worship that were evident in the rival Christian religion of their time.

Notwithstanding the proscription, Persian miniatures are all about images of people and animals. Indeed, some of the scenes we saw on sale in the bazaar were of languorous youths reclining in hedonistic poses and enjoying cups of wine. Others were of voluptuous women in love. None of the subjects wore

Tea house, Isfahan

Isfahan

'Ali Qapu palace

religious garb. But the art form did not, and does not, attract religious opprobrium. The reason is that the inventive and pious Iranians have rationalised the paradox by characterising the work as too small to be representative in the prohibited manner. It is merely an expression of imagination, not of reality. Nevertheless, it seemed incongruous to me that the images, which were so human and natural, such a joyous exultation of the sensuous – completely at odds with the stern fundamentalism of the present – were allowed to be distributed.

I was keen to arrange an interview with another cleric, for Isfahan is an important religious centre, noted for its piety. I wanted to see if there would be any contrast with the ayatollah in Shiraz, any inconsistency. Our guide, despite protestations of having connections at the highest level, had a difficult time finding someone willing. After a couple of days in the search, he could only come up with a mullah. I didn't mind; indeed, there was merit in speaking to someone who had not yet reached the learnedness of an ayatollah. His views might be closer to what most people felt. Again, it was necessary to go to a medresa. After virtually no waiting, the mullah came out of the courtyard to the anteroom and greeted us warmly. It was discreetly indicated by our guide, who had spoken with the mullah previously, that it would be best if Anna-Maryke did not attend the interview. I found that surprising, as the ayatollah in Shiraz had not minded. This man was younger, though; perhaps he felt threatened by a woman, or perhaps it was just that Isfahan was a more pious place than Shiraz. I felt awkward, but Anna-Maryke said she would go for a walk. I promised not to be long.

The mullah had a gentle face with a black beard, flecked with grey, and moved in the unthreatening way of a kind man. He was wearing a white shirt with a grey robe inside a black outer garment, long

Stalactite decoration, Maidan Square

Isfahan

and uncreased. The white turban on his head was like a halo of serenity. While he could speak some English, it was limited to greeting words, not enough to dispense with an interpreter.

What follows is my foreshortened recollection of the questions and answers in the interview with the mullah. We were joined by 10 or 12 university students, who sat with us on traditionally patterned carpets faded with the patina of age. We faced a central courtyard, peacefully leafy and still. A blackboard and chalk behind us showed we were not yet in the information age.

Q: Do you think Iran is a proselytising nation?

A: There are many Muslim countries. Muslims everywhere know the Iranian people have a background of accepting Islam. Faithful people in some countries are frustrated by the failure of governments to foster a religious society. If all governments were the same, like Iran, Muslims would be united and encouraged in their religion. Iran is showing the way; others are taking notice. We see that the principles of government in the East [ex-Soviet Central Asia] are shaken when we send the message of Islam, and in Western countries too.

Q: What is your attitude towards Western technology?

A: We can have a religious society and technology. Technology is not special to the West. The Prophet [here, the students who had gathered around muttered "Sala-lah" ("peace be upon him and his family")] says search for knowledge, even in China, everywhere. If we fell behind in technology, it is because powerful countries like the UK and US exploited us. They would not let us learn. But after the revolution, we gained our independence. We are not dependent on any other country. Under the Shah, we were a colony, and that is why we fell behind.

With some Western countries, we had and have good relations, but not with the United States. They tried to play tricks. If we blocked them one way, they would try another way. Ayatollah Khomeini [the students rumbled, "God bless him"] said we can not trust the United States. They tried to take over our oil, buy it at cheap prices and sell it high. We can not have good relations with the United States, unless of course they change, cease to deceive us and trample on us, become more like Germany and France.

However, during the 20 years since the revolution, the US have shown that they will not change.

Q: Do you think Iran will become a powerful nation again over the long term?

A: Yes, we think we will become a powerful country. But, according to Ayatollah Khomeini [again, the students muttered a blessing] we have to do our duty without thinking about whether we will be powerful. We do not wish to control nations around the world. What we want is an Islamic governmental system throughout all Islam which will do its duty according to the dictates of the *Koran*. Everything stems from the need to adopt the 'straight way'.

Q: What do you see as the principle difference between Iran and non-Islamic countries?

A: The main difference is that we believe in an afterlife and in resurrection day. The teaching of the *Koran* emphasises human responsibility. On the last day, all people will be raised to life and brought before God to be judged. Those who have lived a life that was mainly good will go to paradise; the others will go to hell.

I thanked the mullah for his courtesy in spending time with us. It seemed to me there was not a scintilla of difference in attitude between the mullah and the ayatollah of Shiraz in regard to the role Iran should play in the world of Islam, at least on the macro level.

After leaving the medresa, Anna-Maryke and I went for a long walk with our guide along the main street, Chahar Bagh (meaning 'four gardens'), a tree-lined boulevard constructed at the end of the 16th century. The guide told us that most of the soldiers in the Iraq–Iran war came from the Isfahan region, which is noted for its religious devotion. He spoke bitterly about the different types of chemical weapons used by the Iraqis: some caused horrible blisters, others made the blood congeal inside the vascular system, all carried death on the back of terrible pain. We saw photographs of the victims, young men suffering human ruination in grotesque form.

His face growing concentrated, eyes firing, the guide boasted about the contrast between the Iranian troops and their Iraqi counterparts. The Iranians would vie with each other for the right to lead attacks, he claimed, while the Iraqi soldiers were quick to surrender when the slightest pressure was applied. But notwithstanding the valour, the war was very difficult for Iran, for it had to stand alone against an enemy that was armed by the West and had the support of most of the world. The bulk of the Arab community stood with Iraq, dispatching troops from Egypt, Syria, Jordan, North Africa, and Saudi Arabia to fight alongside their fellow Arabs. While an Islamic umbrella covered the belligerents, ethnic rivalry and doctrinal differences split them tragically. Over a million people died in the war, all appealing to the same God.

Our guide spoke proudly of the inspirational leadership of Ayatollah Khomeini, proud to give an example of the propitious interface between military

Mosque dome, Isfahan

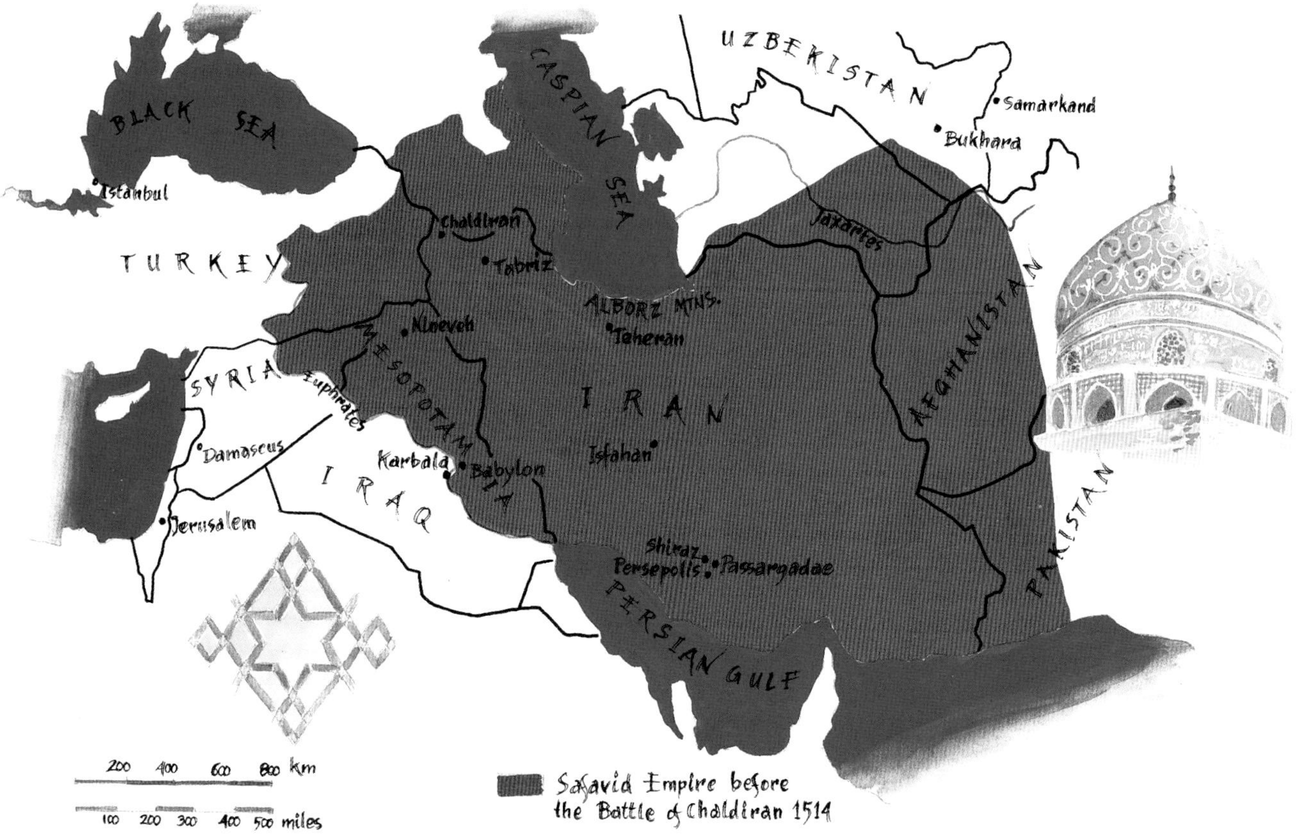

BLACK SEA
Istanbul
TURKEY
CASPIAN SEA
UZBEKISTAN
Samarkand
Bukhara
Chaldiran
Tabriz
Jaxartes
ALBORZ MTNS.
Teheran
Nineveh
SYRIA
MESOPOTAMIA
Euphrates
Damascus
Karbala
Babylon
IRAQ
IRAN
Isfahan
AFGHANISTAN
PAKISTAN
Jerusalem
Shiraz
Persepolis • Passargadae
PERSIAN GULF

200   400   600   800 km
100   200   300   400 500 miles

Safavid Empire before
the Battle of Chaldiran 1514

decision-making and religious guidance. In 1988, towards the end of the war, the Ayatollah had a dream that the Iraqis would attack Fave Island en masse with chemical weapons. When he awoke, he ordered a retreat – a difficult command for the generals to accept in light of the culture of attack and sacrifice inculcated into the troops. The decision turned out to be correct. Many lives were spared. Dream interpretation was a common leadership technique used by the Ayatollah, arising out of his link with the Sufi tradition.

While uncritical enthusiasm for charismatic leaders is not uncommon, although on the wane in the West, the man's animation was informed at a deeper level, beneath personalities. We met many others like him. It reached into the roots of the Islamic mind, and touched the source of commit-ment that alone offers the chance of repelling the perceived menace of world secularism and material-ism. Argument might rage about whether a liberal or conservative trend in Iranian society should be encouraged, but that the *Koran* is the guide rests securely beyond discussion. Even the reformist politician, Mohammed Khatami, who was recently elected prime minister by a stunning victory at the polls, reflecting a widespread call for more personal freedom, is a cleric and deeply committed to the Islamic way of life. While some of the more extreme strictures on social behaviour might be relieved in time, it hard to think that a change in character is on the cards.

Coloured by affronted pride though it may be, the Iranian motivation is more profound than that. It engages the will to survive in a mortal struggle with forces – stemming from the West and, in particular, its undisputed leader, the United States – that threaten to overwhelm the traditional values of its Islamic society, the way of life that provides its identity. The clash of civilisations, now 14 centuries old, will inevitably continue. The only question is what form it will take in the future. If a more engaged understanding between the antagonists can be achieved, there is hope that it will be less violent than it has been in the past.

It appears clear that the revival of Islamic faith in a people yearning to be rescued from national weakness and erosion of identity has created a sense of personal empowerment in contemporary Iran. Individuals feel they have a place in the world that is benignly watched over, and the means, through following the straight path, of gaining power over themselves, for themselves and for others. The sense of inner strength that comes from the conviction of a life lived strictly in accordance with divine revelation creates, they believe, a higher state of being than can emerge from one draped in material affluence and swamped by hedonism, the paradigm they perceive in the West. They would acknowledge their lack of economic and military power, but retort that they do not suffer spiritual angst.

There is no doubt that Iran will acquire modern technology, mostly from the West, but it seems probable that because it and the accompanying materialism are relegated to second rank, the process will be selective. Thus, some elements of Western culture could be adopted and others rejected. In this manner Iran might in time – perhaps a long time – become an important power based on its own paradigm, influenced by but not derived from the West.

I felt we were at the heart of a process of regeneration whose influence was radiating far beyond the boundaries of its crucible. Evidence of its effects we had seen in Turkey, and I suspected it would cause action at a distance farther east. In the days of its imperial past, Iran ruled lands beyond the Caspian Sea so remote that their existence has been known in the West more through poetic reference than through geography. They invoke images of fabulous wealth, heroic conquerors, legendary artistic beauty, great wisdom and scientific learning. One of the Magi to attend the birth of Jesus probably came from this region. Collectively known as Central Asia, these territories reach out over arid, flat and at times mountainous terrain, from the eastern frontier of Iran all the way to China. Part of the Islamic inheritance, they are now awakening from the long spell cast on them by the Soviet Union. We were eager to go there.

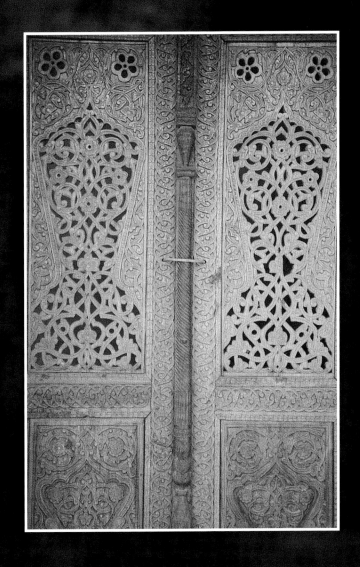

Part IV
CENTRAL
ASIA

Tilla-Kari, medresa

PART

IV

Chapter 13

Heart of Asia

Alicher Novoi

The faraway Oxus River cascades from the roof of the world in the Pamir Mountains, above the Hindu Kush, and slices north through the freeze-heat steppes of Central Asia to charge the Aral Sea, 2600 kilometres in the distance. Its life force generated the mysterious civilisation of classical Transoxiana that has seduced powerful minds since the morning of recorded history. Over time, a change of name was often the fanfare for a new regime. The great merchant cities of Samarkand and Bukhara, on the Indo-European sector of the ancient Silk Road, are today located in what the Soviet colonists dubbed Uzbekistan.

The land between the rivers Oxus and Jaxartes generated the fabled Sogdiana, which at the time of the Achaemenid dynasty stood as the northeastern frontier of the Persian Empire. Sogdians, an Indo-European people, feature on the processional staircase at Persepolis, caps bulging in front where their hair was tied in a knot. The region was known as Transoxiana to the European poets. Now called the Amu Darya and the Syr Darya, these mighty rivers enclose the bulk of Uzbekistan, named after the Uzbek Turkic tribe that forms the dominant ethnic group today.

The Sogdians amassed legendary wealth from trade along the ancient system of caravan routes that cut through their oasis country after passing over the mountain chain that isolated Chinese Turkestan. The fame of the powerful Fergana horses of eastern Sogdiana, said to run so fast that they sweated blood, reached the imperial court in China. In the second century BC, desire for the horses drew the first official Chinese expedition to the lands the Chinese called the Far West, inaugurating the Silk Road.

On either side of the Amu Darya lie enormous deserts, monstrous life-threatening traps for the unwary. To the east is the Kyzylkum ('red desert'), to the west the Karakum ('black desert'), the different colours due to the mineral

Tamerlane

content of the sands. Crossing them was the perilous task of the caravans of camels that brought goods and human contact from East to West and back. From ancient times, human settlement had huddled around a system of verdant oases that stretch across the desert like a string of emeralds strewn on a beige cloth. Without them, it is doubtful whether the Silk Road would have started before the age of mechanised transport. The land out there in the midst of the largest continent breeds a harshness of climate that matches its inherent inclemency – viciously hot in summer and flesh-shrinkingly cold in winter. The best time to visit is in spring or autumn, when the weather is tolerable.

TASHKENT

At half past one in the morning, we landed in Tashkent, remote capital of this distant land. Women in black chador and men with the stubble favoured in Islamic nations shuffled quietly down a dirty corridor to line up in a tenebrous concrete room, its walls spoliating shamelessly. Cigarette smoke billowed, fogging up the air like a London pea-souper – men in the East are like tobacco kilns – and we had to put up with smarting eyes while scruffy officials laboriously processed people's documents in the gloom. Visitors need visas, which can be obtained only inside the country, so we had to appear at the frontier and trust in our travel agent. No-one speaks English in Central Asia; Russian is the lingua franca, amidst various Turkic and Iranian dialects. After two hours of waiting with no agent in sight, a dour clerk opened his visa kiosk. To our relief, when our turn in the long queue came, he found our names in a grubby, handwritten notebook, and mutely issued the papers.

After we had passed the formalities and were on the other side of the customs and immigration barrier, two men with an Asia Travel sign materialised, and whisked us away by car to our hotel along wide, tree-lined streets designed by the Soviets to demonstrate the power of the State.

The hotel was as forbidding as a KGB prison; all lights, inside and outside, had been turned off, but we could just make out a shabby, six-storey concrete building, senescent before its time. With nobody in sight, our guide led us

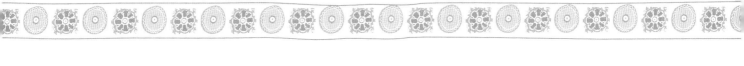

through clanking doors into a high-ceilinged lobby and knocked on a half-glazed partition just inside the entrance. In a few seconds, which seemed much longer in the dark, a raw bulb flared in the room. As we entered, an obese, dishevelled woman with sleep in her eyes shuffled behind a messy desk, groped at our passports and handed us a key, all without a word. As soon as we left, the light went out. While we turned to pick up our luggage, the travel-agency man evaporated silently. We had to make three trips in a tiny, rickety elevator, carrying our bags down a long corridor rank with the decadence of neglect, to reach our room, which was linked by smell to its facilities. A pale dawn light was beginning to seep through the thin, limp curtains as we went to bed.

The next day, we were driven, bleary-eyed, to the offices of Asia Travel. The manager apologised for the hotel, mumbling through a thick Russian accent that the guide, in a sudden burst of unbureaucratic initiative, had made a diversion from the one specified in our itinerary – seeing were not in a group, he had assumed we would prefer a cheaper establishment. Mercifully, the rest of the hotels on our trip turned out to be better, though only marginally. Still, we were not there for luxury.

We met our new guide. His name, Rustan, after the hero of the *Shahnameh*, reached back into the centuries to a time when this part of the world was a literary inspiration. He was from Samarkand, a Tartar whose parents had been forcibly resettled under the grandiose social-engineering scheme Stalin forced upon the nation to break up troublesome ethnic groups and salt the vast Asian hinterland with Russians. Today, 12 per cent of Uzbekistan's 22 million people are European.

The hurricane that knocked down the Soviet empire is blowing historic change across Central Asia. We saw its effect in Tashkent, an unremarkable city of two million with the soul of an administration

centre. Lenin statuary had metamorphosed into images of Uzbek national pride: the bloodthirsty Tamerlane, looking fatherly astride his horse, and Alicher Novoi, the 15th-century Uzbek Chaucer who wrote in the vernacular, giving it status alongside the Farsi spoken by the upper class.

Mosques, once sparsely attended, are now alive with worshippers. The Soviets baulked at prohibiting religious observance, but managed to inhibit the natural inclination of the 80 per cent Muslim population by making atheism a prerequisite for advancement within the command economy. In reaction to the antireligious political correctness of the previous regime, people see the practising their faith not as a burdensome discipline but as an expression of freedom, a release from alien stricture.

After Uzbekistan gained its independence, in 1991, an Islamic fundamentalist movement sprouted up suddenly, mainly in the Fergana valley, driven by encouragement from Iran. Zealots tried to influence government policy, while young women happily began to wear the hejab. Medresas sprang up all over the country, teaching the *Koran* to enthusiasts who knew nothing but the dictates of Marxist atheism. Stonemasons turned their skills to building mosques.

Some things haven't changed, however. Faces in official positions still have Soviet dourness; smiling is considered undignified, suggesting a lack of serious dedication to the task at hand. And the cell-block-style hotels still have floor ladies, invariably fat and cranky, who control the room keys and pass their lives in front of loud television sets.

Uzbekistan is a nominal democracy but, under Islan Karimov, an old Soviet hand, remains as authoritarian as it was under the ancient regime; *plus ça change, plus c'est la même chose*. Nevertheless, a new pride walks in the street. The inheritors of the great Sogdian culture which in its day strode the world's frontiers of art and science have thrown off the shackles of Soviet colonisation that held them in sway for over a century and a half. Liberation from foreign hegemony is a tonic that satisfies their political needs, which have never encompassed true democracy.

Notwithstanding independence, their freedom is exercised within a culture still burdened with overtones of the recent past. Soviet proletarian style dominates the cuisine and the restaurants. We had dinner in a highly recommended establishment, Tashkent's equivalent of a three-star restaurant. When we entered, the place had been darkened for instant atmosphere, so dim that we could not see the food. It was just possible to make out that we were almost the only customers there. Plastic flowers hung on the walls, illuminated by pencil-like spotlights. Starched red serviettes stood upright on the table like phalluses.

We were greeted with conversation-blocking rock music, which played for a while, then mercifully stopped. A tired-looking man with a grumpy face came out into a floodlit area and began to play soupy pop music on a Panasonic organ set up on small aluminium poles. It wasn't as loud as the rock, but the peace we felt whenever he took a break was the best part of the evening.

The Russian-speaking waiter, who could manage only one or two words of English, insisted that we eat the salad he had placed at our table without being asked. We tried to explain that we did not want it, not indicating that the real reason was its rusty condition, which made it singularly unappetising. But he refused to take it away, disappearing for 20 minutes, then coming back to monitor our progress. He did not intend to take our order until we had eaten it. I finally broke the impasse by indicating in sign language that we would gratefully pay for it if only he would remove the baleful vegetation.

He finally did, with a scowl, and we progressed to something edible, but the food was so bland that it wasn't worth engaging one's sense of taste. In fact, we found the food all over Uzbekistan appalling, a disappointment made astonishing by the culinary quality on the other side of the Pamirs, where the culture had not been influenced by the Soviet factor. The people are of the same ethnic group and have similar traditions, including basic recipes, but there is no comparison in the quality of the food.

Rustan packed our luggage into his Gigoli, made in the massive automobile complex on the Volga, and drove us southwest along the old Silk Road towards Samarkand, into land the ancients called the Hungry Steppe. Now, some of it is irrigated to support fields of cotton crops that spread over the desiccated land like huge flecked rugs. Mulberry trees for silk production lined the sides of the road. But soon we passed the signs of cultivation and launched into the mournful desert. It wasn't devoid of vegetation, though; scrub blasted by the winds relieved the monotony of the stony sand. Along the road, a small purple flower called 'saksaul' brightened the way. It seemed so delicate and intimate, a little lamp of life in the hard landscape, mortally threatening in its scorching, lonely vastness. The road was straight and flat, unmarked, but wide enough to accommodate six lanes of traffic. We were far into the vast Central Asia plain that stretches east to the Pamir Mountains just 200 kilometres from Tashkent. All along the way were police checkpoints, where we had to stop and show our passports.

We passed through oil-rich Kazakstan briefly, but long enough to see what must be the most curious service station in the world. For two kilometres along the desert road, scores of tattered entrepreneurs were selling petrol poured from makeshift containers: old vodka bottles, jerry cans, battered 44-gallon drums – anything that could hold fluid. Some were living in dirty tin shanties with burlap doors; others kept old-fashioned beds outside on the shoulder of the road, strewn with soiled sheets. Petrol stains coagulated the sand. All was hot, dusty and dry. It looked like a scene out of *Mad Max*. No-one paid any regard whatsoever to the danger of combustion, even in the fume-infested 28 degrees. Aghast, Anna-Maryke and I shifted hurriedly when we saw a tough-looking tribesman nonchalantly light up a cigarette as he filled our tank, spilling fuel freely on the ground.

We were in what historians call the 'heart of Asia', the crucible where the fascinating mixture of Caucasian and Mongolid races has reached an alchemic form. Its human history has been a violent fusion, tectonic in its force, like the plate boundary collisions beneath the ground that forged the structure for some of the most spectacular epithermal gold deposits ever discovered. The Muruntau ore body, with 100 million contained ounces, equal to the current reserves of the International Monetary Fund, is the world's largest open-pit gold mine. Hidden in the mountains of the Kyzylkum desert, it is an important contributor to the nation's balance of payments.

The Islamic world, founded on Arab armies and brought to the heights of civilisation by a felicitous mixture of Arab and Persian genius, reached its apogee in the 10th century and then began to lose vigour. In Central Asia at around this time, one of the great migratory eruptions of history was taking place. Turkic tribes, on the move in the ninth century searching for new lands to graze their horses or just attracted by the breathtaking affluence they saw in the civilised world, began moving west out of their homelands in Central Asia. Some intruded into southern Russia and eastern Europe, while others infiltrated the porous borders of eastern Islam. While conquerors in wars, the nomads surrendered to the intellectual power of Islam, easily trading their traditional shamanism for the sophisticated religion that offered so much promise. One of these, a particularly warlike tribe, was the Seljuks, who carried the Prophet's banner into Anatolia and battered the eastern defences of the Byzantine Empire. They debouched out of Central Asia in the 11th century, establishing themselves as the dominant power in Iran, and pressed west. Backed by their successful armies, they wrested leadership of Islam from the Arabs, establishing a universal sultanate to replace the ailing caliphate of the Abbasid dynasty. The defeat they inflicted on the Byzantine army at Manzikert in 1071, in Anatolia, resonated so loudly throughout Christendom that it led, a generation later, to the preaching of the First Crusade.

The arrival of the Turks brought the vigour of a new race to the people of the Prophet, the third race of Islam. The new converts rose in power as the political unity of the Arabs and Persians fragmented and their military strength flagged. Over the next five centuries, the societies of Islam were to endure successive invasions of Turkic peoples, mainly from Central Asia, and their cousins, the Mongols, as the age of the nomad took hold. The settled inhabitants of farms and cities, softened by affluence, had no hope of standing up to the fierce horsemen toughened by a life in the elements and constantly on the move. Gun power had not yet arrived to lessen the odds. The difference in lifestyle and strength bred a contempt in the minds of the nomad warriors that led many of them to commit atrocities far beyond any military need.

Over the years, these migrant conquerors mixed with the predominantly Indo-European settlers they encountered in western Asia, forming a Eurasian race. Today in Uzbekistan, over 100 nationalities live together and every fourth marriage is of mixed race.

The most devastating of the migratory invasions

Samarkand

was the onslaught of the Mongols, a people who lived in the harsh northern grasslands above China and Central Asia. They share common origins with the Turks, to whom they are linguistically closely related. So hardy were their troops that they could ride all night, snatching sleep in their saddles while on the march, and so unfastidious that they would eat the lice that covered their bodies. Put on a horse as soon as they could walk, the Mongols were natural riders, able to shoot looking backwards using their composite bow, the most advanced weapon at the time. A feuding, bellicose people, according to one European traveller who visited their lands, they would rather fight each other than rest from battle. Military tactics, practised frequently in their vast co-ordinated hunts, were honed to such sharpness that entire contingents could manoeuvre as one man. No army stood a chance of resisting them.

In the 13th century, their legendary chieftain Genghis Khan led his steppe cavalry into the cultivated Asian heartland from the north, thrusting warfare to hitherto unknown extremes of devastation. For the next 150 years, people lived in nerve-abrading fear of seeing the yak-tail standard loom without warning over the dusty horizon, signalling yet another genocidal onslaught so terrible that the world had to wait until the 20th century to witness its equal. In one episode, Genghis' youngest son, Tolui, sacked the prosperous Silk Road city of Merv, massacring what commentators claim to have been a million citizens in three weeks of incomprehensible terror, an event four times more lethal than the atomic bomb attacks on Japan.

The Central Asian region is an amphitheatre for the classic drama of nomadic barbarians overwhelming affluent sedentary people. The steppe fury wreaked such calamity upon the world that many say it caused the renowned melancholia of the Russian people who were forced to endure it for 200 years. Out of it arose the Western fear of the 'Yellow Peril'. The Mongol dominance throughout Asia survived Genghis Khan's death for several centuries, spreading to China where his grandson Kublai Khan established the Yuan dynasty and entertained Marco Polo at his fabled court.

SAMARKAND

After hours of driving across the monotonous, dusty steppe, so vast it seemed endless, we came to the romantic city of Samarkand, the place that Tamerlane made his capital. Perhaps it was the contrast with the miles of desiccation through which we had travelled, but my first impression was how green it was. Trees were growing everywhere, even on small streets, and all looked clean. The colour took the savagery out of the baleful sun that had beaten down on us all day.

As we drove into town along handsome, wide roads, we began to see the fabled domes of Samarkand, their turquoise and blue tiles flashing in the sun, standing nobly above the drab buildings carelessly thrown up during the Soviet era. In the centre of town, the streets were teeming with people, the women in spectacular traditional dresses, long and in such bright colours they would have looked garish had the light had not been so harsh. The contrast with the dusty steppe through which we had been battling was like drinking a glass of water after a choking thirst.

In lands east of the Hellespont, dust and sun are the bane of human life. The dry monotone of desert and steppe depresses the mood and the pitiless sun drives summer temperatures to enervating heights. The bright turquoise towers and shady gardens of Samarkand were built as the antidote. Its location, where the Zeravshan River brings life to the Kyzylkum desert, attracted settlers at least as early as the Persian Empire, wealth tumbling into its coffers

Registan

Tiles

from Silk Road commerce. But as Tamerlane's capital, it reached a glorious peak, inspiring legends as far away as Europe.

One of the most randomly bloodthirsty of the super-warriors from the steppe was Timur, a shepherd's son whose early leg wound gave him the name 'Timur-i-lenk' ('Timur the lame'), anglicised to 'Tamerlane'. Through his parentage, which was both Turkic and Mongol, he took great pains to develop a claim of descent from Genghis Khan, whose savagery he boosted to a new level. In his sanguinary biographical play, Christopher Marlowe described Tamerlane as a conqueror who "in the furrows of his brow harbours revenge, war, death and cruelty".

Born around 1336 near the small town of Shahr-i Sabz, 50 kilometres from Samarkand, this illiterate military genius who prepared for battle by playing chess defeated the Persian and Turkish empires, two of the mightiest powers of the day, and built a domain that stretched from

Tilla-Kari, medresa, Registan

Tiles

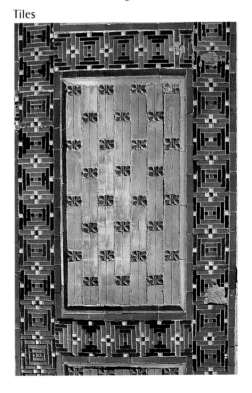

the Euphrates to the Ganges. Driven by a blood lust unusual even by the standards of his day, the self-proclaimed 'scourge of God' shed terror like a lightning storm, wherever he rode. In Sistan, he had 2000 people encased alive in wet plaster and built into a tower. Travellers could tell when Tamerlane had just invested a city well before they got there, by the huge mounds of rotting heads piled high outside to advertise the penalty for resistance. Chroniclers of the time called them Tamerlane's minarets. At night, a ghastly phosphorescence of decay would light up the sky with a pale hue.

Calamity blackened the 14th century like the dust cloud that blocked out the sun in the age of the dinosaurs. It was the period of the Black Death, which in Europe claimed the lives of one-third of the urban population. Identified as the bubonic plague and transmitted by the fleas living on rats, it owes its baleful origin to Central Asia, from where it migrated along the northern trade route to Istanbul. In its homeland, the Black Death was as monstrous a destroyer of human life as it was in Europe. In that century of mortality and desensitisation to suffering, Tamerlane was but a grim continuation of the paradigm, an apparent outcome of fate, cruel but unavoidable. In a morbid way, he was appropriate in that dark age where the lethal plague was so prevalent and random that it seemed like a personality distinct.

Not all people view the 'scourge of God' in the light of European history. The Uzbeks consider him a national saviour who expelled the Chagatai Mongols from Central Asia and left an architectural signature that alone justifies tourism in their country. He was the 'lord of the favourable conjuncture', who seized the times and bent them to his will, forging a glorious empire for his people. Taking a swipe at Soviet domination, the President of the Uzbekistan Republic noted when unveiling a monument to the sanguinary conqueror:

> For many years our people were in the colonial grip; they were deprived of their right to worship their great compatriot, to requite him according to his historical desserts.
>
> They tried to blacken the name of Amir Timur in our history, to bury it in oblivion on purpose, to destroy the national self-confidence of our people so that the people would lose their feeling of national pride and submit themselves to allegiance. But Uzbek people have not forgotten their ancestors, their heroes; the memory of these has been ingrained in their soul.

In two years of frenetic building, Tamerlane engaged the finest Persian architects of his empire to reconstruct Samarkand into the showpiece of Islam, inspiring poets to call it "the lustre of the Earth's face". Talent was imported from Tabriz, Isfahan and Shiraz. The Mongols, to whom Tamerlane boasted he was related, had completely destroyed the city when they swept through a century before, leaving a clear building site, as did the Persians on the Acropo-

lis of Athens. The new Samarkand grew up out of the section where the poor had lived. As a reminder of the extent of his empire Tamerlane named villages around his new capital Cairo, Damascus, Baghdad and Shiraz.

Today, Tamerlane's capital rivals Isfahan as the world's most important centre of Islamic architecture, but its glories reach back to ancient times when it was the seat of the Sogdian empire, famed for its exotic wealth and sophisticated culture. It is a history book written in stone.

After the regicide of the Persian King of Kings, Darius, by his kinsman Bessus, Alexander the Great pushed eastwards in pursuit of the murderer, who had declared himself the successor to the Persian Empire. Passing over the Hindu Kush, the Macedonians emerged onto the vast plain of Sogdiana, where they stifled the last gasp of Persian resistance and entered Samarkand, the key Persian stronghold in their Sogdian province and even at that time a major city. Called 'Marakanda' by the Greeks, it was here that Alexander speared his comrade Black Cleitus in a drunken rage provoked by arrogance piqued. It was also where, during his 18-month sojourn, he succumbed to the opulent lifestyles of the Achaemenids, causing a major rift with the more tradition-bound of his countrymen. The theme of opulence was carried forward by Tamerlane in his majestic building programme.

So much did Rustan sing the praises of the Registan Square on our long drive through the desert that we made it our first port of call when we arrived in Samarkand. He was right. We stood dazzled in front of its effulgent domes; truly, it was one of the most arresting city squares in the world. An archaeological suite of three medresas clad in polychrome tiles, it was constructed over the 15th and 16th centuries. Tall, resplendent minarets decorated with graceful Kufic script set off the medresas in a

Dome of the Tilla-Kari, medresa

Koran–holder,
Bibi Khanym Mosque

visual counterpoint. One of them tilts as crazily as the leaning tower of Pisa. Russian engineers tried to straighten it 75 years ago but managed only a few degrees of correction. No solid ground in the area aids the builder, a reminder that Registan means 'place of sand'. Until this century, it was a giant blotting-paper for blood spilt in public executions.

The sun reflects the blue-green light from the highly fired glaze on the tiles, which are laid in multipatterned facets, giving the assembled structures the appearance of a titan's jewellery collection. On close examination, we observed a paradox: on these Islamic buildings were motifs from the Zoroastrian religion so ruthlessly repressed by the Arab conquerors – the circle (symbolising eternity), the cross (for prosperity) and the swastika (whose rotating shape indicates the wheel of regeneration) were intermingled with Islamic forms. Apparently, the proselytisers who came through in the seventh and eighth centuries tolerated images of the ancient faith, as long as they were not of life figures. Sensibly, they wished to ease the anxiety of the local people in their forced transition to Islam.

Close by stands the mighty Bibi Khanym mosque, built by Tamerlane to celebrate his Indian victory, a feat that inspired his successor, Babur, to establish the Moghul Dynasty. In a lightning booty raid, Tamerlane conquered

Delhi, then withdrew. A gigantic stone Koran-holder sits in the gardened courtyard, constructed for the Osman *Koran*, so large that the imams could read the text from the balconies along the colonnade. We saw a woman crawl under it in the hope that she would be blessed with its reputed fertility powers.

Legend tells another story – Tamerlane's favourite wife, Bibi Khanym, built the mosque to surprise her husband on his return from campaigning in India. And surprise him it did, for it is among the most outstanding examples of Islamic architecture in the world, having taken 500 labourers and 95 elephants to carry out the plans. Indeed, its flashing majolica mosaic decoration, marble carving and colourful papier mâché lift the noble dome and portal into such an architectural paradise that they have been compared to the heavens and the Milky Way. When her husband returned, he was impressed not only by the creation, but also by a lovebite he noticed on his wife's cheek, which turned out to be the signature of the amorous Persian architect in charge of the job. When he heard that his indiscretion had been discovered, the terrified lover fled up one of his minarets and leapt off – though not to his death; the resourceful scamp miraculously flew back to Persia.

Behind the mosque's wall bustles the largest food market in Central Asia, active every day but jam-packed on Sundays. The covered multihued spice display alone spreads over five rows of 100-metre stands, which are actually long concrete troughs, inside which large sacks brim with spices, neatly packed so closely together that they touch each other, forming a continuous line of colourful circles. Coriander, rosemary, thyme, mint, basil, saffron, cloves, nutmeg and cumin (a favourite with lamb in Central Asian cooking) were all heaped into the sacks, giving off scents that drew one to them like a magic spell.

In another section, silver-grey peach kernels, like limestone gravel, formed elbow-deep heaps, covering the brightly clad saleswomen in white dust. People eat the kernels as nuts. Large yellow crystals of raw sugar stood

Above and over: Samarkand market

on wooden counters nearby. Figs wrapped in vine leaves, mounds of red and green grapes, apples, peaches and plums bulged over their wooden stands. Traditionally clad women in bright purples, yellows, reds and greens stood behind their stalls, weighing produce, collecting money and chatting with the customers. The buzz of the shoppers swept around the market at a happy pitch.

On the other side of the emporium, lush lettuces, onions, tomatoes, cucumbers, squash, eggplant, and hot red chilli peppers tempted the shoppers. Sweet-smelling dried grass, used for incense, offered a chance for an impulse purchase. All the produce had been brought from the rich growing fields of the oasis that morning, fresh and unblemished.

Meats of all kinds, preserved and butchered on the spot, rounded out the diet. Men did the butchering, slicing pieces of meat off large carcasses hanging from hooks, then weighing them on old-fashioned counterweight scales. Outside, a gigantic pile of melons stood in the shade. Men were picking others from the back of a truck and tossing them like footballs to their workmates on the ground. The sweet, thirst-quenching fruit is a favourite in Central Asia. Street vendors nearby, many of whom disclosed gold teeth when they smiled, were cooking little kebabs over wood coals. For a customer, they would slip the meat off the skewer, squeezing it into a bun like a hot dog. Clouds of smoke wafted the appetising barbecue smell throughout the bazaar.

The people in this mercantile pageant were lively, friendly and full of cheeky fun. Indeed, whenever we went outside establishments controlled by officialdom, such as hotels, banks or the ticket booths for monuments, the people were relaxed and natural. The severity of visage and dullness of attitude favoured by the Soviets for public comportment marked such an occupational difference that at times it seemed the country was divided into two separate communities. The bright traditional dresses of the women in the market, some in the famous Uzbek zigzag pattern, surged like an undulating rainbow, and the gold thread in many of the fabrics glittered in the sun, a flash of brilliance against dark skin. Most of the faces were Mongolid, but duskier than the Chinese, and many disclosed Eurasian origins. The Uzbeks, endowed with high cheekbones and broad, frank foreheads, are a good-looking people, especially the women. Whenever we had occasion to deal with them in the markets or on the street, we found them very friendly, willing to help and quick to smile. They seemed a gentle people.

The Uzbeks are a Turkic tribe who migrated into the region in the 16th century, pushing Babur and his tribe, the last of Tamerlane's descendants, known as the Timurids, out of Samarkand. He left to found another great dynasty, the Moghul Empire of India.

Just a short walk from the bazaar took us to Shah-i Zinda, the royal necropolis, an eye-catching collection of blue in tiles decorating a series of mausoleums. The complex takes its name, which means the 'living king', from the legend surrounding Kasim ibn Abbas, a cousin of Mohammed who is credited with converting the Zoroastrian population of the Samarkand region to Islam in the seventh century. The holy man is said to have been at prayer when a group of believers in Ahuramazda, resentful of efforts to put down their faith, fell upon him and cut off his head. According to legend, the headless saint finished his prayers, picked up his head and leaped down a nearby well, where he lives still.

Samarkand

Kasim's shrine was rebuilt by Tamerlane in a public gesture of his commitment to Islam. Indeed, Tamerlane went out of his way to gain the support of

Tilla-kari, medresa

the clergy and helped them promote the Sharia as the guide to social as well as religious behaviour. Ostensibly devout, the crafty despot declared in the code he enacted for his people:

> I have learned through my knowledge of life, unless power leans on religion and law, it will not be able to keep its status and force for long ... I have treated the descendants of the Prophet with respect.

A curious psychology that combined savagery with a sense of high culture drove Tamerlane to leave as his stamp on Central Asia a melding of nomad vigour with the civilising tendency of sedentary culture. In the process, he brought the wild Turkic peoples into contact with the sophisticated Persian world, creating a Eurasian model that was to influence Islam for over a century.

Just inside the portal to the necropolis rises the 'Stairway to Heaven', in a series of 36 steps sacred to pilgrims. They are a challenge to concentration, for the faithful must mount them on their knees, reciting a verse from the *Koran* and counting each on the way. It is considered a sin to get mixed up, the punishment being to climb them all again, 36 times, once for each step. Failure to take this opportunity for expiation is to risk not going to heaven. We didn't see any knee-climbers there, though, and were not inclined to try it ourselves.

With the wealth and power amassed by their ferocious progenitor, Tamerlane's successors, the Timurids, gave themselves over to the blandishments of hedonism after his death. However, even though their lives were largely filled with drinking and feasting, at times they extended their concept of pleasure to the expression of high culture. Under

Shah-i Zinda mausoleum

Shah-i Zinda Mausoleum

Ūlūg Beg

Shah-i Zinda Mausoleum

them, an efflorescence of scientific and artistic excellence lifted Central Asia to pre-eminence in Islam and left a permanent legacy, particularly in architecture. The monumental style of Samarkand, its domes inherited from Damascus but raised to give a floating appearance, and its dazzling blue and turquoise tiles, derived from Chinese porcelain acquired along the Silk Road, made a statement that resonated throughout Islam for centuries after. It was the fusion of Turkic and Persian canons.

The torch of architectural design later passed to the Ottomans, who leapt to fill the vacuum left in Timur's empire when he died. Sinan, the great architect of Süleyman the Magnificent, acknowledges his debt to the Timurids

in his masterpiece, the Süleymaniye in Istanbul. The Safavids of Persia adapted the Timurid aesthetic to their constructional showpiece in Isfahan – Maidan Square, described as "the greatest opera set in Asia" and inspired by the Registan of Samarkand. The buildings of Moghul India also reflect the culture of Central Asia, from whence came the dynasty's founder, Babur. The Taj Mahal is Timurid architecture.

Led by the early Timurids, the world of Islam flowered. Talented people from all over Asia were attracted to the community of excellence at the great merchant cities of the Silk Road. This golden age occurred at around the same time as the Italian Renaissance, its Florence and Siena being Samarkand and Bukhara. It, too, owed its life to the patronage of princes, but unlike the Western experience, which was largely a reaction against faith in favour of reason, the Timurid renaissance looked to a revivification of Koranic values in social institutions.

Like those influenced by the Italian Renaissance, the Timurids built their culture on a princely vision of idealised society constructed on principles that extolled the noble. They took inspiration from the characters in Firdausi's *Shahnameh*, the reference text of nostalgic chivalry and heroic action. It was the most popular publication of the times, after the *Koran*, and offered endless opportunity for the art of book illustration.

We took a 25-minute walk through the clean, leafy streets of the old city, wisely kept protected, through the prohibition of new construction, from encroachment by the industrial quarter. We reached a small artificial hill that covers one of the most exciting historical finds of the 20th century: the curved track of the giant sextant built by Ūlūgh Beg, the cultivated grandson of Tamerlane who preferred science to conquest. In the first decade of the century, after years of studying ancient manuscripts, a Russian primary-school teacher worked out where the observatory mentioned in the manuscripts was likely to be situated, and he was right. So important was the discovery that the gifted teacher requested in his will that he be buried alongside it. The arc of the sextant was 63 metres long, the radius 40 metres, and it was housed inside the three-storey, 30-metre-high observatory. With this gigantic instrument, he accurately plotted the positions of over 1000 celestial bodies, which he published in his *Catalogue of Stars*. He calculated the length of the year to within 58 seconds, and made observations consistent with the concept of the Earth revolving around the sun decades before Copernicus introduced the concept to Europe. In fact, Europe knew nothing of his work until two centuries later, in 1648, when the *Catalogue* was discovered, dusty and neglected, in the Bodleian Library at Oxford.

The struggle between religion and science was as fierce in the East as in the West. Echoing his teacher's maxim, "Where knowledge starts, religion ends", the astronomer Khan mortally provoked the Muslim clerics with his questioning approach to truth. His sponsorship of debates on the existence of God were judged to be crossing over the line that separated the legitimate pursuit of knowledge from the impious. In a backlash of orthodoxy mixed with personal ambition, he was murdered by his own son and his observatory demolished by religious fanatics. Two hundred years later, similar heresies pushed Galileo to the brink of death.

The ghost of Tamerlane is in the dusty air of Samarkand and in the majesty of its monuments.

Buried at the age of 70, his mortal remains inhabit a turquoise-tiled mausoleum he caused to be built for his favourite grandson. A graceful ribbed dome rises 30 metres into the sky beside a square courtyard, which is entered through a double-arched portal, the higher arch canopied with a stalactite ceiling. Turquoise tiles are set in intricate and varied geometric patterns. A drum supports the huge dome, giving it a floating appearance. On it, a stylised Kufic inscription in turquoise glaze announces: "There is no God but Allah and Mohammed is his Prophet". Under the vaulted dome intricately decorated in blue and gilt stands an octagonal hall, with walls of green alabaster tiles and niches whose ceilings are festooned with stalactite carvings. Light diffuses through the stained glass of apertures on high. The interior contains Timur's stone, a huge slab of dark-green jade, said to be the largest in the world and given by a Chinese princess. A wooden pole hung with yak tails stands in the hall, a chilling reminder of the appalling fear instilled by the sight of the nomad warriors' standard emerging out of the dust on the horizon. It is now a symbol of holiness.

The crypt below the floor hides the grave of the fearsome conqueror. A Soviet anthropologist opened it to verify the traditional view of the cause of Tamerlane's lameness. In the course of the investigation, he discovered that the great warrior, at one metre and 70 centimetres, was a tall man for his times. But he also found, underneath the tombstone, an epitaph warning that if the emperor's peace were disturbed, the whole world would hurtle into calamity. The next day, on 22 June 1941, Hitler unleashed Barbarossa onto an unprepared Soviet Union. The anthropological investigations took almost two years. As soon as the bones were placed back in position and the lid of the grave closed, the Russian army won its pivotal victory at Stalingrad.

Chapter 14

Pillar of Islam

On the way out of Samarkand, we drove past the high, windswept mesa near the Hungry Steppe that housed the old city, so devastated by Genghis Khan that it was forever abandoned. Now, the dusty site where the beguiling Sogdians seduced the mighty Alexander is preserved as a barren outdoor museum of eroded earthworks.

BUKHARA

No portal or caravanserais remain, but we knew we were on the Silk Road connecting Tamerlane's capital across the Kyzylkum desert to another merchant city of learning, the legendary Bukhara, called by Marco Polo the greatest city in Persia. Small green-spiked bushes about a foot high, called karagach, relieved the dust-brown of the landscape. The snow-covered Pamir Mountains rose in the distance. Mud-brick houses lined the bumpy asphalt road, interspersed with trees painted with white socks. They were mulberries, hosting the descendants of the silkworms brought clandestinely to Samarkand by a royal Chinese bride around 420 AD, so that she would not be without her beloved fabric in her new life. In doing so, she incurred a huge risk, for the Chinese authorities guarded, on pain of death, the intellectual property that underpinned their monopoly of sericulture.

Caravans laboured for seven days to make the journey from Samarkand to Bukhara, caravanserais built at one-day intervals along the way. Now, automobiles take four hours, but at a cost in pollution. Trucks, buses and cars belch out particulates in clouds so dense they sometimes obscure the sun. Near Bukhara, they pass under a shoddy natural-gas pipeline that bends up over the road like a crooked bridge, its insulation flaking off in filthy swatches. The danger of an explosive rupture waits to ambush the passing traffic.

Central Asian countries are hugely endowed with petroleum resources. In addition to its oil riches, Turkmenistan hosts the world's fourth-largest gas

Kalyan minaret

Miri Arab medresa

Main street of Bukhara

Nadir Dvanbegi Khanaka

reservoir. Once natural gas comes into its own, the Central Asians could become the Arabs of the steppes. It's a coincidence discomfitting to the West that both peoples are Islamic.

Bukhara, with its library of 45,000 books, was one of the great intellectual centres of the Middle Ages, its name, etymologically linked to the Sogdian phrase 'source of knowledge'. Under the Samanids, who made it their capital, Bukhara was the most important city in Islam. Its favourite son, Avicenna, composed a medical encyclopaedia in the 11th century that remained the standard reference for 800 years, even in the West. The city's 250 medresas attracted religious scholars from all over the Islamic world, inspiring the faithful to call Bukhara the 'Pillar of Islam'. Even the climate is enlightened:

Bukhara boasts an average of 300 sunny days per annum. The holiest city in Central Asia, it is said that the light there radiates upwards to the sky instead of downwards from the sun.

In the old section, which remains bustling and fully inhabited, we strolled along crooked stone-block roads sandwiched between straw-reinforced mud walls, some recently constructed but still fashioned in the same manner as the originals, no abrupt change in style disrupting the harmony with the past. The façades of the buildings on the narrow, intimate streets were discreet, hiding the wealth of their owners from the gimlet eye of the tax collector. Large patterned doors of solid wood hid the secrets of the families living behind. The doors of Bukhara are worth a study in themselves; there must be 100 different designs, all intricate and old. Every now and then, the maze of unnamed streets revealed a square, whose space allowed us to see a beige horizon of domes standing like round stones worn smooth by the weather. Alongside, slender minarets punctured the dusty sky. All the shapes and colours seemed natural together, nothing out of place, as in a master work of art. The continuity of atmosphere suggested a stage set or museum exhibit, yet this was a real city, brimming with people leading their everyday lives.

Nadir Diranebi, medresa

A giant stork's nest perched on the medresa opposite the blue-tiled mausoleum that houses the body of Ūlūgh Beg, his heretical head lying beside his torso. The nest was a reminder of the annual avian migration from Egypt, a pilgrimage that lapsed when the plague-ridden ponds of the city were filled in.

Throughout history, the wonders of Bukharan monuments have impressed all who saw them. Even Genghis Khan felt their power – as the brutal invader was sacking the city, he stopped in front of the Kalyan minaret, ringed with 14 belts of intricate brickwork whose design never repeats, and looked up at the skyscraper in amazement, his cap falling off, exclaiming, in probably the only concession to humility he ever made: "I am the conqueror of the world and have taken my hat off to no man. This minaret is more powerful than I." It is

Mosque, Bukhara

possible that he was impressed mainly by its lethal utility: customarily, victims were thrown to their deaths from its prodigious height, the practice ending only in 1884.

Minarets rise all over Bukhara, staking out mosque and medresa complexes with a vertical dimension that constantly encourages one to look to the heavens. The word 'minaret' comes from an Arabic word meaning 'platform of fire' (such as a beacon, often used in ancient times for signalling). The lofty form was meant not only as a place for the call to prayer but as a signal of power, both secular and religious. The minarets of the Bukhara oasis are shaped like cylindrical pillars, with a castellated turret at the top mounted by a flame-shaped cupola. Their intricate brickwork gives an intriguing textural quality that draws the eye to them.

Bukhara is a city of shapes and shadows constantly redefining their space. The open-pointed arch portals of the mosques and medresas framed changing pictures as we walked past; yet not all seemed revealed. Dark entrances opened into intricately faceted domes that looked like pomegranates freshly cracked open. They were the stalactite ceilings.

We were being oriented to the inner sanctum of Islam's past, spectators to its aesthetic nobility and its unbending cruelty. It seemed at times that we had pierced the veil of mystery that has separated this puissant and fearsome culture from the West since the Middle Ages; yet on a deeper level, so much remained cryptic that we felt we would never penetrate beneath the surface. How could we fully relate to the mortal cataclysms that shook the souls of these remarkable people over the centuries? The poignancy of the moment was honed by the thought that access for Western travellers is so recent here. Before the collapse of the Soviet Union, our visit would have been unthinkable.

The Russians have had a long and tempestuous relationship with Central Asia. The marauding horsemen of the steppes turned the Middle Ages into a long night of fire and brimstone for the Slavic people. Following the conflict with the Mongols, a religious divide kept the denizens of the vast Eurasian lands locked in mutual suspicion and antipathy. The longest border between Christianity and Islam stretched along the edge of Central Asia and the Slavic societies. Trade and commerce on the northern Silk Road, however, made contact inevitable. Russian furs, hides, nuts, honey and walrus tusks from the northern forests found canny buyers in the bazaars of Bukhara and Samarkand, who paid Samanid silver dirhems to the Russian traders. The Central Asian caravans braved the harsh northern climate and raiding bandits to bring dyestuffs, cotton fabric, wool and silk, along with dried fruit and metal utensils, to the emerging tsardom of Muscovy and its dominions.

Commerce distracted the mind from deeper currents that fed the long-lasting animosity, but not entirely. From the beginning of the 17th century, an issue arose that was to dominate the diplomatic agenda in that part of the world for the next 200 years, eventually providing the casus belli that opened the way to Russian colonisation of the East: the use of Russian slaves by the khans of Central Asia, particularly in Bukhara and Khiva. Talk in Russian society rose to outrage as news seeped across the steppes that thousands of Russian prisoners taken in raids were languishing in servitude, having been snatched from their caravans or in skirmishes with Tartar tribesmen. The thought of Christians in Muslim bondage offended religious sensibilities, tarnishing the image of a burgeoning and self-sufficient nation that the Russians were seeking to promote in Europe. The assault on self-esteem provoked a desire for aggressive intervention, in order to teach a lesson to people they viewed as unenlightened.

Official attempts to free the slaves began with the efforts of the Russian ambassador sent to Bukhara in 1620 by the tsar. Despite persistent diplomacy, the ambassador succeeded in freeing only 31 slaves, and their emancipation had to be bought with a large sum of cash. Frustration dogged Russian diplomacy during the whole century. Gradually, the diplomatic emphasis changed to matters of espionage, military and economic. Russian officials began to foment dissension, arranging alliances with rival factions, in order to weaken the defence capability of the region. Fortified outposts popped up all over Central Asia, allowing the Russian military to reach far from their home base.

A gap in the solidarity of the Central Asian khanates opened up when the ruler of Khiva sent an emissary to Peter the Great suggesting a treaty with Moscow. In return for measures leading to freer trade, such as lifting of the Russian embargo on the export of steel and lead, and a mutual defence alliance, he offered to become the vassal of Muscovy. The excited tsar replied with alacrity, forgetting about the subject of trade, which was probably the real purpose of the overture, with a lofty command that the khan submit himself forthwith. Silence dissipated the diplomatic overture, and until the 19th century, relations between the two regions bogged down in sporadic attempts by Tsarist diplomats to extend Russian influence and free the slaves. But as the economy of Silk Road cities declined, hit by the competition of alternative trade routes, the balance of power tilted inexorably towards Muscovy.

After the disastrous Crimean War, in the early 19th century, the Russian tsar turned east with thoughts of expansion, setting a course of intrusion into lands said to be endowed with rich agricultural and mineral potential as well as being a still-attractive market. The voices proposing a policy of systematic conquest won the day at court. In response, in 1865 Russia sent an expeditionary force against Tashkent to secure it for Russian interests before it fell to the emir of Bukhara, who was showing signs of heeding the entreaties of the Muslim clerics for protection against the infidel. After an easy victory, the Central Asians hopelessly outclassed by the modern weaponry lined up against them, Tashkent was proclaimed annexed to the Russian Empire. The policy of the conquerors was to develop Tashkent into the commercial capital of Central Asia, draining influence away from Bukhara, which they feared as a spiritual generating force. This policy carried over into the Soviet era. The colonisers went to great pains to siphon away the vital fluids that would sustain a jihad against them. They were as successful as they had hoped.

Driven by the insistence of Russia's emerging commercial and industrial classes, who could see the growth in business that stemmed from the annexation, new expeditions were mounted in Central Asia, bringing Samarkand and even the recalcitrant Bukhara under Russian dominance. In a few years, the whole of Central Asia, with its agricultural and mercantile wealth, was incorporated into the Russian Empire, much to the consternation of Victorian Britain, increasingly alarmed at the prospect of Russian forces turning south towards India.

Folk dancing, Bukhara

While we were walking around the old section of Bukhara, we stumbled upon an open-air Uzbek folk concert being performed in the Gaukushon medresa square. The mosque and its graceful minaret nearby created an atmosphere of grand solitude, ideal for a concert. The performance started in daylight, and continued while a cloudless sky faded into light blue and declined into darkness. Lights in the niches brought the medresa into the scene and provided an unmistakably Islamic backdrop. Although the music from the bowed and plucked strings, the tambourines and xylophone, was thoroughly Eastern, I thought of Rimsky-Korsakov's *Scheherazade*.

Traditional costumes and varied musical themes brought home to me the richness of the multicultural society of which they were an expression, in place long before the postmodern West discovered that peoples from distinct backgrounds can create a vibrant community without submerging their origins. The coquettish upsweep of the girls' eyes, the horizontal sliding of the head, the belly dance, made plain the Mongolian, Indo-European and Turkic roots. Over 100 nationalities live in Uzbekistan. There, the human clashes of the past have been horrific, and on a scale possibly matched only by the German–Russian war, their ferocity fanned by the vast differences between the competing forces – Turk opposed to Caucasian, nomad versus sedentary dweller, poor against rich. Now, the peaceful co-existence is so secure it seems eerie.

The global rise of the tribal ethic through the ebbing waters of nationalism that has marked the post-World War era is also in evidence in Uzbekistan. People there are rediscovering their roots and feeling the pride of practising their own culture. Since language is the principal carrier of culture, they are insisting that Uzbek be spoken on the job, particularly at the lower levels of the employment pyramid. Russians, who seldom bothered to learn

Medresa

the language, are finding the requirement a form of discrimination and are fearful of its consequences. The revival of the local people's faith, because it, too, was downplayed under Soviet atheism, manifests the reawakening of tribal instincts. In Uzbekistan and in other parts of Central Asia, as elsewhere in the world, political orientation has shifted from a composite to an individualistic paradigm. The willingness to belong to a grand nation-state such as the Soviet Union, comprising several tribal groups, some of which must submerge their individual identity in order to make possible a cohesive political whole, has given way to a preference for the self-actualisation made possible by tribal sovereignty. Such sovereignty is accepted to include the varied nationalities that live in the country.

On the other hand, Islam is a unifying force across tribal boundaries. It is more than just a tribal badge to be displayed in celebration of freedom. While not as tightly binding politically as the model of the nation-state, it has a similar tendency towards universality. While no-one can foresee to what extent the tribal instinct will be submerged in the global resurgence of Islam, it does seem clear that, at least in Uzbekistan and throughout Central Asia, both pressures – tribal and religious – are being directed towards a deepening separation from their former overlords.

After the concert, we walked into a poet's night. A crescent moon beside a minaret lit our way, tinting the sky's darkness a deep azure. No streetlights competed with it. Retained heat from the mud-brick walls softened the temperature as the desert night took over. The day's dust seemed to have disappeared from the cobblestones, and the famous Labi Khaus bathing pool sparkled coolly, hugged by 300-year-old mulberry trees, their foliage looking massive in silhouette. Behind them, the street led darkly away to the old Silk Road.

Only two medresas, both in Bukhara, are func-

tioning in Uzbekistan, but that is likely to change. We found one, and arranged an interview with the local mullah. This time, there were no problems with Anna-Maryke being present. The Uzbeks are not as strict as the Iranians. The mullah and a few colleagues had the daunting task of teaching Islam to a population that had belonged to an atheist State for 70 years. Although naturally religious, the people know not the *Koran*. In his white turban and dark robes, the mullah was an arresting figure, confident in his manner, lofty but friendly. I could sense that he was used to being in a position of authority. No notion of self-doubt or diffidence diluted the certainty of his views. He had the deep peace of mind that comes from the acceptance of absolutes.

Opening with, "We begin of Allah and we end by Allah", he explained the fortunes of Islam using the metaphor of an eternal journey of peaks and valleys. The present climb out of Soviet godlessness, he passionately believes, will lead eventually to the re-establishment of Bukhara as the centre of Islam, as it was in the 11th century. He claimed that the president of the republic speaks of this. In the presence of traditions and architecture that so inspire the spirit, I did not find his prediction outlandish, particularly since he deemed it unnecessary to place it into a specific time frame.

Clearly, he was delighted with the demise of Soviet control over his people. He saw the release as an expression of Allah's will and a stage in the cadence of Islamic life. "In the Soviet days," he said, "religion and State were separate. Some say they should be combined. Today, they are separate. Only Allah knows whether this will remain the case. Maybe they should remain separate. I don't know. Anyway, Islam is stronger than governments. Everyone has Allah in his heart."

I asked him about the presence of fundamentalism in his country and about the influence of Iran.

He hitched up his robe and replied in measured tones, "Fundamentalism is not strong here. The *Koran* is really more liberal than the way Iran practises it. Everybody is responsible for their own behaviour. Mullahs should not be politicians. Godly concerns are different from worldly ones. We are Sunnis and Iranians are Shiites."

With that comment, suggesting moderation, he was positioning his people alongside Turkey, which has ethnic roots intertwined with his people and is also Sunni. However, in an excursion into mysticism, he went on to say that Iran is closer to Mohammed than is Turkey, because it is nearer where the Prophet died. In forceful tones of pride, he concluded,

"Under the Soviets, it was difficult for the people to practise their religion. They forgot the wisdom of the *Koran*. Step by step, we are going to open more medresas, to teach the people their religion again. Bukharans are naturally pious."

There was a quiet confidence in the mullah's eyes. He clearly felt that Central Asia was recovering the sensation of its soul, anaesthetised for years by the Soviet system. We thanked the mullah for his kindness, then went for a long walk in the city.

Most of Bukhara's bright tiles have slipped off their surfaces to reveal a mass of earth beige, which now colours the urban landscape, the wonders of the architecture demonstrated essentially by shape. An exception, though, is the Miri-Arab medresa, whose twin Timurid floating domes sparkle with turquoise tile. By the 16th century, Central Asia had moved from the violence of a military society, through the civility and cultivation of the Timurids, to a period of clerical domination of the State. Besieged by internal divisions and hostile neighbours, the Uzbek rulers looked for support to the sufi orders, or 'tariqats', particularly the Naqshbandi, whose headquarters were at Miri-Arab, in Bukhara. Soon, the Bukharan emirs took on the characteristics of dervishes, seek-

ing to meld the cares of governance with the guidance of the spirit. The order of dervishes was named after Baha' al-Din Naqshband, a charismatic teacher who found acceptance of his message in the gloomy days that followed the Mongol invasions. His tomb, close to Bukhara, is considered so sacred that making three pilgrimages to it relieves the believer from the duty of the haj.

The Naqshbandis were the Islamic equivalent of the Jesuits in the West. Emerging from a reforming base, they were institutions geared to internationalising their basic religious message. They grew so influential that in the mid-16th century, an Englishman on a visit to Central Asia, the first of his countrymen to travel there, remarked that the chief cleric was more powerful than the king. From Central Asia, adherents fanned out across the Islamic world – south to India, where they ministered to Central Asian immigrants (who were flocking to the Moghul Empire to take advantage of job opportunities in the army and civil service), and west to Ottoman Turkey. There, they multiplied, growing to account for close to one-third of all dervishes in Istanbul and establishing most of the largest religious lodges. As with the Jesuits, teaching distinguished their activity.

In common with all Sufis, the Naqshbandis saw the human state in a paradoxical dimension, regarding what passes for popular wisdom as folly and clothing a deeper wisdom in the appearance of idiocy. They often used the device of the short tale to convey their message, such as in the story of Baha' al-Din Naqshband meeting the wanderer.

The great sufi master Bahaudan (Baha' al-Din Naqshband) was teaching his disciples in the grand square of Bukhara when a wandering Kalendar sufi came up to them. As was common among sufis, Bahaudan asked the newcomer where he was from. The traveller's face opened with an idiot's grin and he replied insouciantly, "I have no idea."

Tiles

Hodja Nasruddin

The discourteous answer was not well received by Bahaudan's respectful disciples, but the teacher then asked, "Where are you going?" "I do not know," was the reply.

Changing tack, Bahaudan inquired, "What is good?" "I do not know," came the answer.

"Do you know what evil is?" "No, I do not."

"Tell us what right is." "Whatever is good for me."

"What is wrong?" "Whatever is bad for me."

By this time, a crowd had gathered. The people became so incensed at the dervish's disrespectful foolishness that they drove him out of town. Without complaint, the traveller strode confidently away in a direction that seemed to lead nowhere.

After the stranger had gone, Bahaudan's agitated disciples pressed for an explanation as to why he had remained so calm during the insulting performance. The sage quietened them with a raised hand and smiled, "You are fools. You do not see that this man was merely holding up a mirror to humanity. He was showing you the lack of awareness and unthinking selfishness that all of you display in your lives every day."

Sufism was repressed during the Soviet tutelage, for its mysticism was seen as superstition and a barrier to modernity. Besides, its emphasis on spiritual values flew in the face of Marxist materialism. In the post-Soviet era, sufis are beginning to emerge, although not yet as a potent force. They are considered dangerous by Islamic fundamentalists, principally because of their worship of tombs of the famous, perceived to be an idolatrous act, and their veneration of saints, probably derived from the mediaeval Christian practice. Fundamentalists believe that the basic imperative of the *Koran* to accept no other God but Allah implies a prohibition against accepting any intermediary who might lessen His omnipotence. The heresy was compounded by the outlandish personal behaviour of some of the wandering dervishes whose idleness, womanising and addiction to wine were as much an affront to decency as the shenanigans of many mediaeval Christian monks.

In essence though, Sufism speaks to a universal sense of the unknowable that marks all religions and delves into the personal orientation that appeals to the introspective seeker of truth. So in certain countries it is on the rise; clearly it is not favoured in fundamentalist Iran or secular Turkey, but it can be seen among Muslims in Pakistan and India, and even in the West. Shops in Europe and the United States sell CDs of music derived from the passionate sounds of sufi devotion, on mainstream recording labels no less. The great Persian muse of sufic poetry, Rumi, can be found in translation on Western bookshelves. The appeal is not limited to Muslims; it is finding a resonance with others to whom Eastern mysticism offers an alternative pathway to religious experience as traditional Christianity wilts under the pressure of postmodern society. The Internet is the host not only of sufi home pages but also of vigorous debates among proponents of different sufi views.

The most impressive temporal building in Bukhara is the fortress at the old

Bukhara
The Ark, Bukhara

entrance of the city, called the Ark, first built in the third century BC, at a time when the Bukhara region was called Sogdiana and its people were still Persian. The glories and the tragedies that have clothed Bukhara with such texture over the centuries have their echo in the story of its founding, which is associated with the legendary characters of the *Shahnameh*. A young prince, Siyavush, fled his tyrannical father, taking refuge with Afrasiab, the overlord of the region. The great monarch was so impressed with the young man that he gave him his daughter in marriage and showered him with money and land. Anxious to make the most of his good fortune, Siyavush had the Ark built. There he lived in such ostentation and arrogance that he engendered the envy of certain powerful nobles and, eventually, incurred the enmity of Afrasiab. Accused of slander, he was put to death. He is said to be buried under the eastern gate of the citadel. According to a 16th-century chronicle, the people of Bukhara commemorate the killing of the talented prince with a sad ballad called *Lament of the Magi*.

The same chronicle speaks of the ancient monument:

> Do not think this is a fortress, it is a lofty mountain
> Well beyond the reach of man's fantasy.
> Its height stretches out to such extremes
> That the hands of imagination are too short for it.

The ancient origins of the fortress are hidden in the many later constructions, spanning 2000 years, and most of the interior is in ruins. However, the old grandeur lives on in the 18th-century gatehouse that rises in oriental splendour on top of a 20-metre hill, twin-domed towers standing on either side of the entrance. The graceful shape of a Timurid arch covers a massive wooden door studded with iron roundels. Crenellated walls, thick and high, spread outwards from the towers to enclose the four-hectare complex that housed the emir's residence, the police

department, various mosques and mausoleums, the armoury, the mint and, most grisly, the prison. It gives off a macabre atmosphere, with its dungeons and torture chamber, and ghoulish history of victims suffering the cruelties of bloodthirsty emirs.

From the roofed gallery on top of the gate, the emir and his courtiers would listen to music and watch unfortunate wretches being dragged out of the dungeons for execution in the square below. In the 19th century, the heads of two Englishmen fell in the dust there, players in what Rudyard Kipling called the Great Game, the shadowy contest between Russia and England for dominance of Central Asia.

One of the victims, a Colonel Stoddard, had journeyed to Bukhara to explain to the emir that Britain's recent invasion of Afghanistan should not be interpreted as evidencing any hostile intention towards Central Asia. Underestimating the vanity of the emir, who was merely a local potentate but endowed with a hyperdeveloped sense of his own importance, the colonel failed to bring any gifts and presented his credentials in the form of a letter from the Viceroy of India, not Queen Victoria. The slight was inflamed by the haughty emissary's riding up the ramp to the Ark, rather than following the local practice of walking. The touchy emir flew into a rage, throwing the visitor into the dungeon that had earned the nickname the 'bug pit'. There, he suffered life-threatening neglect and the attentions of vermin for three years, until his brother officer, Captain Conolly, arrived for the purpose of obtaining his release. But the suspicious emir formed the view that Conolly was plotting with his rivals in Khiva and Kokand, so threw him into the bug pit too. When news of the disastrous retreat of British forces from Kabul reached Bukhara, the emir concluded that their power was on the wane and had the two luckless emissaries beheaded.

The aura of power and violence seemingly emitted from the Ark, even today, faded gradually into the dusty streets as we walked away, and disappeared completely by the time we arrived at the leafy park that houses what has been described as the gem of Central Asian architecture, the Samanid mausoleum. It stands fully restored among the trees, relieved of a two-metre layer of sediment blown in from the desert that had until recently stifled it. The masterful style of the building incorporates the pre-Islamic tradition of the Sassanids, redolent with symbolism, and integrates it with the geometric patterns of Islam. The form is a basic cube structure, with a hemispherical dome resting on top. The cube represents stability and is cognate with the Earth, while the dome symbolises heaven. The two motifs are combined in a unity that is evocative of the universe.

Central Asian architecture is distinguished by its unique use of brickwork, the designers rendering the medium as flexible as the painter's brush. Arguably, it has taken the art of brickwork to its highest form. The Samanid mausoleum is its apotheosis. The intricacy of the brick design gives the façade a sense of texture and creates a diverse community of patterns. Within them are hidden meanings that disclose the thoughts of the local society going back to its roots. Above the double arches that form symmetrical entrances on each of the four sides are discs symbolising the sun and the planets, bodies that played such an important role in the science and religion of the region. Brick rings form a chain frieze that encircles the mausoleum above a series of arch windows on high. They are a throwback to the Sassanid pierced pearl design that was carved on the walls of pre-Islamic buildings.

From ancient times, the economic engine of Bukhara has been trade. The oasis town was a marshalling yard of caravan tracks that converged from the four cardinal points of the compass. Bazaars sprouted up where the main highways crossed, alongside supporting caravanserais. Over time, the merchants built domed structures over the chaos of the market stalls. Reflecting the wealth and importance of their function, these covered bazaars appeal as much to the aesthetic as to convenience. Three remain in Bukhara and have just been renovated.

The largest is the cupola of the jewellers, where precious metals and costly gems were brought from all over the world – lapis lazuli from Afghanistan, rubies from India and Burma, sapphires from Ceylon. Today, as the relative wealth of the world has shifted elsewhere, the goods for sale are of a more modest nature. In Timurid style, the emporium's cupola floats high on a drum resting on an octagonal hall encircled with a multidomed gallery. The shops are cooled naturally by air flows coming in from the street and carried up and out of arched windows set high on the periphery of the cupola. Light shines down from the top. The second dome is devoted to luxury headgear: caps embroidered with gold thread and beads, fur hats and turbans of expensive fabrics. Money-changing and lending are carried out at the third dome, called the Taq Sarrafon. This was often the first stop for merchants coming into the city. The inside of the cupola, which rises high over the hall, giving it a generous spaciousness, is gracefully composed of intersecting arches that reduce the roof to a small skylight at the summit. Timurid brickwork adorns the arches.

Next door, a pattern of pentagonal and hexagonal halls interlinked with resting niches form the Sarrafon public baths, an indispensable feature of urban life. Throughout the ages, the medicinal and hygienic properties of baths were highly esteemed. In his *Canon* of medical science, Avicenna extolled their virtues, advising that they be spacious, of moderate temperature, with bright light and pure air and water. In reaction to the crowded popularity of the

Around Labi Khaus

Domes of the Covered Bazaar

Samanid Mausoleum, Bukhara

Carpet selling

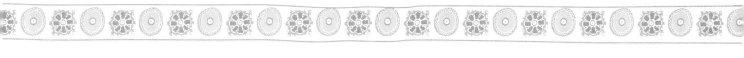

institution, an 11th-century code of conduct noted wryly "Men of wisdom consider deserted baths to be the greatest fortune".

Water in the Bukhara oasis was the life force of the city, but in the past it was also a savage killer. The ponds and waterways bred deadly bacteria and insects. Most notorious was a parasitic worm that infected those who drank from the river flowing through the city centre. An English traveller of the 16th century, Anthony Jenkinson, observed people who had worms he described as elbow-long living in the foot, between the toenails and the body tissue. He saw them being extracted through the ankle by skilful surgeons, very slowly, for if they broke, the toxic ooze would poison the patient.

Today, it is said, the water has been cleaned up. That may be so, but it still looks lethal, even though some of the ponds that remain are quite beautiful. Especially so is Labi Khaus, surrounded by centuries-old plane trees. Its banks consist of benches of limestone blocks that rise out of the water into a green park that housed the tea bazaar of ancient times. Now it is gone, but a teahouse, old and atmospheric, remains. We had lunch there and watched old men wearing traditional Central Asian skullcaps playing chess at the water's edge.

Dome in covered bazaar, Bukhara

After lunch at Labi Khaus, we went shopping for carpets. Bukhara is the best place in Central Asia to buy them, although most of the prized ones are woven in neighbouring Turkmenistan. The Bukhara colour is generally a rich red or brown. The carpets are for sale everywhere: in the street, in the monuments, even in private houses. Superb examples of the traditional nomad artisanship, they are rich in symbolic abstract designs and are tribe-specific. The vendors are usually personable and not too pushy. Bargaining is a jocular exchange and, because the prices are low by Western standards, not stressful.

It is illegal to export anything over 80 years old, and guidebooks warn visitors to expect trouble at the border, even with new carpets. Most difficulties, however, can be resolved with a bribe. When we left the country, a customs official haughtily moved to confiscate the carpets we had bought, claiming they were hand-woven – a new one on us. The man was standing in such an open area that he did not seem to expect an offer of money. He demanded to see certificates showing the weaving dates. When I produced them, he suddenly changed his manner, asking me in a soft, supplicant voice if he could keep them. Since I had expected to be required to hand them over anyway, I was happy to oblige, a little mystified by the importance he appeared to attach to these bits of paper. It was only later that I realised the scam – he wanted the documents to sell to dealers smuggling out antiques. That was bribe enough.

Our guide took us walking, through cobblestone streets closed in by changeless mud-brick buildings, to an old house in the ancient Jewish quarter. Bukhara has had a thriving Jewish community down through the ages, but with free emigration since the Soviet collapse, many Jews are leaving for Israel. The building was run as a backpacker hostel. The owner of the establishment was a gruff-faced, corpulent man from Turkmenistan with a drooping moustache and loose clothes. He led us into a large, smelly room strewn with empty beer cans and Coke bottles surrounding a half-eaten melon with a knife sticking out of it. Two sleepers lay motionless, heads against the wall, their sleeping bags open. Ignoring it all, the paunchy proprietor pointed to the carpet on the floor and mumbled grumpily, "Very old." I asked him, through the guide, how old, to which he responded, "Over 100 years." It appeared to be a good-quality Bukhara red, thin, as it should be, and large. I told the man that Customs would not allow us to export carpets that old, whereupon the piece suddenly became some 30 years younger. We didn't buy it, not just because of its dubious age but also because the fellow was asking too high a price.

Our guide suggested we go to another residence, telling us that private houses were better places to go for carpets, because they did not have the overheads of shops. This one was more salubrious, the home of a wealthy trader, proud of his new shiny car, a Lexa,

parked outside. We went through the door into a courtyard cooled by greenery and a fountain. Rooms stood off it all around, as in a Roman peristyle. Ushering us courteously into a room with several carpets stacked up in the corner, he offered us chai (tea) and raisins. This time, we bought a carpet – after a spirited bargaining session that spanned several cups of tea. The process of coming to a deal is a cultural pleasure in the East, as well as a means to maximise profit. To cut it short by paying too much earns no respect.

I left Anna-Maryke at the house while I went to a nearby bank to cash some travellers' cheques. The infuriating plethora of bureaucratic procedures involved at least four people and took almost an hour. The woman who seemed to be in charge asked me repeatedly whether I would accept 'sum', the local currency, instead of dollars. She lectured our poor bemused guide on the merits of insisting that shop vendors take sum, giving them dollars only if they refused.

Besides carpet-dealing, Bukhara was prominent, until the Russian Empire consolidated its hold on Central Asia, in 1868, as the hub of the slave trade. At one time, three-quarters of its population were in bondage, large numbers snatched by raiders from the caravans that plied the Silk road. The slavers often attacked in the greyness of dawn, when the caravaners were kneeling in prayer. For three hours every morning, Monday to Thursday, manacled unfortunates, their features ranging from Caucasian to Turkic, were displayed in a filthy backstreet courtyard. They would stand glumly in 30 or 40 stalls while buyers prodded and squeezed them like cattle. The deals that fixed their lamentable fate were discreetly made in self-indulgent comfort at nearby caravanserais.

Chapter 15

Of Treachery and Massacre

The cobra-infested Kyzylkum desert stretches towards Turkmenistan, the independent republic encompassing the other principal Silk Road city, Merv, seven hours away from Bukhara by car. On either side of the thinly asphalted, jolting thoroughfare, cotton crops unfold to the sandy horizon on land where rain hardly ever falls.

The peaceful acreage dotted with white puffs looked so benign that it was mind-wrenching to think that here, people are perpetrating one of the most egregious environmental devastations in the world.

When the outbreak of the American Civil War, in 1861, choked off the South's cotton exports, Russia turned to its eastern frontier lands, which had, for centuries, demonstrated cotton-farming capacity. Engineers tapped the waters of the mighty Amu Darya and Syr Darya arteries, which feed the Aral Sea, and a world-class fabric industry sprang from the desert. Uzbekistan produced two-thirds of the cotton grown in the Soviet Republic and is still one of the world's top three producers. For years, the environment supported the intrusion, but eventually, the gigantism of the Soviet system overwhelmed nature's capacity to cope.

Between 1960 and 1980, central planners doubled the annual water plunder, even though the irrigated area grew by only 20 per cent. The marginal increase in cotton production was earned at the expense of a 75 per cent reduction in the volume of the world's fourth largest lake. The open Karakum canal, which takes one-quarter of its erstwhile supply, loses 12 per cent of its load by evaporation into the parched air and seepage into the thirsty sand. Ports regressed landward, leaving slumped ship hulks rusting on arid flats. By 1987, the Aral Sea's shrinking surface split into two. A further divide is expected in a decade.

The exposed seabed harshened the local climate and bred a plague of salty dust storms that ravage the area. Surrounding soils choke on a toxic brew of salt and agricultural chemicals. Tens of thousands of bemused people succumb

Cotton harvest

each year to an aggravated incidence of respiratory diseases, throat cancer and other ailments attributable to pesticides, defoliants and fertilisers borne on the unwholesome winds.

As the Amu Darya crossed into Turkmenistan, it disclosed unmistakable evidence of the hydro-pillage. Most of the pontoons that made up the road-bridge lay disconnected on the dried sand of the riverbed and over two-thirds of the railroad viaduct was on land. We lurched across the moving pontoons that were left in place, sandwiched in the thick, smoky traffic, which consisted mostly of large trucks stuffed with cotton bales. An unpaved road greeted us on the other side of the shrunken river. The authorities had not yet extended the paved section of highway to the exposed bed, for that would be an admission that nothing could be done for the dying river.

Demand for fresh water rises in direct relation to rising living standards. As long as economic development continues, pressure on water supplies will increase, often at the expense of environmental values. Arguments over the damming of water flows are commonplace today across the world. In Uzbekistan, protesting voices, swelled by the support of global environmental groups, are calling for a review of water use to save the Aral Sea. But the cost of this would have profound economic consequences to a nation that is struggling to pull itself out of the international cellar. The issue is complicated by the fact that more than one country claims rights to the river bounty. Throughout history, many wars have flared up over access to resources that hold the key to

Amu Darya

economic development. While in the past, these have consisted of the hard commodities and energy, the future holds the risk that water could join the ranks as a casus belli.

We had to pass through customs and immigration at the little village on the riverside. Uniformed officers sitting behind a small, dirty table at the side of the road checked our documents, and told us we had to purchase new visas to get back into Uzbekistan. Because we were to be out of the country for more than a day, they closed them. They said there was a visa office at Merv, our destination in Turkmenistan. Under the Soviet system, it was possible to travel freely throughout Central Asia, but now that the republics are sovereign states, red tape has grown like a weed.

We drove through the depressing, very Soviet-looking river town. It was a jumble of warehouses, dirty concrete apartment buildings five storeys high, wide streets and a railroad terminal, all laden with dust and exhaust fumes. The verge of the road leading out was littered with discarded inner tubes and worn-out tyres left to degrade slowly in the sun.

MERV

After stopping at so many checkpoints along the highway that they seemed like traffic lights, we arrived at Merv, famous throughout the world in the heyday of the Silk Road. Contemporary Merv was built in the Soviet era and shows it. Like others of its ilk, it is an inducement to dejection, dressed in drab,

Merv,
Turkmenistan

medium-height blocks of badly mixed concrete, with the sounds of heavy machinery hammering the polluted air. The city was designed to deliver utility on the cheap. Our hotel was in the same vein. The accommodation was spacious, though, with two chairs and a sofa in one room and a separate bedroom. Most of the lights had no bulbs. In the bathroom, which at least had a cold-water shower, a large girlie poster graced the mirror.

Old Merv is a treasure trove of history and one of the most important archaeological sites currently under investigation in Central Asia. We learned from the chief of the British expedition, who invited us for some green tea, that it was founded by Zoroastrians around the sixth century BC. This date places it at the beginning of the Achaemenid dynasty, the succession of warrior kings, founded by Cyrus the Great, that lifted the nomadic Medes and Persians into the greatest power the world had yet known.

The Greek geographer Strabo wrote about the Merv area, impressed by its vineyards and the lushness of its vegetation rising abruptly out of the desert. The city was an important entrepôt on the Silk Road throughout classical times, and endured the attentions of conquerors from the Persians to the Russians, mixing its genetic material in a great Eurasian cauldron. After the Roman general Crassus lost his battle with the Parthians, in 53 BC, 10,000 legionnaires were marched there across the desert to a life of slavery.

Near the city was discovered a trilingual stone, which yielded up the secrets of the ancient Akkadian language of Mesopotamia, spoken by the famous lawgiver Sargon, in the manner that the Rosetta Stone divulged the key to Egyptian hieroglyphics.

Merv was a vital link between West and East, more Western than Samarkand or Bukhara. The great merchant rulers of those cities would have exerted influence over the Merv oasis, but the city was probably independent.

In the foothills not far from Merv, ephedra still grows, the plant from which the Zoroastrian priests extracted the intoxicating drug used in their sacred rituals. Under its influence, the pupils of the practitioner dilated, bestowing on him a supernatural air. In fact, the enlarged human eye was one of the commonest symbols of Zoroastrianism. The Chinese have used ephedra, which they call Ma Huang, for more than 5000 years to treat asthma and other bronchial disorders. In the West, it is currently used as a starting material for the clandestine preparation of methamphetamine.

Merv reached its zenith in the 11th century, under the Seljuk Turks. The nomad horsemen made it their capital, building it into the most influential city in Islam, after Baghdad. The artisans, craftsmen and sophisticated merchants of Merv were renowned throughout Islam. Its epicurean culture is supposed to have been the inspiration for Scheherazade's *Tales of a Thousand and One Nights*. Under their charismatic leader, Alp Arslan, whose moustaches were so long that he had to tie them behind his head, the Seljuks built a domain that spanned the Asian plains from Afghanistan to Egypt and laid the foundation for the Ottoman Empire. Their defeat of the Byzantines at the battle of Manzikert, around the time of the Norman invasion of England, opened the way to the global supremacy of Islam that lasted until the Baroque period.

In its golden age, Merv was famous for its advanced state of technology. Mediaeval chroniclers wrote of the high quality of Merv cotton, which had been produced since the fifth century AD, when Rome was in its death throes. We saw the site of a kaolin brick-lined furnace dating to the Middle Ages that smelted carbon steel at 1400 degrees. It has been tested and found to be capable of making steel equal in quality to the pride of 19th-century Sheffield.

But Merv's glory was destined to be to so eclipsed that the famous city took centuries to recover from the gloom that descended over its ramparts. From the grasslands of Mongolia, Genghis Khan marched his forces over the Pamir Mountains and into the Muslim heartland of Central Asia in a series of campaigns that earned him a reputation as one of the most brutal destroyers of civilisation in history. After conquering Bukhara and Samarkand, the ferocious invader demanded that the leading citizens of Merv pay a heavy tribute in grain and beautiful young women. Outraged by the severity of the levy, the Mervians killed the Mongol emissaries sent to extract it. Predictably, the response was incandescent rage. After some delay, as Genghis Khan was preoccupied elsewhere, the yak-tail standards appeared outside the hapless city. Tolui, the most bloodthirsty of Genghis Khan's savage sons, had been sent at the head of an army to exact retribution. Tricking the terrified population into surrender without a fight, he proceeded systematically to slaughter every man, woman and child. Each soldier was given a quota of 300 people for decapitation. It is estimated that upwards of one million people were massacred in a frenzy of brutality that cast such a pall of dread over the oasis that no-one dared to inhabit the city for over a century. Even when settlement began to seep back into the oasis, it took centuries for Merv to regain even a semblance of its former prosperity. Then, at the end of the 18th century, disaster struck

Top: Kyz-Kala fortress,
Merv

Above: Turkmenbashi

again, when the envious emir of Bukhara invested the city and breached its life-supporting dam. From then on, only wild Turkmen tribesmen inhabited the region, using it as a base for slave-raiding expeditions against caravans along the Silk Road.

We clambered up the sun-baked clay slopes of the Erk Kala, the oldest of the five ancient Merv fortresses, built one after the other, centuries apart, as the city passed through its many cycles of rise and decline. From the top of the citadel, the fortress looks like a giant caldera half a kilometre wide, standing high over the desert. A constant wind swept across the flat dusty vastness and quickly dried the perspiration we had generated on our climb up. A sense of desolation filled the air. In its baleful past, each time a new stronghold was built, another invader would ride across the plains with devastation on his mind. Time and the elements completed the task of ruin. Now, the only inhabitants of the once-thriving merchant city, to which five caravan roads led for most of the life of the Silk Road, are long-legged sand ants that scuttle among antique potsherds half-buried in the caked earth. Birds have pecked holes in the ancient walls, now so weathered that they are friable enough to allow the chiselling out of nests.

The outer wall of Erk Kala melds into a later redoubt built by the Sassanids in the third century BC. The mounds that can be seen rising from the walls are the slumped remains of towers from which the terrified Zoroastrian citizenry vainly defended their city against the messianic Arab armies. The invaders

Karakum Desert near Merv

called the place Giaur Kala ('fortress of pagans'), in response to the many fire temples they saw there.

Like many travellers to vestiges of ancient civilisations, we had, simultaneously, a feeling of belonging to the glories of human achievements past and a feeling of third-party detachment from the cadence of rise and fall. We took comfort in knowing that the fall had happened to them, not us. But the baleful north wind that was wearing down the bricks of the mighty Erk Kala knew that the barbarians who rode into the thriving city and out again leaving a million dead are not without recurring analogues elsewhere.

We walked across the dusty earth to see the Kyz-Kala, a windowless castle built by a Sassanid governor. It was called 'the house of maidens' tears' after it began to be used by Sultan Sanjar, a grandson of Alp Arslan, as a venue for his famous bacchanals, to which he would bring pretty slave girls to entertain himself and his friends. The walls of the castle are pockmarked from the missiles catapulted against them by the conquering Arabs.

As our local guide took us through the Sultan Sanjar mausoleum, the tallest in Central Asia and a fitting tribute to the glory of the Seljuks, she complained about the lack of tourists. The last ones she had escorted were a week ago. Numbers were one-quarter what they had been under the old regime. Facilities are declining with the slumping economy. We didn't have the heart to say how much we appreciated the dearth. Fed up with the poor economic conditions, she longs to go back to her native Russia, but that depends on her husband getting a job there. Turkmenistan is so poor that many of its Russian citizens are leaving and returning home, not withstanding the economic chaos there. Additional motivation comes from a discrimination against them that is born of revanche.

Some express the view that part of the economic anaemia is due to the corruption of President Turkmenbashi. Asked on television about his Swiss bank account, he replied insouciantly that yes, he had one, but it belonged to the State. After the Soviet collapse, the upsurge of nationalism convinced the ambitious politician that it would be best if he divorced his Russian wife. He set the wheels in motion while she was on a visit to Russia. Hearing about it, she rushed back to Turkmenistan and promptly marched into a cabinet meeting to confront the astonished president. Most of the ministers left the room in embarrassment as she shouted: "I put you there and I can remove you." He recanted.

Turkmenbashi took over when the Soviets left and runs the country as a dictatorship. He seems to be suffering from the political disease Lord Acton identified. Reputed to be one of the richest men in the world, he appeared on a Moscow television interview programme, where he was asked, "Why are your shops so empty, with no food to buy?" In reply, he scoffed, "I do not wish my people to be spoiled."

Not particularly religious, Turkmen society is nevertheless Muslim and is in the process of rediscovering Islam. The government is steering a course that keeps both Iran and Turkey in view, playing one off against the other. The Turkmen people don't like the haughty demeanour of the Turks, who seem to treat them as poor relations in a pan-Turkic domain, and feel uncomfortable with the strict behavioural rules of the Iranians. But still, they are taking part in a resurgent Islam. Mosques are being built; more and more people observe the rules of prayer.

Just outside Old Merv, small mud-brick domes appear out of the desert, which is studded with camel thorn. Some are squat and others high pitched. They were like buttons on a giant coat strewn over the land. We were told that some were the tops of cisterns for drinking water, while others were the lids of underground icehouses, used as communal refrigerators since ancient times. The intriguing structures are typical throughout Central Asia.

The road was bumpy near town, but in the countryside, it wasn't too bad. It was wide enough for three lanes of thinly based asphalt, plus shoulders, a mixed blessing, for drivers are tempted to use the centre lane and play chicken with oncoming traffic. We only just avoided a few accidents waiting to happen. Saksaul, which looked like small weeping willows, grew wild along the sides of the road, its feathery leaves painting the desert with patches of pale green. The landscape was like that of the Australian outback, but beige, wide and flat, its desiccated expanse thinly carpeted with scrubby plants. Little tamarisk flowers caught the eye with their purple in the sun. We passed camels standing singly in the sand chewing their thorn, imperious heads in the air. As we went by, they would fix our car with contemptuous stares and lope off into the dunes.

Camels, dust and the sun constantly beating down without respite are the essence of the Silk Road in Central Asia. The history of this region is of time moving slowly in long periods of low energy, suddenly punctuated by savage action. We were travelling along a peaceful mercantile road, but one that had been constantly vulnerable to cruel raiders suddenly materialising out of the tranquil haze without warning. These days, the territory is safe. In the distance, we could see the long goods train of the trans-Caspian railway puffing in the desert heat.

After hours of driving, we came back to the Amu Darya crossing, where we again stood between heavy trucks on the pontoons as we waited for the slow traffic to move across the wobbly bridge. Whenever the truck in front of us started up, a huge black billow of smoke would belch across our windshield, blocking out the light like an eclipse. There was a constant stream of trucks all day long, many of them from Iran. It took us 45 minutes to cross a couple of hundred metres.

At the Uzbekistan border, we ran into trouble, a problem that we knew was a possibility but were told would not arise. The officer who looked at our passports said curtly that our visas had been closed when we left the country for Turkmenistan and we now needed new ones. At the visa office in Tashkent, we had been told we would have no problems leaving Uzbekistan and getting back in. We had quizzed our guide, Rustan, who concurred. But all were wrong. The guard was adamant, even in the face of a stream of voluble pleading from our embarrassed guide. After arguing for half an hour, Rustan gave up and told us we would have to get visas.

We were in the soup. The nearest place to obtain a visa was Bukhara, two hours' drive away, but we could not enter the country to go there. The only solution was for Rustan to go by himself and leave us at the border, without passports, since he needed them to support the visa application. As he drove off into the heat haze, Anna-Maryke and I felt a sudden sense of exposure, vulnerability. We were completely in the hands of people from another world, a place that had been, in the past, uncompromisingly hostile to travellers from our background. Everything depended on Rustan and his willingness to stick to the case. The timing would be tight, for it was already half past three in the afternoon. He didn't know whether he would be able to get there before the visa office closed. He could not even phone us, for it was one of those days when the telephone at the border didn't work. If he got there too late, we would have to stay the night in the border office, or outside, for

without documents, we would not be allowed to go to a hotel. We ascertained that much before Rustan left. It was infuriating that the authorities had found it necessary to close out our visas when they knew we were planning to return to Uzbekistan in a couple of days. It was petty bureaucracy rejoicing in its power.

Under the Russian regime that fell in the early 1990s, the tribes of Central Asia, which had been at each other's throats for centuries, were subjected to a *pax Sovietica* that ensured a measure of cooperation across borders. With the withdrawal of compulsion, the new countries that encompass them are now left to their own devices. We seemed to be the victims of a trivial power play between Uzbekistan and Turkmenistan, which don't particularly like each other. Driving an Uzbek car ensured that we would be stopped frequently at Turkmen checkpoints.

The border office was stark, a small hut built of concrete blocks, flanked by a continuous stream of belching trucks and cars slowly passing by in a stop-start rhythm. We could walk around freely, as long as we stayed between the two countries, in no-man's land. Whenever we got too close to a border, armed guards would begin to walk slowly towards us, not saying anything or even gesturing. After about an hour, one of the guards came over and said in sign language mixed with one or two words of English that, if we wished, we could go over to a little shelter standing in the gully nearby. Made from three old truck tops and a scrabbly concrete block wall, this was where the off-duty guards relaxed. We walked over to it, but decided to pass on the invitation. The place was small, and crowded with men watching television in a darkened room.

To while away the long hours, we went for a walk in the desert. It seemed we could go as far as we liked, if it was in a lateral direction. As we came back, a crescent moon began to rise from the horizon, casting a ghostly light on the feathery saksaul growing out of the sand. The long lines of trucks were still there, smoking and noisy, their headlights competing with the moon. Different guards were on duty now. I supposed they must have been informed about the two foreigners who were being kept in no-man's land, for when we approached the block house, no-one paid any attention. The boredom got worse after dark, for there was nothing to see and, there being no place to sit inside, we couldn't even read. We were unable to communicate with the guards, for they couldn't speak English and we had long ago grown tired of attempting sign language. Apart from the boredom, our heaviest feeling was the vulnerability of our position – completely in the hands of Rustan, whom we hardly knew. Being stranded without papers in a land so remote is no fun. At least he belonged to an agency.

Finally, car headlights veered out of the truck line and came towards us. They stopped, and a harried Rustan appeared. What a relief! He rushed over to the blockhouse with our passports and newly minted visas. Mercifully, the official on duty immediately saw them to be in order and stamped our entry into freedom. It was now well into the night, six hours

after we had been refused admission into Uzbekistan. Rustan told us he had driven as fast as he could, but still got to the visa office after it had closed for the day, so had tracked down the appropriate bureaucrat at his home and persuaded the fellow to open up the office especially. Had he not done so, we would have spent the night and most of the next morning walking around the border post.

Back in Bukhara, we drove over to Labi Khaus to pick up carpets we had bought, then set out again on the Silk Road. Ahead of us was a 480-kilometre drive through the Kyzylkum desert, north towards the Aral Sea.

KHIVA

Our destination was Khiva. It was the Khorezm city that struck dread into the hearts of the Victorian English, whose Eastern imperial ambitions brought some of their more intrepid adventurers into contact with the xenophobic Silk Road post that dominated the northern caravan route to Russia. There, they had the opportunity to develop what Lord Curzon, the English Viceroy of India, called "the frontier school of character". In the 18th and 19th centuries, Europeans began to venture into these remote lands, but at great peril, for Christians there were hated as dangerous infidels. Usually, a gruesome death in the public square would be their reception if discovered. Often, they would disguise themselves as dervishes, for odd behaviour, which could cover any linguistic deficiency, would go unnoticed in a sufi.

The old buildings of Khiva, moulded from the stone, mud, fired clay and wood of the harsh mid-continent land, still speak the language of diplomatic intrigue mixed with high culture that formed the character of the Silk Road entrepôt in the 19th century. Khiva was the focal point of the tussle between England and Russia for hegemony over Central Asia, the one seeking to protect its imperial power in

Khiva

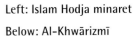

Left: Islam Hodja minaret
Below: Al-Khwārizmī

India and the other trying to expand its commercial interests eastwards after the Congress of Vienna blocked its westward ambitions. Judged from the perspective of these purposes, the match ended in a draw, for Russia eventually incorporated Central Asia into its empire, while England held on to India.

It was a cautious, surreptitious joust in which espionage and feinting were the techniques of battle. Every traveller was charged with obtaining as much information as possible about anything that could be of military or diplomatic use. I wondered whether a cultural memory of the times has influenced the minds of Eastern Europeans who so easily suspect visitors to their countries of spying. The Russians called the competition the 'tournament of shadows', and were to play it again during the Cold War against the United States. A new version of it could spring up again in Central Asia, fomented by covetousness of its outstanding mineral and petroleum wealth. Already, major Western oil and mining companies are operating there. In some of the hotels, we saw Americans who had the unmistakable can-do demeanour of engineers.

The road from Bukhara was flat and straight, like all roads in Uzbekistan, and seemed to never end. For miles, we passed mud-brick farm buildings huddled in groups and separated by expansive cotton fields. Small villages and informal communities set far apart seemed to be swallowed up by the immensity of the featureless space. There was a curious form of intimacy in the vastness, for low-lying bushes sucking water out of the oasis around Bukhara, sometimes two metres high, tended to break up the vista, bringing the horizon closer to the road. But as the water presence faded, the vegetation shrank into little scrubby runts eking out a living at a competitive distance from each other and the green cast of the landscape turned into the usual beige. A small fluffy-tailed animal scampered along the side of the road, stopped for a while, disoriented, and disappeared into the sand. I asked Rustan what it was and he replied that it was a gopher. Falcons, their feathers variegated with brown and beige, circled effortlessly overhead, inscribing wide arcs in the dusty sky as they searched for the little lives of the desert. Every few kilometres, twisted black strips of broken truck tyres littered the roadsides like carrion. The surface stability of the landscape started to decline with the thinning out of vegetation, ceding place to shifting sand dunes as the real desert took over. Winds became more constant as barriers to their sweep disappeared. Sand began to blow across the road like the powdery drifts at the beginning of a snowstorm.

In ancient times, the river system feeding the Aral Sea from the south formed a wide marsh delta ample enough to support cultures which took pride of place in the march of history. Wild animals and birds abounded. It was the home of the Caspian tiger, until the fierce beast was driven to extinction by human encroachment. Today, the salt bush and feathery saksaul plants are all that keep its wide expanse from barren dust. Enveloped in the vastness are isolated oases that meander over the landscape, chasing the capricious changes in the river courses. In such a one stands Khiva, mud-walled scion of ancient Khorezm, the old name for the delta region. Rustan told us that the name means 'sunny country', for the sun shines 300 days a year. To the east, the red hues of the Kyzylkum desert stretch into eternity. There is nothing to moderate the space-like extremes of seasonal heat and cold.

In Biblical times, a legend emerged that Noah's son Shem, leading his nomadic tribe through the Karakum desert from the west, came upon a fertile oasis ideal for settlement. For protection against marauding bandits, he ordered his people to build a fortress. As thirst took hold, they dug a well in the sand. The diggers struck an aquifer, extracting water that surprised them with its purity. After drinking it, the nomads exclaimed, "Khey-vakh!", and so the town was named. Today, you can visit the well in a corner of the old city.

In the days before Cyrus the Great, the lands of Khorezm, which encompass Khiva, belonged to the wild Scythian horsemen called the Massagetae. The Persian conqueror incorporated the region into his empire as a satrapy, where it acted as the eastern frontier of the Achaemenid heritage until Alexander arrived. Civilisational decline drove Khorezm into the grip of nomadic invaders for centuries, until the coming of the Arab armies. By the 10th century, Khorezm had risen again, and along with Bukhara, joined the vanguard of the Islamic cultural efflorescence of the Middle Ages. Al-Bīrūnī made accurate calculations of specific gravities there, and the region gave its name to the mathematician al-Khwārizmī, who inspired our word 'algorithm'. A monument to him stands proud in Khiva today. Avicenna also spent time there.

The capital city of Khorezm in its heyday was actually Kunya-Urgench, not far from Khiva, and the location of Central Asia's tallest minaret, a magnificent remnant of past glories. Urgench took the brunt of the Mongol onslaught when Genghis Khan swept down from the northern steppes, only to be crippled again by five assaults from Tamerlane, who wished to eliminate this commercial rival to his Samarkand. After the decline of the Timurids, Khiva rose to prominence again, in a revivified Khorezm.

After the era of destructive conquest ended with Tamerlane's death, Khiva was allowed to remain intact to the present day. Its mud-brick fortified wall still surrounds the city, so well preserved that it looks like a film set. Its majolica-façaded palaces and mosques stand in such profusion that the city seems like an urban museum. People live there, but avoid the monument areas. Their residences are made from wooden frames covered with baked clay, laced with straw for extra insulation. The houses of the upper socioeconomic classes are designed around an open courtyard, which is surrounded by the living quarters and wood-canopied terraces ('ayvans'). Family and friends relax in the ayvans, which are richly decorated with slender hand-carved wooden pillars, ornamented ceilings and highly glazed ceramic tiles. The wood carving, particularly of the columns and doors, is astonishing, like that in Bukhara, the patterns intriguing one to follow their intricacies to the point of dizziness, while the brickwork on the graceful minarets is poetic geometry, endlessly variable. A minaret is built for each

mosque, of which there are 50, in a city that today has only 40,000 people. The combination provides the skyline with a texture of domes and vertical intrusions.

We entered the city through the impressive twin-turreted west gate, built of sun-dried clay brick, which connects with the Ichan-Kala ('old town'). Less than one square kilometre, it beckons the traveller to explore its mysteries on foot. The khans who ruled Khiva for over four centuries until the Russians enveloped it were of legendary cruelty, controlling their domain by terror. European travellers to Central Asia in the 19th century, fascinated by this remote and dangerous branch of Islam in the Aral delta, were aghast at the severity meted out to enemies of the khan. An Anglophile Hungarian orientalist, Arminius Vambery, who became an expert on Central Asia through searching there for the roots of his people, reported to a breathless Victorian London accounts of gruesome executions by impalement where unfortunate victims took days to expire. On one occasion, he witnessed a executioner calmly gouge the eyes out of eight elderly men, then nonchalantly wipe his knife clean on their beards.

Looking like a carbuncle protruding from the side of the old citadel, the macabre Zindon bears witness today to the horrors that befell those who offended the khan. Once the jail, it is now a museum of torture. Effigies of chained prisoners holding begging bowls set the doleful atmosphere. Those on death row were held for seven days, given water but no food, washed, then dragged in manacles to the public square, where they were beheaded. A solemn drumbeat would alert the townsfolk to the advent of the spectacle, which usually took place on bazaar day, when the biggest crowds congregated. Prisoners lucky enough to have access to money could usually buy a reprieve, unless they were thieves. Pictures of minaret jactation display one of the com-

monest forms of execution, where the offender is thrown off the top of a minaret.

If a woman was unfaithful, her punishment was to be stuffed into a sack of wild cats and scratched to death in public. As late as 1912, a European witness reported that a woman who refused to marry in accordance with her father's wishes was half-buried alive, then stoned to death, while her lover was hanged.

A young Russian officer arriving in Khiva on a solo mission to put out feelers for an alliance told of the Khan's method of enforcing his decree against smoking and drinking alcohol, which he had just given up himself: offenders had their mouths slit open to the ears. The weird grin formed by the scar was

Above: Kaltar-minar minaret, Khiva

Left: Kunya Ark, Khiva

supposed to express the foolishness of the sin against the Sharia.

Tales of treachery extended the sinister reputation of Khiva. In the days of Peter the Great, stories of gold discovered at the river Oxus began to excite the attention of the court. Peter's wars were draining the treasury, so ears were open to any financial solution. Khiva's old overture of offering to become the Tsar's vassal now seemed a useful pretext for an adventure into that remote and poorly understood land of opportunity. Besides, Khiva lay halfway to India, which reports indicated abounded in riches that could, under the right circumstances, be snatched away from its British rulers.

The Tsar dispatched a heavily armed force of 4000 men, supplemented with artillery under the command of Prince Alexander Bekovich, an officer in the

Life Guards regiment. His orders were to march to Khiva, and offer Russian protection to the khan in return for possession of the region. In the event of non-compliance, Bekovich was to use his artillery to smash down the mud walls of the city. The wily khan received the Russian expedition with apparent courtesy but explained that his city was too small to accommodate a force of that size. He claimed himself anxious to be hospitable, suggesting that the size problem could be solved by splitting the men into small groups, which could be billeted separately. Against the advice of his second-in-command, Bekovich agreed.

As soon as the men dispersed, the Khivans overwhelmed them in a sanguinary massacre. Bekovich was slashed to death in front of the khan and his head severed. The ghoulish khan had it stuffed with straw and sent to his neighbouring ruler at Bukhara as a boast of his triumph. Some of the men were spared death to become slaves, while a sorry few were allowed to escape across the Karakum desert and back to the Caspian Sea, to bear the news to a shocked St Petersburg (although there was not sufficient shock to prompt the dedication of resources to vengeance). The tsar's geologists never got the chance to explore the region's gold-mining potential. That had to wait. Uzbekistan is now in the top 10 gold producers in the world.

When the Russians took over Khiva in 1873, they collected all the gold and silver coins in circulation and prohibited any further minting. The economy turned to paper for its currency, using the more durable silk for higher denominations. Silk banknotes are on display at the local mint, which has been converted to a small museum.

We walked over sun-drenched cobblestones to the complex of residential extravaganzas, enclosed by a high brick wall, that make up Tash Havli, or Stone House, built over eight years in the 19th century. The original architect had the lack of diplomacy to warn the khan that his palace could not be constructed in the two years allotted for the task. The disappointment of the monarch was quickly followed by the execution of the architect.

The formidable walls yielded to a graceful, pointed arch portal flanked by majestic minaret-like towers built onto the mural structure, their brickwork disclosing the geometric patterns common to Central Asia, with a hint of blue tiles. The wide double door displayed intriguing carvings held in place by three rows of iron studs.

The portal opened into a large courtyard emblazoned with walls of bright majolica blue tiles set in panels. It contained the secret world of the harem, complete within itself. Inside lived the khan's wives and concubines, snatched, bought and contracted for from as far afield as the Silk Road caravans could reach. On three sides above the first level, high ayvans looked down, supported by single columns of involutionarily carved wood. The wooden cross-beamed ceilings of the ayvans were brightly painted with floral motifs. The interior of the palace rooms was richly ornamented with colour and geometric patterns, giving an overwhelming impression of stylish opulence. Outside, the blue majolica flashed in the sun, smooth and clean against the textured beige brick.

We visited the hammam, or Turkish bathhouse, which has been in continuous use since the middle of the 17th century until recently. The entire complex is built underground with its 'smoke canals' supplying heat from well water heated in the boiler room. From the outside, all that can be seen is a series of picturesque domes standing low in the dusty street. A contrasting vertical dimension is supplied by a nearby thicket of minarets reaching skyward. One of them, the Kaltar-minar, which has a base diameter of over 14 metres and is clad in blue tiles, was to have been the tallest in Central Asia. Romantics claimed it was to be high enough to have been seen from Bukhara, almost 500 kilometres away. It stands unfinished, squat and a little sinister, like a cooling tower for a nuclear power plant.

We climbed up on top of the walls for a view of the old city. The rooftops were so close together that it would be possible to jump from one to another in a chase. It could be a scene for a romantic novel or a movie. The beige colour of the mud plaster in the various building structures blended them together into a cohesion of textured unity. Television aerials standing up like crooked sticks looked incongruous, a modern intrusion on the past. A haze softened the angles of everything and the wind cut the cruelty out of the heat. In the distance, trees with dusty green canopies looked like they were growing out of the mud roofs, relieving the dryness of the cityscape. The blue tiles of the rounded shapes and majolica panels scintillated in the moving air. Nasal sounds of Central Asian music wafted up from speakers in the bazaar. They were topped for a while by the long-winded call to prayer of the muezzins, starting up one after the other in a tortuous fugue. We looked down into the square to where the khan used to pitch his ceremonial yurt on top of a round brick platform. Receiving guests there permitted him to claim that he had not lost touch with his robust nomadic origins in the Turkic steppes. Besides, in winter, the yurt was easier than a palace to heat, its felt walls an excellent insulator.

On one side of the city square, a lone camel was tethered in the sun, a colourful carpet draped over its back. Eyes half-closed and snout lifted high, underslung lip suffused with white saliva, it looked disdainfully past the people walking by. Abruptly, it would swing its head around like a gun turret to look at some distant object. Nearby, children walked through the streets, sucking on sugar cane. Women in the traditional gold-and-red zigzag dresses of Uzbekistan pulled wheeled carrying carts laden with yellow melons from the oasis. Old men in astrakhan hats ambled by alongside the younger generation in tracksuits and Reeboks. A bicycle glided by. The pace of life was languorous. Many men were just sitting around, not bothering to talk. Dogs were everywhere, white and beige, all small. After dark, we heard them barking and fighting in a constant counterpoint.

A soaring blue-tiled dome signalled what has been described as the most beautiful architectural complex in Khiva. It is the mausoleum dedicated to a 14th-century wrestler so famous that Iranian professional exponents of the sport say prayers to him before their matches. Pahlavan Mahmud's fame was based not only on sport; his athletic prowess paralleled talents in poetry and medicine. He became the patron saint of Khiva, despite the rumour that he wrote anticlerical poetic satire under a pseudonym. Inside the dome, a breathtaking cupola, scintillating with varied majolica designs, rose into a panoply of glistening blue and white. On the walls, in beautiful script, the plaintive strains of ego ask: "Will they remember me above my remains?".

Not far from the opulent buildings constructed by Khan Allaquli in the mid-19th century from the burgeoning profits of the trade with Russia furtively lurks the old slave market, in use until the arrival of the Russians in 1873. Khiva was one of the most notorious entrepôts for the dismal traffic, and a target since Peter the Great for Russian efforts to free their unfortunate citizens. Not all slaves were Russian, although Russian males were most highly prized. Persians and Kurds made up the majority, with Persian females particularly sought after. In the twisted logic of the Great Game, the English sent emissaries to Khan Allaquli with entreaties to free the Russian slaves, in the hope that this would

Outside a medresa wall

remove the pretext under which Russian military expeditions were penetrating further and further into the steppe towards Khiva. The khan received them in a bemused state of mind, for he hardly knew who the British were. Some of his advisers thought they were a subtribe of the Russians, or at least their vassals. The khan asked how many guns the British army had, boasting that he had as many as 20. A dashing 28-year-old Indian army officer, Richmond Shakspear, managed to free several hundred Russian slaves, an event greeted with public joy in St Petersburg, but with private fury by the tsar, whose excuse for marching on Khiva was effectively removed. Khiva's fall was delayed for a generation.

The Shergazikhan medresa, where some of the most prominent intellectuals of Khorezm were educated, was built by slaves, some Persian and some Russians, captured from Prince Bekovich's expeditionary force. The khan promised to free them on completion of the medresa. The project dragged on for so long that the slaves, having lost faith in the prospect of freedom, rebelled and assassinated the khan. A local historian installed the inscription over the entrance: "Alas, save me from the slaves".

Mohammed Rahimkhan, medresa

Amin Tura medresa

I was impressed by the aesthetic care devoted to the learning establishments of Central Asia in the days before the socialist realism of the Soviet hegemony stifled creativity. The mellifluous and grand proportions of the medresas and their beautiful blue and white tiles, integrated with calligraphy – the artistic symbol of knowledge – disclosed the conviction of their planners that elegant physical surroundings can inspire the educational process. In the West, notwithstanding contemporary affluence at a height never before experienced, utilitarian architecture now dominates the university environment.

By the time we left this fascinating city, which had survived so many natural disasters and human cruelties with its magnificent and distinctive architecture intact, I felt proud that UNESCO has included it in its register of monuments of the heritage that belongs to us all.

In travelling through these vast Eurasian lands, I was struck constantly by the burgeoning influence of Islam. The 55 million people living in an area about the size of Australia have firmly turned their backs on Marxist atheism and are relearning their traditional religion. The Islamic revival we saw in Turkey and Iran is now engulfing the 'heart of Asia'.

Central Asia is contiguous with Iran and Afghanistan, both countries with strong commitments to Islamic fundamentalism. Partly because of racial solidarity, but also because they belong to the Sunni sect, whose world centre was the Ottoman caliphate, Central Asians look more to Turkey than to Iran as a paradigm. They see Islamic revival as a social rather than a political movement, a return to a moral and spiritually enriched life guided by the Sharia. For Iranians, the goal is more than that; it is the creation of an Islamic State based on a theocracy run by the ulema.

Whether the liberal model will continue to be followed in this strategically vital part of the world is not foreseeable. Certainly, it should not be taken for granted. Iran, imbued with proselytising zeal, is considered a friendly nation, with whom cultural and economic ties go back along the Silk Road over 2000 years; most of the trucks that ply the great commercial and ideas artery today have Iranian licence plates.

We flew in a Tupolev from nearby Urgench to Tashkent, over the Amu Darya choking with sandbars that looked like scabs from the air. The vast expanse of desert gave way to the green pastures of the capital. A father let his five-year-old son sit on his knee to look at the scenery as we landed, not bothering about the seatbelt. We stayed just long enough for another Russian flying cattle car to take us into the Central Asian skies that extend east over the Pamir Mountains.

On the other side of the peaks lies the Chinese sphere of influence, exercised over people with the same ethnic and cultural origins as we had encountered. One group of people had been dominated by the Soviet system in recent times, the other by the Chinese, for a longer period. What would the differences be? Both are Islamic societies whose religious ideals have been suppressed by secular overlords. But that is changing. What drew us most was the opportunity to travel the Chinese portion of the Silk Road, arguably the most fascinating section of the venerable trade route, for it contains relics of the Buddhist migration from India, one of the most important propagations of ideas in history.

Part V
XINJIANG

Buddist cave, Kyzyl

PART
V

Chapter 16

The Silk Road

Suddenly, in the midst of battle beyond the eastern frontier, a shimmering wall of supernatural light flashed in front of the seven Roman legions commanded by Marcus Licinius Crassus, blinding their dreaded troops. Already hard pressed, the disciplined ranks faltered and then broke in panic. The famed eagle standards fell to ignominious surrender and 10,000 legionnaires marched off to a life of slavery in the East. Their general, the richest man in Rome, whose name is cognate with the word 'crass', was captured, and held while his Parthian enemies poured molten gold down his throat.

The Parthians, from what is now Iran, had acquired their secret weapon from Chinese traders in exchange for an ostrich egg. It was silk, sewn into long banners, its smooth surface reflecting the high-wattage desert sun. The battle of Carrhae, in 53 BC, east of the Euphrates River, was the West's introduction to the diaphanous textile invented in China during the Neolithic Age, probably 4000 to 5000 years ago. Soon after the defeat, samples of the fabric made their way west, and within decades, noble families in Rome were wearing it.

XIAN

We flew to Xian (pronounced Hsi Arn). The nation's capital during six dynasties, it was the eastern starting point of the network of ancient caravan tracks that the 19th-century German geographer Baron von Richtoven named the Silk Road. It is perhaps best known in the West as the site of the terracotta warriors grandiosely entombed with Qin Shi Huang Di (pronounced Chin Shir Huarng Di), first emperor of a united China and the man whose name was given to the country.

But the ancient city deserves greater fame. Its archaeological treasures, which when fully explored may well rival those of Egypt, corroborate the story of a metropolis under the Han dynasty (202 BC to 220 AD) as powerful in the East as Rome was in the West and as glorious under the Tang dynasty

(627 to 918 AD) as was Constantinople. It is a heart-land of the Chinese intellect. Sino-communism began there, as did the standard Chinese script. The reverence for writing that informs Chinese culture is implicit in the fact that the word for 'civilisation' is the same as that for 'script'. The silt-filled Yellow River valley of the surrounding Shaanxi province is called the 'cradle of Chinese civilisation', and the famous discovery here of a skull and jawbone indicate that *Homo sapiens* inhabited the area 800,000 years ago.

A Chinese scholar we met introduced us to the popular saying: "If you wish to understand China in the last decade, go to the Shenzen special economic zone; if you wish to understand China in the last century, go to Shanghai; but if you wish to understand China over the last 3000 years, go to Xian".

Extraneous forces have isolated China. For centuries, the ferocious Turkic tribes, known to them as the Xiongnu (pronounced Hsiung Nu) and to us as the Huns, sealed its northern and northwestern frontiers. Further south and west lies the vast tectonic crunch that curbs passage into the plains of Central Asia and India. The cataclysm happened about 15 million years ago when the crustal plate that carries India rammed into the southern edge of Tibet, thrusting up huge areas of Central Asia into the largest mountain system in the world and re-directing river courses away from China. It cut the western region off from the widespread inland waterways that were to provide the main communication matrix in later years, when Chinese society emerged. Alexander the Great reached Afghanistan, but it appears that his geographical knowledge was stunted by the mountain barrier, now called the Pamirs and described by Marco Polo as the "roof of the world". West and Far East were fated to live in ignorance of each other during their formative centuries. It remained the case until a formal trade route arose to connect the two segments of the world.

In 138 BC, hearing that the Yuezhi (pronounced Yeweh Jir), a Scythian tribe and traditional enemy of the Huns, had been driven west in a series of sanguinary battles and might be fostering revenge, the Han emperor Wu Di dispatched a mission of 100 men led by Zhang Qian (pronounced Jarng Chien) to solicit an alliance. For centuries, the aggressive Huns had been marauding China from the northwest and were a constant preoccupation of Chinese foreign policy. It was to contain them that Qin Shi Huang Di built the Great Wall in the third century BC.

After 13 years of perilous adventures, during which he was captured by the Huns, married one of their princesses and escaped, the indomitable emissary returned to Xian – without the support of the Yuezhi, whose vengeance had dissipated in their new land west of the Taklamakan desert. But Zhang Qian brought back tales of 36 fabulously rich kingdoms in the shadowy west. Many of these were in the oases of Central Asia: Samarkand, Bukhara and Merv, the lands of the Sogdians, not yet overrun by the Turkic tribes.

Best of all was intelligence of a heavenly breed of horses from the fertile valley of Fergana (the eastern province of modern-day Uzbekistan), more powerful than the smaller Chinese species. The horses ran so fast that enthusiasts claimed they sweated blood. More careful observation disclosed that the species was prone to a parasite, which caused a skin irritation that sometimes erupted in bleeding. The superb form of these stalwart horses was to inspire Chinese artists for centuries to come; the famous Tang horse style is derived from it. Smelling military advantage, the emperor forwarded trade delegations to acquire the superior mounts, inaugurating a mercantile link that would internationalise the world. Added to the fêtes and material rewards that were lavished on the observant emissary was the title 'Great Traveller', bestowed on him by the emperor.

For commerce to flourish, peace must reign. Gradually, the increasingly warlike Han armies subdued the fractious tribes, no doubt aided by the Heavenly Horses, and despite periods of dynastic decline, Chinese trade was relatively secure in the Silk Road region until Genghis Khan imposed his pax Mongolica in the Middle Ages. However, the xenophobic Ming dynasty that followed closed China off from the outside world, ringing the curtain down on the epic commercial drama.

The human drive to obtain what somebody else has can be expressed by theft, force or trade. While examples of the first two appear in its record, the Silk Road is arguably premodern history's paramount case study of the latter method. The earliest trade was in pigments, jade and religious articles. Later, from the East appeared silk, furs, bronze weapons, iron, rhubarb for medicinal applications, porcelain from highly fired kaolin, not produced in the West, and rag paper. The West exported textiles, metal, glassware and gold to finance its current account deficit, as well as ivory, tortoise shells and rhinoceros horn, which traders sourced in Africa, giving a triangular dimension to the commercial route. Rhinoceros horn was much prized in China for its aphrodisiac properties, more supposed than real, for the true reason that such attention was focussed on the poor beast was that its horn resembled a human phallus.

It was a business of middlemen. Merchants would not complete the arduous journey of 14,000 kilometres themselves, but would sell their goods at trading centres along the way, then return home. By the time the products reached their destination, they had been marked up many times. In Rome, silk became so expensive that Emperor Tiberius, who ruled at the time of Jesus' crucifixion, sought to ban its use as a plague on the economy, synchronously condemning it as an invitation to lasciviousness. At the time, the Romans had only the vaguest idea about China, their name for which was Seres, and probably would have been amazed at the sophistication of its capital city, which we were about to visit.

We arrived at the Xian airport by way of one of China's 38 airlines, all controlled by Beijing but operated individually. As we filed off the clean, new Boeing (China is Boeing's largest customer), we were greeted by a large sign reading, "Civilized Performance, Satisfactory Service". With access to millions of native English-speakers, I found it droll that, throughout China, translations are always awkward, often comical and sometimes downright ludicrous.

Close by the modern city, to the northwest, are the remains of Chang'an, built as an opulent imperial statement by the Han ruler 50 years before Zhang Qian went on his epic journey. It also had the good fortune of being situated in the most important silk-producing area. For years, the caravans enriched this magnificent city with luxuries from the fabulous West, and gold and lacquer appeared with fine silk to adorn the life of the inhabitants.

Under the golden age of the Tang dynasty, during which, in the seventh to 10th centuries, China reached its highest cultural glory, Chang'an was the largest city in the world, covering an area more than five times larger than that of Rome at its height. The grid pattern of its streets, similar to those of Hellenistic cities, inspired the Japanese architects who designed the sacred cities of Kyoto and Nara. With the Tang descent into the chaos of the Five Dynasties period, the glory of Chang'an faded into provincialism, until the Ming emperor Zhu Yuanzhang rebuilt it in the 14th century, giving it a name that expressed the aspirations of the time: Xian ('western peace').

During the Tang period, Xian rivalled Byzantium in its cosmopolitan diversity. Scores of nationalities

Left: Big Wild Goose Pagoda
Below: Garden of Little Wild Goose Pagoda

from the Chinese empire and tributary states mixed with the local people, and foreigners from as far away as Persia made their way along the Silk Road to seek their fortune in the Tang capital, or to escape persecution, particularly after the Arab invasions. Exotic religions flourished in the expansive and liberal environment. Nestorian, Zoroastrian, Manichaean, Judaeic and Islamic places of worship sprouted up alongside the temples of Buddhism that represented the dominant religion, a faith that had migrated there along the Silk Road. It was under the Tang dynasty that Buddhist art reached its highest form of expression and the silk its finest quality. Buddhism, so vital to the soul of China, captured the imagination of Chinese rulers and architects, acting as the inspiration for some of the most impressive buildings in the nation.

In Xian, two imposing pagodas, called the Little Wild Goose and the Big Wild Goose, encapsulate the Buddhist legacy. During the Tang period the wild goose was revered. As soon as we walked into the pomegranate garden of the Little Wild Goose pagoda, I felt the noise and tension of the city's bustle slip from my shoulders, like the sensation of a soft massage. In the enclosed space, my attention was focussed on the particular: the orange flowers of the pomegranate trees, and the wooden staves propping up the old locust trees, whose branches drooped with memories of dynasties past. Single-petal roses brought to mind that the flower, now so complex in the West, originally came from China. The layered 15-storey pagoda, which formed part of a disappeared temple built in the Tang period, rose out of foliage where the light formed changing patterns as the branches slowly moved. Chinese flute music floated through the slightly perfumed air from somewhere unseen, and a light breeze moved silently through the leaves, making them glitter in the sun. Swoops of swallows in constant movement around

the pagoda emphasised the peace and stillness elsewhere, in a classic Chinese duet of contrasting forces, yin and yang.

The contemplative atmosphere seemed to be informed by the Buddhist texts in Chinese translation that we knew were stored on each floor of the tall pagoda, whose steadfast composure had endured 70 earthquakes. All religious sanctuaries express a tranquil atmosphere, but somehow, the ideal of serenity, of sloughing off all worldly desires, that lies at the heart of Buddhist aspiration elevates its shrines to a higher level.

Under an old locust tree, a wizened calligrapher sat working quietly with his rice paper and ink, using the nail of his little finger, which he had allowed to grow very long, to inscribe the elegant cadences of his art. Beside him, a notice in unaesthetic English script proclaimed the man to be a "World Well-known Artistic Person". Calligraphy, echoing the importance the Chinese place on writing, is the most prestigious of the art forms in China. Because the Chinese ideographic script lends itself to the beauty of shape, it can be combined with poesy to give two dimensions to the same artistic idea. The best calligraphers do not sell their work as a matter of course. Usually, they are salaried employees of cultural institutions, practising their art part time. They might, however, sell you a piece, if they are in the mood and consider you capable of appreciating their work. A month's notice is required for an appointment.

We walked over to a discreet little kiosk that housed a gigantic drum, said to be the 'luck drum'. A sign next to it advised: "The stroking of the Drum can dispel the Evil, crack down the Evil, can make you encounter peace, keep you away from disaster". Superstition has always run deep in the Chinese character, something with which religion has had to contend. One of the greatest of these, one that has never left the soul of the Chinese, is Buddhism. Paradoxically, this was a foreign religion, coming east to China along the Silk Road from India.

The intellectual cargo of the Silk Road was the religious thought of the ancient world. Persian Manichaeism, Nestorian Christianity, Islam and Buddhism, reckoned by Sir Aurel Stein to be "India's greatest contribution to the spiritual development of mankind", all journeyed east towards China, but of these, Buddhism was the only one to be taken up by a majority of Chinese.

Trade flowed over the Karakorum Mountains both west and east from north India, but the Buddhist monks who travelled with the caravans found a market for their ideas mainly in the Far East. Perhaps it was because the prevailing thought structure there was Confucian, which dealt with the appropriate moral order of society rather than with a system of spiritual evolution. Even though Taoism explored a mystical connection with nature and ventured onto the metaphysical plane, the spiritual field was, essentially, left open. West of the Pamirs, it was occupied by Christianity, Islam and Judaeism.

In the first century, the Han emperor Ming Di converted to Buddhism after seeing in a dream a vision of a flying apsara (Buddhist angel), and established the Indian import in China. For centuries, Chinese Buddhists were troubled by the problem of authenticating the stories and revelations from India communicated to Chinese novitiates, until a Tang monk, Xuan Zang (pronounced Hsuarn Dzarng), embarked on an epic pilgrimage to India, bringing the sacred sutras, which were written in Sanskrit, back to Xian. There, he translated them, in a tour de force of literary accomplishment. Of comparable importance is the nature of his 16-year voyage to the source of Buddhist wisdom. It was one whose danger, solitude and extreme physical hardship enhanced an inner journey of the soul in a manner

similar to the quest for the holy grail by Western idealists a few hundred years later.

Xuan Zang started his pilgrimage from Xian as a young Buddhist monk of 27, aware that travelling to the western regions was forbidden by imperial edict. Riding a skinny roan horse, he managed to dodge the tall watchtowers that guarded the roads of the kingdom, making it through the Jade Gate in the northwest. It was the outpost that separated the sedate, civilised world of the Tang from the barbaric lands of the western mountains and deserts, infested by hostile tribes and bloodthirsty bandits. His path traversed dust storms and waterless heat, snow-blasted mountains and endless desert, sometimes with only the bleached bones of his unfortunate predecessors to guide his steps. He was often alone with his spavined mount, indomitably pursuing his dream of reaching India. The spiritual epic earned him a place in Chinese lore that inspires people even in the modern age. Mao Zedong wrote poems about his travails. The stories of Monkey from the 16th-century humorous novel based on Xuan Zang's travels are part of the Chinese cultural repertoire from opera to television series and comic books. Thoughts of Don Quixote spring to mind.

When Xuan Zang returned to China, the emperor had the Big Wild Goose pagoda built to house the Buddhist texts he brought – more than 500 of them. There, he spent the rest of his life working on their translations. When we visited the arresting seven-storey building in a commanding position overlooking the city, I wondered whether any state in modern times would ever award a scholar such an honour.

Outside the pagoda, we noticed a disturbance in the street. People were talking aggressively, and more began to gather. When we walked over to investigate, we found a confrontation raging between three motorcycle policemen and a group of about 20 people. We discovered that the police had towed away a truck that was illegally parked, but this provoked so much protest from the crowd, which was sympathetic to the truck driver, that the police had to allow it to come back. The people then laughed and jeered as the crestfallen policemen started up their motorbikes, stony-faced, and roared off up the street.

We were invited to lunch by the rather serious but very friendly Shaanxi museum director and several of his curators. The restaurant to which he took us was famous for its dumplings – little meat and vegetable delicacies known in the West by their Cantonese name 'dim sum'. They were the favourite cuisine of the last empress. The establishment produced 200 varieties, with the tradition that staff would note which ones you ate, serving you new dishes at each visit until you had tasted all 200. We had 12 servings, each one different and, thankfully for our capacity, quite small, much smaller than the Cantonese version. I thought them the best I had ever tasted.

During lunch, the director talked very authoritatively about the wealth of archaeological discoveries still to be made in the environs of Xian, particularly of artefacts from the fecund Tang period. Digging is interminably slow, due not only to the lack of resources but also to a reluctance on the part of Chinese authorities to expose perishable treasures to the atmosphere. They are hoping that improved methods of protection will be developed. Bad experiences of important paper manuscripts disintegrating to the touch are driving this caution. Also, the cost of maintenance, restoration and housing is a barrier. But the Chinese relate well to the slow rhythms of time. While we were eating our shrimp dumplings, the director's mobile telephone rang. He pulled it out, and talked animatedly for a while, excusing himself with a little shyness. I asked our translator what the learned academic was saying. "Oh, he is just talking to his broker, getting the latest prices on the Shang-

hai Stock Exchange." The diners at the table laughed when he quoted the current stockmarket index. Everybody buys shares in Xian – even the restaurant was listed on the local stock exchange.

After lunch, we went to the museum, where we were ushered into a high-ceilinged private room furnished in brightly polished mahogany. We sat on sofas with hard red-leather cushions that encouraged good posture. While we were given an orientation to the establishment, tea was served. The beverage originated in China, probably reaching India along the Silk Road.

The director escorted us down into the vaults of the museum, where the famous Tang frescoes were kept, not accessible to the public. They were like a bank vault, secured by a large steel door opened with a key. As we walked along the corridor, a huge roller door came up automatically, like a scene from a James Bond movie.

Without saying a word, the director rolled out a massive vertical panel a metre and a half thick, three metres high and four metres wide. On each side was an eighth-century Tang fresco. He then pulled out others, each on rollers, until he had about 10 open, a mere fraction of what was held in the vast storeroom. Archaeologists are digging up more each year to add to the collection, although the pace is slow. The fresco pieces, which had been carefully excised from the tomb walls they covered, were made from a layer of mud and straw, plastered over to form a surface for the paint. It is just as well the Chinese authorities are keeping them away from the light, because many are already in faded condition.

Each fresco displayed a different scene: two horsemen, a mountain in the background, painted in an almost abstract way; ladies of the court, with huge fans. One fresco that seemed to typify the innate sense of superiority that led the Chinese to think of their country as the Middle Kingdom

Terracotta warriors, Xian

depicted a procession of foreign courtiers – a Mongolian dressed in deer shoes and round fur hat, a Korean and a Persian – all gesturing in supplication to three Chinese mandarins in voluminous sleeves, who were chatting among themselves, their backs to the emissaries. A painting of a polo game disclosed another influence that had migrated along the Silk Road. These images are famous throughout the world, copied endlessly in books. Western department stores even sell placemats adorned with them.

We went for a long late afternoon walk in the old part of the city, which is enclosed by a fully intact fortified wall built in the Ming period. The streets were teeming with active and voluble people, clearly friendly, often calling out in English, "Hello! How are you?". They seemed happy, content with their life, which is better than in the recent past. Food is everywhere, and cheap. The people are well dressed; especially the young women, who all use make-up, a huge contrast from the days when it was forbidden and everyone wore Mao uniforms. I wondered whether the cheerfulness stemmed just from the newness of the better times, and if so, whether it would last as the current lifestyle became familiar and gaps opened up between the rich and the rest.

While we were standing in a huge crowd, bicycles flashing past in mad confusion, a policeman came rushing over towards us, blowing his whistle shrilly and stopped the traffic in half the street. Motioning to us he then led us across the street, stopping the traffic in the other half, smiling all the way. Not all traffic controllers are in uniform. Near our hotel a man, blind in one eye, with a cigarette drooping from his lips (the Chinese are inveterate smokers), was employed to stop the bicycles in their path at the intersection by pulling up a red string tied to a tree on the other side.

For many people, their whole life cycle seems to be spent in the street, transporting on bicycles or in bicycle-drawn carts the goods they buy in the morning and sell throughout the day and night. They have their own territory on the pavement, within regions that specialise in various products – shoes, shirts, artwork, stamps, old books and so on.

We passed through forests of food stalls. Food was all around, all the time. On the roadside, people were chopping, tossing stir-fried things around in woks over open-fire braziers, coal- or propane-fuelled, barbecuing satay sticks, selling dumplings from wicker steamers and offering various cold delicacies. A man at a fish stand was skinning a living frog. Smoke and cooking smells swirled around us.

In the backstreets, everything was crowded. A row of barber shops ended right next to a grocery stand where a woman was chopping cabbage with a meat cleaver. People spat on the footpaths, and honked their noses as they sped by on bicycles. Some of the shops were squalid. We passed one where three fat fish lay upside down in a tank filled with dirty water, their gills flapping slowly as life oozed out. Eels lay gasping, their heads close to the surface of the water, too exhausted to move.

Air pollution was as heavy as a dusty cloak, due mainly to the amount of coal that is burned for cooking, heating and electricity-generation and exacerbated by the growing encroachment of the automobile on roads once ruled by bicycles. Natural gas, which burns more cleanly than coal, has been discovered not far away and is being harnessed in power-generation, but coal will continue be the primary source of energy for a long time.

TOMB WARRIORS

At Lintung, just east of Xian, the terracotta army of Qin Shi Huang Di, the first emperor of China, stands on guard. We visited the site along with hundreds of other tourists, all Chinese. The emperor's tomb area covers 56 square kilometres, a complex larger than the pyramids of Giza. The tomb itself, which contains, according to the records, archaeological treasures too big for grave robbers to take away, has not yet been excavated. The authorities are taking their time, perhaps made a little cautious by tales of automatic crossbows and other booby traps set by the cunning artisans who built it.

Recently, archaeologists have dug three immense pits to uncover the warriors, made from terracotta, that stand ranged in military formations, ready to protect the soul of the forceful man who united the warring states into a national entity for the first time and who built the Great Wall against the northern barbarians. It has been estimated that there are 7000 of these warriors, some 1000 of which have been unearthed so far. The faces bear distinctly individual features – some with moustaches, others with beards, most clean-shaven – but all demonstrate the stoical demeanour of the doughty warrior. There is no effigy of the commanding general, for he is the spirit of Qin Shi Huang Di.

To protect the emperor's protectors from the elements, a vast shed, like an aircraft hangar, has been built over the excavations. The enclosed space, faintly illuminated through side windows, adds an eerie dimension to the silent presence of the lifelike figures, many of which are stained with the smoke of war, for shortly after the emperor died, the nation erupted in rebellion and angry forces burned down the giant vaults of rammed earth and wood-beamed roofs. The mausoleum was neglected, and eventually receded under a ceiling of earth that grew over time to a thickness of five metres. In the spring of 1974, a local farmer digging a well uncovered the first of the ancient soldiers to see daylight for over 2000 years. The discovery changed his life as well as history. Relieved of hard labour on the land, he now spends his time in a private office, signing autographs for tourists, an honoured treasure of the nation. We saw him there, but didn't have the patience to stand in the long queue for a signature.

On our way to the airport, we passed mounds that rose out of the flat wheat fields, from 100 metres off the road to the horizon, like pyramids slightly flattened by weathering. They were the 300 Tang dynasty and 72 Han dynasty tombs that have been identified but not yet explored. So far, 48,000 beautifully painted Tang period figures, much smaller than the terracotta warriors, have been discovered, and this is but a fraction of what is expected.

URUMCHI

Our flight to Urumchi, capital of Xinjiang, was cancelled while we were at the airport, a vicissitude quite common in China. Eventually, we got on a rickety Tupolev and shoehorned ourselves into the cramped quarters. The one-class aircraft was jammed with people and hand-luggage. The carpet was soiled and the armrests worn to the metal. Smells of stale food and sweat choked the atmosphere, already stuffy from poor air circulation. There did not appear to be too many more journeys left in the old crate; I hoped this would be one of them. As we clambered up the steps, we noticed a sign in English on the worn fuselage of the Russian aircraft: "China Xinjiang Airlines – Rented". I wondered who was responsible for the maintenance.

Formerly called Chinese Turkestan, Xinjiang (pronounced Hsin Jiarng) is the furthest the Chinese writ extends and is thought of by the civilised Chinese as their Wild West. A vast land of steppe, desert and oasis one-sixth the size of the United States, Xinjiang is bounded by the Altaic Mountains to the northeast and the Kunlun, Karakorum and Pamir mountains to the south and west.

The Kunlun range is famous for jade. Although now an autonomous region within the administrative system of China, it has been historically more associated with Central Asia than with the Han Chinese. Its indigenous people, who are Muslim, are of Turkic stock, related to the Huns who ravaged China's north in the past and whose multifarious tribes pushed west in a series of warlike migrations to terrorise the Indo-European flatlands. It is the cradle of the Turkic race. From the vast area protected by mountain walls, successive tribes fanned out to the north, to the Mongolian grasslands, and west across Central Asia to Eastern Europe. Attila the Hun could trace his ancestry to this part of the world; his name is commonly given to boys today from Xinjiang to Hungary. The inhabitants of Turkey trace their linguistic roots – and many, their racial ties – to the region. The Mongols are closely related. Within a few days, Turks can pick up enough of the local dialects to converse with people throughout Central Asia, creating a continuous 6000 kilometre language chain from Istanbul to Urumchi.

Chapter 17

Today in the Middle Ages

KASHGAR

We didn't stay long in Urumchi, for we wanted to get to Kashgar, in western Xinjiang, and start our journey back along the Silk Road towards China. When we arrived at the Urumchi airport, joking about the decrepit condition of the aircraft in this part of the world and how it seems a triumph of determination over technology that they fly at all, we were greeted with a large sign over the door: "Grasp the Opportunity, Consolidate the Enterprise, Strike for the Third Takeoff – Xinjiang Civil Aviation". The mind boggled. We hoped that on this occasion, the pilot would make it at the first attempt.

From Urumchi, we flew back in time to Kashgar, west over the snowcapped Tian Shan range (which means 'Heavenly Mountains'), as far west as it is possible to travel before leaving China. The name 'Kashgar' comes from the words for 'brick kiln', a proud reference to the fact that the town was the earliest brick-making centre in the region. Marco Polo, who travelled there when it was subject to Kublai, the great Mongol khan who ruled China, spoke of the fine orchards and vineyards of its surrounding oasis, and of the vast cotton plantations. It is still a lush growing area. Each oasis town along the Silk Road is famous for a fruit. For Kashgar, it is the pomegranate.

The airline lost our bags in Xian. We had reason to suspect that the porters had deliberately failed to load them because the aircraft was too heavy with passengers. Other people were missing their bags, too. No-one seemed perturbed, as they expected them to arrive on the next flight. They did.

The old caravan town is the junction of the two main Silk Roads that passed north and south of the fearsome Taklamakan desert, said to have devoured more lives than any other in the world. The name comes from the Turkic words meaning 'enter and never return'. Marco Polo, who encountered the desert in the 13th century, wrote with dread about the spirit voices that lured countless travellers into the lethal maw of its endless wastelands.

Kashgar

The Chinese section of the Silk Road stands chiefly in Xinjiang, whose name means 'new territories', conjuring up images of a remote and wild land. Its population is predominantly Uighur, a Turkic people related to the ancient Xiongnu or Huns. The name 'Uighur', meaning 'united', refers to the many tribes making up the society. The vast area is largely covered with loess, windborne soil deposited with the capriciousness of nature. It is astonishingly fertile when watered, but most of the region enjoys only 10 millimetres of rainfall a year.

At the frontier airport, which had the casual atmosphere typical of outposts, our guide, a cheerful, plump Uighur woman who learned English at the First Experimental Foreign Language School for Minorities in Xinjiang, was waiting for us. Her name was Parida. Guides are virtually the only English-speakers in this faraway land where Europeans are still a curiosity. Our hotel was concrete-block basic, but the local food was palatable – mutton spiced with cumin and chilli, laghman noodles, and clean, fresh greens. And even though we were in a Muslim region, beer was commonly available. It was amazing how much better the cuisine was than what passed for food on the Soviet side of the Pamirs, even though the staples – mutton and bread – were the same. I could only think it was due to the influence of the Chinese, with the consummate importance they place on good food.

One evening, we drove to the outskirts of town, to a restaurant set in an orchard of apricots and mulberries ripe for the picking. Before dinner, we wandered through the burdened trees, tasting·the sweet fruit at random. Outside in the garden, enclosed with a low brick wall, a pit dug one and a half metres deep and lined first with brick and then with salt crystals served as the establishment's oven. A sheep, hung from a metal crossbar attached by wire, was cooking in the pit. The wood at the bottom was

white-hot, radiating an intense, even heat up the sides of the pit and roasting the meat at a slow, steady pace. No turning mechanism was needed. Cumin is the distinctive spice in Central Asia, and the cook told us that before roasting, the mutton had been rubbed with flour, eggs, pepper, salt, onion and cumin mixed together into a paste. When the meat was served, it was so tender that no knife was needed and the taste was superb, the best I had ever experienced. We drank beer, which somehow seemed to go well with the spicy flavour. Anyway, the wines in Central Asia are more for historical interest than for drinking.

Kashgar is full of archetypal Turkic buildings: intricately carved wooden balconies overhanging the street, supported by finely chiselled posts. To the west of the town, in a small oasis, is another example of the public reverence accorded in Central Asia to men of letters: the towering statue of Mahmed Kashgari, an 11th-century Uighur scholar who compiled a seminal Turkish-language dictionary. In the West, by contrast, our principal statuary is almost always limited to political or military celebrities.

We went on an aimless walk through the Sunday bazaar, reputedly the largest open-air market in the world. More than 100,000 people saunter through each market day, as they have done since the heyday of the Silk Road when Kashgar was called its pearl. We were time-warped back into the Middle Ages; only the outdoor television sets blaring out the din of action movies, full of guns and martial-arts fighting, disclosed our generation. Except for electricity, the atmosphere was exactly as it must have been in the days of the great caravans. Today, the donkey was the engine of choice. There are so many donkey carts that peak-hour roads are blocked by donkey jams. Instead of honking horns, drivers call out, "Posh, posh!" to clear a passage through the surging crowd of pedestrians. They are unwilling to slow down or deviate from their path. While we were walking down the main track in the bazaar, I failed to move out of the way fast enough and got slashed on the leg by a load of wood.

Products were grouped together as in a sprawling department store, sound and smell marking the boundaries. Tinkers beat their pots and pans, which sounded like Caribbean steel drums, and slumped sacks of colourful spices perfumed the air. Long dried grass, used for basket-weaving, was stacked high next to brooms made from the karagach we had seen at the edge of the desert. As to be expected in a Turkic society, carpets flew at us from every side as we walked through their section. They were not as fine as the proud work in Bukhara, but were nevertheless bright with simple, commonplace patterns. A common design incorporated the pomegranate, the motif of Kashgar and a symbol of happiness and good fortune. Anargul, meaning 'pomegranate flower', is a popular name for girls.

High-cheekboned men in the process of being shaved bald for reasons of hygiene sat under red, yellow and navy umbrellas. Men were buying and selling with gusto; the merchant strain runs deep in these people. Few women ventured into the main part of the market. A cluster of about 500, most of them wrapped in the brown shawls of Islamic fundamentalism, loitered down by the muddy river, chatting; none was engaged in commerce. A huge statue of Mao Zedong erected in 1953 stood pointing the way for the people to go; it was not in the direction of Mecca. The Uighurs pay no attention to it.

Birds in cages were singing so loudly that they could be heard 50 metres away, above the babble of the crowd. Their impetuous voices mixed in with the baaing of sheep, the braying of donkeys and the lowing groans of cattle for sale down by the river, which ran murky brown for a kilometre at right angles to the main thoroughfare of the bazaar. Small

billiard tables set on rickety trestles were everywhere, groups of men crowding around them to play the popular game. I joined in at one, making a few shots, but found it hard to get the ball to move over the rough felt. The game ended when I leaned on the table to get a better reach and the table collapsed, tipping the remaining four balls into the pockets and pitching me into the dust amidst raucous laughter.

The aroma of cooked food – barbecued satay sticks and oven-baked bread – dominated the bazaar. Dumplings were moistened and stacked on trays inside mud-brick ovens glowing with wood coals. Eggs filled huge wicker baskets sitting on the ground, the hard-boiled ones painted red. Sheep heads bubbled in murky water, until suddenly, a swarthy cook would pull one of them out and hack it in two with an axe. One 'thwack' and the two halves would fall outwards on the wooden block. The cook would toss a serving onto a plate, and put it on a rough table for the customer. Eager eaters in traditional garb demolished steaming eyes, brains and cheeks. Other establishments sold large curved lumps of bright-yellow meat – smoked sheep lungs, which quivered on the plate as the diners sliced off bite-sized chunks.

Succulent melons, famous throughout Xinjiang, were sold from piles heaped up on stands, but not the ones most sought after. Out of season when we visited, the beshak shirin is the king of fruits. Shaped like a cantaloupe and twice as big, it is yellow with green striations, its skin when ripe so thin that the juice oozes through. The fruit's flesh, which is white or pale yellow, is considered the ambrosia of the oasis.

A circle of men in embroidered skullcaps squatted around a contingent of fighting cocks; the shoulders and thighs of the fierce birds were pecked bare from the sport, which is banned in most parts of the world. The tail feathers were all intact though, some

Bazaar, Kashgar

Kashgar

blue, some red, all a brilliant iridescent. The red-faced gladiators were crowing and strutting aggressively, angry, with pride engaged. Every few seconds, the hand of an owner would dart out to restrain his bellicose bird. They were there to be sold, not to fight; that occurs in winter.

Xinjiang lives in the charms of the past. Near Kashgar, in the small oasis of Toyuk, we were the first Europeans to have been seen since 1989. But life is changing for the indigenous Turkic people, who look to Central Asia for their roots, not to the Middle Kingdom that has incorporated them.

In local affairs, Xinjiang retains autonomy, but in matters of national importance, China has the say. Racial tension stalks the land that the Uighurs have owned in a tradition that goes back to the third century and, through their kinsmen, to times before history. Though still a minority, at 23 per cent, the Chinese population (universally known as Han, not to be confused with the dynasty) has burgeoned from just four per cent 50 years ago. Uighurs do not mix with the Han, unless they have to, and even then, the contact is more out of politeness than warmth. In a gesture of chauvinism, the Chinese call the non-Han people throughout China 'minorities' rather than using the proper names of the various ethnic groups.

A Uighur we met in Kashgar told us a story about the relationship. An American who was sitting in a train travelling across Xinjiang took a couple of puffs of his cigarette and casually threw it out of the window. Then, he tossed the whole pack out. A Uighur sitting next to him asked why he had thrown out the pack as well as the butt. "We have too many cigarettes in the USA," he replied. A Japanese in the compartment did the same thing with his Walkman, explaining, "We have too many of them in Japan." Suddenly, the Uighur stood up and threw a Chinese out of the window.

In 1990, local anger at birth-control restrictions suddenly flared into anti-Han demonstrations. Seeking to stem the impoverishing tide of population increase, the Chinese government imposed a restriction of one child per couple. Even though Uighurs were allowed to have two, they were outraged. The locals tell the story of a foreign tourist who was visiting a Uighur family in a village at around this time. He asked how many children they had. The father said they had 12. "How can you have so many in the face of the government policy?" he asked the Uighur man. "When I found out about the policy, I already had 10 children, so I had another two."

Three years after the protests, a fatal explosion in a Kashgar public building signalled that the build-up of frustration with Chinese dominance was at breaking point. The authorities clamped down fiercely, and a reduction in civil liberties followed. Now, People's Liberation Army stations bestride every large town. The atmosphere, though calm on the surface, is fragile, the two peoples never having been really compatible. Over the last 2000 years, Chinese armies have conquered the Kashgar region five times and have been violently expelled on four occasions.

Nevertheless, the races get along on a functional level, and in the absence of a specific grievance exploding in the presence of laxness by the authorities, there seems little danger of widespread rebellion. Economic growth, accompanied by an abundance of food, is calming the savage breast. The Chinese are wise enough not to interfere with local agriculture, whose bounty, grown underneath the violent waves of marauding armies, has enabled the hardy oasis people to endure the dominance of the conqueror until he is absorbed or goes away.

Religion remains a problem for China, however, in this region to which merchants travelling along the Silk Road brought Islam in the Middle Ages. Banned during the Cultural Revolution, attendance at mosques is now permitted. When Ayatollah Khomeini visited Kashgar, he prayed ostentatiously in the 15th-century Aidka mosque, the largest in China.

Still, official policy disapproves. Children under 18 are denied religious education and just two medresas struggle to serve the needs of several million faithful. People are resentful but afraid to speak out. They are not especially pious, being more aligned to Central Asian moderation than to Iranian theocracy, but nevertheless are deeply attached to the social dictates of Islam. In Kashgar, which has the greatest proportion of Uighurs of the major Xinjiang cities, the presence of Islam pervades.

The graceful Timurid architecture of the Abakh Hodja mausoleum, tiled in green jadeite, stands as a reminder that the Kashgar oasis is related to the great Islamic cities of Samarkand and Bukhara, on the other side of the Pamirs. In it reside the remains of the sufi ruler, or khoja, who governed Kashgar and its surrounding oasis towns in the 17th century. He became a saint, and stood next to Mohammed in the hearts of the people in these eastern reaches of Islamic influence. His grand-daughter was the famous Fragrant Concubine who was snatched by a Chinese expeditionary army after defeating the Uighurs in a nearby battle, and brought to the Forbidden City to regale the emperor. That she did in style, becoming his favourite wife, so honoured that when she died, her family was allowed to bring her body back to Kashgar. It was borne in state in a colourful palanquin, for burial in the mausoleum. In keeping with the tradition of support for Koranic learning that marks Islamic States, a medresa was built nearby. Motifs of Bukharan style distinguish the building, particularly the carved-wood pillars and ceiling of the loggia. The khojas' century-long attempts to regain power in Kashgar after the Chinese toppled them in the 18th century are an indication that Islamic theocracy here is deeply rooted.

Just outside Kashgar, we visited the old British consulate, Chini Bagh. The grand piece of Victoriana has faded with the glories of empire, declining into an unkempt restaurant hugged by a few neglected rose bushes struggling against invading weeds. It was the residence of the long-serving British diplomat Sir George Macartney, who carried on there the intrigues of the Great Game. His prime adversary, the Russian consul, was installed a short distance away, at what has been converted into the Seman Hotel, the best in Kashgar. Macartney's hospitality was prodigiously praised by the European cultural adventurers who came through on their way to the Buddhist caves to explore and take away their priceless treasures. They all stopped over – Sir Aurel Stein, Albert von Le Coq, Sven Hedin – heroes in the West and 'foreign devils' in China.

Nearby, bales and crates were being packed in a courtyard and loaded onto trucks. In rudimentary English, the Pakistani boss told us that he buys cheap Chinese sewing-machine parts, dinner sets, calculators and clothing and hauls them from Kashgar in a four-day trek over the Karakorum Mountains to Peshawar, where he keeps a shop. In the winter, the highway is closed for three months. The products are different and the camels are gone, but the Silk Road still operates comme il faut.

We set out from Kashgar east along the northern route of the Silk Road, the branch that passes north of the Taklamakan desert under the shadow of the great Tian Shan mountains. Once we got past the Kashgar oasis, the land lost its life, changing into a vast panorama of moonscape shapes and shadows. Drainage channels scratched scars deep into the tissue of the rock that formed the mountains, beige sand spreading endlessly out from their base. Buddhism and Islam, both brought to this region by the caravans, competed for the souls of the population. It is recalled that the local king saw a group of Muslim merchants praying by the side of the road while their camels were left unattended. Asked why they did this, they replied, "Allah will look after them". The monarch was so impressed with the depth of their faith that he converted to Islam and imposed the faith on his kingdom.

Buddhism had its day earlier in the history of the Silk Road. We passed a stupa and pagoda built of mud brick so eroded they looked like natural features blended into the surrounding sandstone escarpment. This was hard country, imbuing traditional caravan travellers with the fear of running out of water, of being cruelly taunted in the throes of thirst by vestiges of its presence in the chiselled passages of the dried flood plain and its caked crust. Small pebbles, smoothed and shaped by the tossing water when it flows in flood, formed scree pavements along the dry riverbeds, which branched out like trees on the ground and on the rounded sand-

Mosque, Kashgar

Mosque, Kashgar

stone formations of the mountain foothills. Torrential water flashes off the range, and most of its charge sinks into the ground, where it flushes through subterranean aquifers. People dig wells, called 'karez', to find it, and then drive adits to divert the precious life-giver to their use. They have been doing this since the days before the warlike Huns controlled this part of the Silk Road.

We stopped along the way to stretch our legs and absorb the stillness. All was quiet except for the constant slow breeze and the sand flies. We heard a donkey driver singing in the distance. Before long, he passed us with his cart, along with others, plying the short distances just as their predecessors did in a past not very different from today. It takes half a day to cover 20 kilometres. But that did not matter to a people who accepted it as normal. Our sense of time, too, was becoming elongated; everything was being slowed down to Silk Road pace. We began to notice the little things: the white roses on the small wild tree, and the diminutive lizards darting around in the sun, camouflaged against the sand made from tiny stones. As we got used to it, the great mountain range to our left seemed a comfortable presence, always there, reliable, a point of reference.

After we were on the road again and had driven a few kilometres, a bus that had blown a tyre blocked our path. The road was too narrow to get around, so we had to wait until its driver changed it. While we were stopped, a donkey cart pulled up behind us carrying an eight-year-old boy with a finger wrapped in a dirty bandage. The top had been cut off, and his father and elder brother were taking him to a hospital in the nearest village, about three hours away. By now, the hand was black. Once we got going, we gave him and his brother a lift. The boy was impressively stoical, neither crying nor saying a word, his face impassive. Anna-Maryke gave him a mint, which he didn't like. The poor child started to cry, not because of the lost finger but because the unfamiliar taste was just enough to overwhelm his ability to cope. As we left, the father passed a small package in tissue paper to his elder son; it was the finger. They were hoping to find a surgeon who could reattach it. After driving for half an hour, we stopped at a small oasis town, where the two boys got out and disappeared into a crowd of people. We never saw them again. It was pathetic to see the hopefulness of these young boys, when their chance of finding a microsurgeon in the wilds of Xinjiang was as close to zero as the laws of probability would allow.

We were now travelling within a few hundred metres of the Heavenly Mountains, which stretched all the way to Urumchi, 1500 kilometres in the distance. Glacial melt flows down from them to the Taklamakan, creating sporadic oases along the way. But since the last Ice Age, the capriciousness of the water courses, which mysteriously appear and disappear like leprechauns, has depopulated dozens of once-thriving cities, leaving them lost under a mask of sand. Legends hang in the air about sudden Gomorrahan collapses into the mouth of the desert by cities caught in the retributive grasp of moral punishment. But all the evidence points to a mechanism of gradual decline as desiccation caused by the melt-

ing of the mountain ice-cap choked out dependent life. Archaeologists salivate over the thought of the ancient treasures that may be hidden out there in the lost cities in the sand.

As we drove along, from time to time we could see in the southern distance patches of green on the vastness of the stony soil, watered by an unsteady tributary of the Tarim River, too small and too ephemeral to act as more than a temporary grazing stop. On our left stood the endless wall of the Heavenly Mountains, with its red haematite layering, white salt patches and green chlorite inclusions splashed on the beige landscape like a giant abstract mural. Textural patterns altered as run-off channels intensified, from wrinkles at the top to deeply etched drainage rills lower down the slopes. Flood-control levees made from stones and set in wide shallow arches by the road, like contemporary sculptures, gave an idea of the tumultuous volume of water that rushes down from the mountain range in season, reaching a peak during July and August.

It was hard to imagine water at all, as one looked at the dry, brown camel thorn that littered the grey, stony soil as far as the eye could see. Trucks, half a kilometre apart, thundered past our minibus in the 30-degree heat, their drivers struggling against lassitude on the straight, featureless road that carries just enough traffic to pose a risk. Some of them succumbed: we saw the aftermath of horrific collisions – burnt-out behemoths clutching each other in the ditch, twisted into macabre sculptures of death.

Willie-willies like puffs of smoke darting around on the desert began to warn us that the baleful Taklamakan dust storms appear as suddenly as did the devastating Golden Horde 800 years ago. Wild winds suck up fine-grained dust from the desert and swirl it high above the ground in a devastating torque action. They sometimes whip up hurricanes so dense that the Chinese call the events dust rain.

Over time, the dust deposited as the storms decline builds the loess formations that characterise the landscape. Darkness descended over the desert as the winds grew angry. We could barely see through the windows of our vehicle. What we could see was the desert beginning to look like a sea whipped up into little wave formations.

We stopped for lunch at a ramshackle village that had sprouted up around this section of the road, dependent on business from truckers. Rows of dirty, squat flat-roofed buildings faced with squalid plaster and topped by television aerials lined the road. Turkic music, competing with static and the howling wind, blared from speakers attached to the tops of electricity poles. No-one was outside. A double oil tanker was parked nearby, surrounded by trucks grubby from days of desert driving. Oil stains splotched the hard-packed road shoulder. As we got out of the vehicle, we were hit by a violent blast of wind. Bending over, we struggled to the restaurant through clouds of dust particles so fine they seemed to invade our pores. In the gloom, where visibility had plunged to snow-blizzard level, the little settlement looked depressing and bleak, like a frontier mining town in the dark, relieved only by the knowledge that shelter was available. We learned that the place used to be a caravan stop, where travellers would pitch their tents in the small surrounding oasis, the only one between two vast stretches of desert.

In the restaurant, which served reasonably good food, we were nearly blown off our seats by Turkic pop music. When I asked to have it turned down a bit, I was surprised (and a little embarrassed) to discover it was a piece sung by Parida's brother, a celebrated pop star in Xinjiang. Inside, in a little alcove built with concrete blocks, rubbish on the floor, a huge blown-up photograph of the Sydney Harbour Bridge graced the wall. I was going to ask what the picture was doing in such a far-off place, but got distracted when Parida reminded us that we had to get back on the road.

We crossed the Tarim River – or, probably more precisely, one of the many strands that comprise it, since it is a collection of water passages. The name of the bridge, Achal, means 'control', indicating that this had probably been a military post at some time in the ancient past. We got out for a stretch and walked around in the wilderness for a while. I tasted the river water; it was slightly brackish, but the local villagers drink it. It would be sweeter during the flood season. The Taklamakan desert is referred to as a 'gobi' desert, which means 'stone' in Uighur. On close inspection, we could see that it was composed of countless small stones, each of which had a distinctive colour: black serpentinite, red and yellow haematite, white quartz, pink granite, green chalcopyrite and lumps of beige loess.

KYZYL

We drove on towards Kucha, to the oasis valley of Kyzyl, where some of the most important Buddhist caves in Xinjiang slumber in the modern era. On the way, the mountains form structures like flying buttresses attached to castles large enough for titans. Sometimes, if you allow your vision to fall out of focus, you can see gigantic faces appear on the steep slopes, their eyes narrowed with the epicanthus fold. We stopped and clambered up the friable hillside to visit a recent discovery, an ancient bronze-smelting site, metalliferous spoil still in place. We looked down on a massive beige flood plain, now completely dried out and patched with white saltpans and struggling camel grass. A crow was calling in the distance. Nearby, a sign announced: "One Spring Drop Bronze Metallurgical Site Put Under Protection April 1 1997". It was typical of the newness of Chinese interest in archaeology that such an important

Tian Shan Mountains,
Kyzyl

site was so close to the road and recognised only such a short time ago. I wondered why the authorities had found it necessary to put the sign in English.

After lunch, we did not have far to go before we turned off the main road into the Kyzyl valley. The form of the mountains began to fade into the dust haze, leaving just the outline. The huge range turned flat grey against a two-dimensional horizon, slightly jagged like torn paper. Sometimes, at their base, erosion patterns formed the shape of Sogdian caps.

The mountains were completely devoid of vegetation, rising naked out of the barren soil, their haematite staining giving them a red hue as the sun

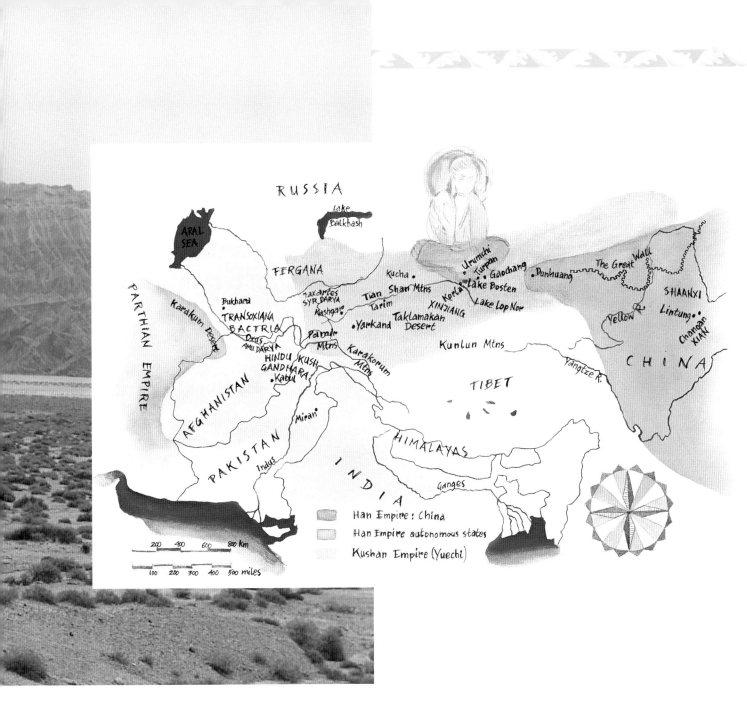

cooked the rock. 'Kyzyl' means 'red'. On the flat ground, saltpans and isolated tufts of scarred camel thorn formed a desiccated pattern within the stony sand. It was an otherworldly place, a retreat for ascetics. Then, the miracle of the oasis appeared. A small tributary of the Tarim shed enough water to create a pocket of vegetation on the valley floor, sufficient to support a community. Poplar trees, the staple of Central Asia, and crops gave life to the mineral scape. Wide-leafed plants used for making paper hugged the riverbanks like papyrus groves.

Deep in the valley, where the rocks form a gorge, Buddhist monks chiselled caves out of the soft and friable loess high up on the face, in some cases so difficult to reach that rope ladders are needed. For 600 years from the third century, caves were carved by the industrious ascetics, until the hurricane of Islam blew over Central Asia. When the locals became Muslims, they destroyed the statues that stood outside the caves but left intact the paintings adorning the walls. The valley was too remote for foreign carriers of the Islamic banner, who probably would have been more zealous. However, in the 19th century, Russian archaeologists discovered the caves, which had been neglected for centuries, and published a book about them, which was circulated in the West. Before long, other Europeans began to investigate the fascinating artworks, including the German archaeological adventurer Albert von Le Coq. Recognising their value, he took camel loads of mural treasures back to Berlin on the pretext that they would be safer in a Western museum. Most were destroyed by the explosions of the Second World War.

Others, too, tramped through the oasis towns and made off with the cultural treasures of the desert. The most famous of these was Sir Aurel Stein, who filched thousands of priceless Buddhist manuscripts from Dunhuang, having bribed the simple monk guarding the cache to let him in. He is considered the prime 'Foreign Devil' by the Chinese, because of the work he did, ironically so revered in the West until recently. Contemporary sensitivities about the appropriation of national heritage have inhibited the museum community. At the British Museum, which houses the priceless relics, almost none of Stein's 'acquisitions' are on display in the Central Asian collection.

The construction of the murals facilitated their removal. The artist would prepare the surface of the rock wall with a paste of camel dung, clay and chopped straw, over which he would spread stucco. Art plunderers merely had to cut the frescoes off in

sizes that fitted into their camel packing cases. To them, these were interesting and exotic works of art. However, for hundreds of years, the inhabitants saw them as being much more important than that – they were holy objects, representing the new insight into the human condition brought to their land by the Buddhist revelation.

Buddhism, founded in the sixth century BC and adopted three centuries later by Emperor Ashoka of India as the State religion, was the most influential of the ancient religions to pass along the Silk Road. Following on the conversion of Emperor Ming Di, in the Han period, interest erupted in the teachings of Prince Siddharta Gautama, who had left the earthly pleasures of his little kingdom at the foot of the Himalayas to gain understanding, through concentrated thought, of the inevitable cycle of life. Gautama evolved into Sakyamuni and 'Buddha', the Enlightened One. Monks, missionaries and pilgrims flocked along the Silk Road, banding together with the merchants in caravans, the convoys of the desert. One of them was Kunajiva, a monk from Central Asia who came to the Kyzyl valley in the fifth century. The earliest Chinese translations of the Buddhist sutras were through intermediary languages from Central Asia, such as the dialect of Kucha. Like Xuan Zang, he helped to set Chinese Buddhism on a more central path to theology, translating the Indian sutras, which until that time had merely been passed around by word of mouth. Employing what he called "matching the meaning", he used Chinese forms of speech and thought to express the conceptual subtleties of the foreign religion necessary to form a theological base for his own culture.

At oases along the way, the industrious monks carved small caves out of the permissive loess, decorating them with religious frescoes painted from local earth pigments. They used the excavations both as living quarters and as devotional centres, while the frescoes served as a teaching medium. The 236 caves, 75 with paintings, extend along the rock face for a kilometre. Set 30 metres up the cliff face, they display some of the finest Buddhist art in Central Asia. We had to go on a winding walk to get up to them.

The murals at Kyzyl, like the many others along the Silk Road, depict the mythological Buddhist tales known as the Jataka stories. These tales illustrate the law of karma, which requires all living creatures to undergo a cyclical series of reincarnations the only escape from which involves attaining the state of absolute transcendence, nirvana, that comes from enlightenment. They tell of the 500 former lives of Buddha, who was reincarnated, as Sakyamuni, as a bear, a deer, a rabbit and other animals before he reached nirvana. Buddha, who formulated the doctrine of the four noble truths, appears on the cave walls preaching the principles of life through the myths. All life is suffering. Desire is the cause of suffering. Suffering can be ended, since its cause is known. By following the eight-part path of thought and behaviour, desire can be suppressed. The stories illustrate the eternal verities that underlie the path (universal fraternity, equality, faith, truth and self-sacrifice) against an antagonistic background (of hate, greed and savagery), to be avoided. The Jataka stories appear throughout southern Asia, mostly in the form of reliefs and sculptures, and China, usually through painting.

The frescoes in the Kyzyl corridor of caves are considered among the finest in China, many of the others having suffered the ravages of defacement. The earliest paintings, dating from the third century, were composed in the Gandhara style, from what is now Afghanistan and the Peshawar valley. Influenced by Greek culture brought to the region by Alexander the Great, the style incorporates Hellenistic features. Bushy eyebrows extend to the bridge of the nose, and moustaches appear. Garments flow over the figures in graceful pleats. The vogue changed as Chinese ascendancy grew, with faces becoming more oriental. By the seventh century, blue and turquoise pigments announced the arrival of the efflorescent Tang dynasty, when the quality of the artistry in the caves reached its apex.

Small figures at the bottom of many of the cave paintings, placed discreetly underneath the celestial beings, are reminders of the symbiosis of art and commerce. In exchange for donations, wealthy merchants were immortalised on the walls.

The caves are not large, most measuring about eight metres by 15 metres, and have a wide pillar three-quarters of the way towards the back. The ceilings are gracefully arched. Every surface is painted with beautifully crafted human and animal figures inside interlinked diamond-shaped frames called lozenges. The outlines looked in some like a series of petals and in others like the fingers of a magic hand. They represent Mount Meru, the sacred mountain of Buddhism. Each lozenge, which was painted a different background colour from its neighbour, contained a separate Jataka story immediately recognisable to the initiated. In the past, a stone statue of Buddha would often stand in front of the pillar, but none was left in the caves we visited. In some of the caves, we noticed that little square sections of the paintings had been excised from the walls, evidence of the bygone days when cultural filching was commonplace. Fortunately, most of the artwork survives.

The Chinese government supervises the caves, which are all officially numbered. It is obligatory to hire a government guide to accompany the visitor to each cave, armed with keys to unlock the roughly constructed wooden doors that have been installed in the openings of the better endowed. Photography is officially forbidden, though a few yuan will sometimes (not always) produce a lapse of vigilance from the caretaker-guide. Even so, it is very limited. Our

Buddhist caves, Kyzyl

guide was a young, rather pretty girl with a flirty hat and clothes that seemed suited to a disco, a place she perhaps would rather have been, for she seemed studiously bored and impatient, becoming petulant when we wanted to go into caves other than those she had been programmed to show us. It was necessary for Parida, who accompanied us on the entire journey, to hire a local guide in Kucha as well. The rules required it. So, at the caves, there were up to three guides. Fortunately, their individual charges were minimal in Western currency.

Most of the paintings express an aspect of Buddha, usually one of his former lives – as a person or as one of many animals. In cave 38, painted in the Tang period with blues and turquoises, a stag is stretched over a river, a rabbit on his back. The story of the image is that a forest in the mountains caught fire, forcing all the animals to run for their lives. They were blocked by a river impossible to cross. The stag, who was Buddha, formed a bridge with his body to save them. The constant trampling injured the stag, but it held out until the last animal came, a crippled rabbit. Holding on just long enough to allow the rabbit to cross the river, the noble saviour died. The scene is economically and elegantly expressed within the lozenge, immediately recognisable and evocative to someone who knows the lore.

The principle of self-sacrifice, which seems to be one of the most prominent motifs of the stories, takes a curious twist in some of the Jatakas. One of them tells of Buddha in his former life as a young Brahmin priest. Along with two other priests, he went into the forest to gather wild fruit. They encountered a tigress who was ready to give birth. A spirit of generosity led them to agree that they would try to feed the tigress, since they expected she would be hungry after her ordeal. When they approached her, she bared her teeth and roared, frightening the Brahmin's companions who promptly ran away.

Staying behind, the young Brahmin lanced his arm to give blood to the tigress, then allowed her to eat him. While the meaning is plain in the context of the Buddhist ethic, the situation might cause someone with a Western cast of mind to wonder at the passivity implied and to question whether the moral of the story might encourage people to excuse weakness by interpreting defeat as self-sacrifice.

Compassion figures strongly in the Buddhist pantheon of values, both for its own sake and for the utility of its consequences. In many of the scenes on the walls of the caves, the mythical garuda appears, dominant and majestic. The giant bird needed to eat 500 snakes a day, most of them poisonous. Eventually, the toxic build-up in its stomach killed the mighty hunter, but Buddha took pity on it, bringing the gluttonous predator back to life. Moved by the mercy of Buddha, the garuda became the guardian of the law.

The artists were often inspired by the rich animal life that used to inhabit the oases and northern grasslands of Xinjiang. The Xinjiang tiger, last seen in the 1940s, appears with two magic tails, each with a forked end, usually in a violent, jumping form, demonstrating the unpredictability of power that frightens all living things. The deer is a favourite, sending messages of love and self-sacrifice. The curved lines of the beast that has turned around to lick the fawn feeding underneath her expresses the maternal love that drives the cyclical continuity of life. The beautifully proportioned horse of Fergana, whose importation to China opened up the Silk Road, also features on the walls, drawn with clear lines and painted with ochre. The animal tradition in art reaches far back into regional history. Rock paintings of sheep, oxen, horses, camels, wolves, boar, tigers, deer, dogs, eagles, wild geese and fish dating back to 1000 BC have been discovered in the Tian Shan mountains.

The draftsmanship exudes the fluidity of confidence. A thorough understanding of animal anatomy allowed the artists to give their subjects a human cast, within the essence of their form. In one of the Jataka stories, a lion is sitting on his haunches, head up, a paw crossed over his shoulder, in a pose suggestive of a person giving a lecture. He is talking to a monkey in a supplicant mode, while a vulture is suspended in the sky, listening. Each figure is drawn so as to be in conversation but still true to its natural shape. The monkey has asked the lion to look after her son while she goes out to gather food. The lion fell asleep and a vulture snatched the baby. When he awoke, the distraught lion pleaded with the vulture to let his charge go free. At this, the ravenous bird changed his choice of menu and declared he would prefer to eat the lion. In order to provide the substitute, the lion ran to the side of a steep gorge and prepared to jump down to his death. Relenting, the vulture gave up the prospect of his dinner and returned the little monkey.

Sometimes, the paintings in the Kyzyl caves are simple representations of animal life without Buddhist references. The profound cultural understanding of the animal form that informs all the paintings gives them a liveliness and a grace that are quite extraordinary. And when they do express a religious insight, they entice the viewer into a reverie of imagination. In their natural surroundings, they create a utopian atmosphere of the pure world far away from the distractions of urban competition and material imperatives. Only there can the ethereal figures of the Buddhist imagination live, to inspire the faithful to lives of ascetic dedication to the ideal. The sense of isolation, created by the single-theme stories within their own discrete frames, connects to the Buddhist doctrine of self-cultivation, of escaping from the entrapment of personal desire.

It is no wonder that the Chinese communists reject Buddhism, for it preaches that the roots of human misery lie in the self-conscious, not in the class structure of society. Notwithstanding a discomfort with the themes, the modern Chinese consider the caves a vital part of their heritage. This perception, though, is recent, for no attempts were made in the 19th century to control the Europeans from taking what they willed from this heritage, nor until the last few decades was any interest shown in maintaining the treasures.

After picking our way carefully down the slopes from the caves, we went for a long walk through a densely vegetated valley. We walked along the floor, which was parted by a stream and lush with poplar stands and ripe mulberries, in the direction of a low rumbling sound. Soon we found ourselves in the company of a group of young local people walking in the same direction. The path began to narrow into a defile, then a gorge formed by high cliffs. Little wild roses grew white on the side of the stream amidst purple tamarisk flowers. The path was now muddy, virtually inundated by running water. The local people were holding their shoes. They were going to a dance, the young women in colourful traditional dresses and the men in clean, patterned shirts. The gorge ended in a cul de sac formed by a circular rock face rising 50 metres into a wooded crest. The face was streaming with a myriad of little rivulets glistening in the sun. A wide sandbar stretched out at the base, pockmarked with small holes formed by the high-heeled shoes of women who had walked through there in the past with their shoes on.

We were at the spring of a thousand tears. Legend, which has found its way into a famous Chinese opera, speaks of a princess of Guici who met and fell in love with a handsome young mason in the oasis forest. The young man asked the king for her hand, offering what he could in simple presents. Affronted

Above: Tian Shan Mountains

Left: Buddhist caves

by the presumption of one of such low social status but cornered by his impetuous daughter, the king told the mason he would give permission, but only if the young suitor would undertake the ordeal of carving 1000 caves out of the surrounding hills. The penalty for failure was to be extreme. The challenge was accepted and the young mason began to carve. After three years, he managed to complete 999, but then collapsed and died of exhaustion. The grief of the bereaved princess falls in endless tears from the rock face. The water, which comes from a glacier, is crystal pure, but if you drink it, you will supposedly turn into a rabbit, one of Buddha's incarnations.

We followed the villagers past the grieving face to a clearing in the poplars which hosted the social gathering. Men were drinking beer at wooden tables, while a few paces off, the women huddled together in groups on the ground. A portable fridge stood under a tree, next to a cassette machine loudly playing Uighur music.

Some people danced in a group on the grass, waving their arms in graceful, set movements; then all together, they would do a hesitation step, clapping their hands in unison. No-one seemed to mind that we were there; in fact, many of them gave us friendly smiles as we walked past. By now, we were only about 20 minutes from our hotel. It was time to go back there for dinner.

The hotel, which was suffering from premature degeneration, was built for tourists and sited to look towards a breathtaking vista of the mountains in isolation, far from any other habitation. However, the first third of the view was blocked by a hideous concrete wall and the rest by poplar trees that allowed only glimpses through their fronds. Wires were strung obtrusively outside the building and a large garbage skip was placed close to the main entrance for ease of removal. Everything was designed for low maintenance, a duty in all cases negligently performed. The inside was soulless and cavernous, desultorily decorated with plastic flowers. Often, there was no water in the bath (no showers were provided), and when there was, it was cold, except for a period from 10 at night until one in the morning. The good news was that we were the only visitors and the food was tolerable.

After dinner, we walked away from the hotel into a sinking light that was painting the loess cave mountain with magic, changing the shape of its contours in alliance with a soft dust haze. The face of the mountain was like a giant altar. Silence crept around us as we walked from the oasis in its direction, defined by the sounds of a distant cricket carried on the quietness of the dusk air. It was still fairly light after half past 10 at night, for all China is ruled by one time, set in the capital of the Middle Kingdom. Ethereal billows of fine dust rolled up the valley like a scotch mist and a desert coolness descended on a slight breeze. Dark clumps of tough karagatch bushes formed silent shapes against the arid beige. I felt the otherworldly sense that the monks must have experienced in the remote valley, protected by its high rock walls. There, expansiveness of the mind came not from the width of vista but from nature's purity of colour and form. Two stars broke through into the hazy sky, now a robin's-egg blue. On the ground, dried mud cakes, delineated by cracks like pack ice, sat on top of the permadust. They formed clean, geometric shapes, as in a Mondrian painting, and crunched underfoot like hard snow. The dust that blows into the valley in a daily cycle, through the entrance, settles into the land during the night, permitting the morning to open into a clear day with a sharp blue sky.

Chapter 18

Silk Road Culture

We drove out of the monk's valley back onto the Silk Road, heading towards the next oasis. The Tian Shan mountains rose higher now that we were entering their foothills. As we came through a pass, we could see snowcapped peaks far away across a wide flood plain suffused with light green from patches of semisucculent camel thorn growing in a shaggy rug. We drove onto the high plateau, flat for miles and up-thrusted amongst the bare stone mountains that ringed it in the distance. The range set far in the background gave a sense of expansiveness and of being, as Marco Polo said, at the top of the world.

A herd of double-humped Bactrian camels, the *Camelis bactrianus ferus*, grazed insouciantly a few hundred metres off the road. Central Asia is the last refuge of the endangered beast that originated there. Only about 900 remain, 50 to 80 in the Taklamakan. Through natural selection, they have developed to endure up to 10 days without water and to close their nostrils to the fine dust driven by the fierce windstorms of the region. In time, we came to a tributary mountain range that looked like a giant wrinkled dragon as we approached. In Xinjiang, the differentially weathered mountains and their outliers take on fantastic shapes, supernatural forms that seem to move and stimulate the imagination. The remoteness and isolation remove any reference points, so that impressions can roam without any check for reality. As we wound our way through a pass to a serpentine river, a huge barren sandstone plain opened up, its surface in sculpted shapes like waves whipped up by the wind on an angry sea. Jagged low-lying shores edged it and high sandstone tables rose up like islands, the whole a remnant of ancient depositions on the floor of a lost inland lake.

On the horizon, a Han dynasty beacon tower came into view. From the first century AD, expanding Chinese sovereignty in the Western Region was secured by mud-brick watchtowers, built 30 metres high and sited every five miles along the Silk Road. Fires were set on the top, accessed by wooden stairs, in a linked communication line that gave instant warning of incursive trouble. The fuel used was wolf dung, regarded as producing the tallest and straightest columns of smoke. The practice gave rise to the expression used in classical Chinese literature to refer to widespread fighting: "Wolf dung bonfires have sprung up all over the land".

JAOGULI

We came to the Jaoguli Buddhist temple complex, constructed in the third century to house a remote community of 5000 monks in the desert. Xuan Zang stayed here on his way to India. It was in one of the 36 kingdoms of the Western Region through which he passed on his pilgrimage to the font of Buddhist wisdom.

We climbed to the top of a tall mud-brick pagoda that stood high on an arid hill, its form worn smooth and friable by hostile weather. The view overlooked a vast beige plain that held a cluster of six or seven oases, separated like islands by the gobi wasteland. Far away, large trucks with loads of stone passed slowly along dried streambeds to a destination beyond the hazy horizon. The central river, which gives life to the barren region, fills only after the annual glacial melt, spreading its body confidently against the pebbled flood levees we could see in the distance. But it was dry now; not a trickle wetted its tumbled stones. The land was totally devoid of vegetation, except for the distinct oases far away, sharply etched in green. In the vastness of Central Asia, life-denying desert, not vegetation, is the natural state. Anything green comes almost by accident, through the caprice of the water god. Little willie-willies moved across the desert floor, changing direction like sails tacking in the wind. It was a spiritual place, far removed from the plane of competitive survival, a world of a different reality, for rounded thoughts and generous feelings.

KUCHA

We arrived in Kucha, a Silk Road oasis not far from the caves of Kyzyl and capital of the largest of the 36 kingdoms. Enriched by Silk Road trade, the town reached its peak of affluence in the Tang dynasty and directed its wealth into promoting the arts and financing the development of Buddhist thought. Kuchean musical forms and instruments were favourites in the imperial court at Chang'an, playing a seminal role in the formation of Chinese music. We saw evidence of this at a concert in Xian.

In 1890, a British army lieutenant tracking the murderer of a Scottish trader along the Silk Road arrived at Kucha. While he was there, some local people offered to sell him an ancient manuscript written on birch-bark, discovered in a dilapidated Buddhist monastery nearby. Intrigued with the novelty of the strange document, he bought it, and sent it to the Asiatic Society of Bengal in Calcutta for translation. It turned out to be written in Sanskrit, in the old Indian Brahmin script of the fifth century, and demonstrated how deep into eastern Silk Road civilisation Gandharan influence had spread.

Perhaps the penetration was made easier by the fact that before the Uighurs came, in the ninth century, the people in the Kucha area were predominantly Indo-European. Through French translations of the works of Xuan Zang, Western scholars had learned of the Buddhist communities that existed in the region. They knew that monks had erected two statues of Buddha, 27 metres high, to guard the road to Kucha, but had no idea that language in a living form had migrated so far from its source. What more evidence of Graeco-Buddhist culture might there be in the endless desert wastes on the other side of the Pamirs? The manuscript lit a conflagration of interest in Orientalist circles, stimulating an archaeological frenzy to look for cultural treasure in the lost cities of the Taklamakan. Von Le Coq (the German),

Paul Pelliot (the Frenchman), Aurel Stein (the Englishman, originally Hungarian), Sergei Oldenburg (the Russian) and Kozui Otani (the Japanese) all scrambled in fierce competition to Kucha and beyond. It was the start of the great cultural raids by scholars whom the Chinese call 'Foreign Devils'.

The Silk Road fruit that denotes Kucha is the apricot. Our guide led us to one of the lush orchards that girdle the built-up area. An elderly farmer, his hard face expressing the weathering of the arid climes, assailed the branches of his apricot-laden trees with a long stick, showering us with ripe fruit, then invited us to tea. Inside his cool mud-brick house, caparisoned with tribal rugs on the floor, a low, wide table was heaped with oasis produce – peaches, walnuts, miniature dates that tasted like citrus, and more apricots. Round flat loaves of Uighur bread were placed nearby. His wife brought out steaming tea flavoured with allspice, along with bowls of fried noodles, some crisply coiled like springs, others wide and crinkly. They were light and tasty. We ate so much that we had to skip dinner, a lapse in routine that offended the staff at our hotel, who were counting on us, for guests were few.

The old section of Kucha still expresses the ancient oasis world – narrow unpaved streets hemmed in by continuous houses walled with mud brick, all dusty and close. Fragments of the old fortified walls built to fend off nomadic invaders slouch between the buildings like tired sentries. Small boys followed us as we walked towards the Grand Mosque, calling out a friendly but persistent "Hello" like cockatoos. The mosque, with its two imposing minarets and large hypostyle prayer hall, stood at the edge of the old city, a reminder that this was a Muslim place, freely and openly practising its religion, notwithstanding its location in China. Built in 1923, the mosque's interior disclosed the Persian influence that was still in the hearts of the people so

far east of Iran, a swastika fret design appearing on the ceiling and in the mihrab.

The bazaar surged with traditional life; wooden carts and aggressive donkey drivers pushed through the crowds, churning up the dust in billows. A section was set aside for the sale of donkeys. Food was everywhere: shish kebabs smoking fragrantly on open fires, and round bread-like bagels emerging from brick ovens and bustled on trays to kiosks, where they were piled up in stacks. Sheep lungs, yellow and quivering, were being wolfed down with gusto. Small pigeons, three to a cage, were on sale to be eaten for breakfast. They are a delicacy, despite the fact that killing the birds has not always been met with approval. At the tomb of an Arabian hodja who came to Kucha as an Islamic missionary in the Middle Ages, the story is told that the saintly man negligently killed a pigeon. The next day, he suddenly died.

Sacks of aromatic tobacco clustered on the ground, the weed doled out in small doses, enough for a single smoke. It was smoked in newspaper, neatly cut pieces of which were also available. People were walking around slowly, stopping for a chat, looking at the goods for sale. Life there was relaxed. The bazaar was a place to enjoy, to feel good in; the buying and selling seemed of secondary importance, so unlike the purpose-driven shopping in the West. Too soon, it seemed, we had to leave, although we always enjoyed driving through the vast wastes of the Taklamakan.

The desert has many moods, and they can be mercurial. On the move again, east towards Korla, we were faced with a frown: a beige-out of dust fog slowed our driver to a crawl. Suddenly, the air was wiped clean, revealing the snowcapped Heavenly Mountains on our left. Han dynasty beacon towers beaten by the wind marked the way. A green pasture opened up in the middle of the vastness, which was

Shopfront, Kucha

now becoming more sandy than stony. Horses and cattle grazed on a carpet that seemed to roll down from the foothills. A railway emerged out of the distance, a black train with its 20 freight cars slowly toiling near one of the paths the caravans had taken, the train's whistle replacing the sound of camel bells. Salt patches that resembled drifts of early winter snow covered large sections of the land.

Oil rigs began appearing on our right, the open desert side. We were passing the north–south road recently built through the Taklamakan to access the prodigious oil and gas reserves discovered in its vast anticlinal centre. A Chinese poet once said, "The soldier with the least words has the strongest determination; in the most barren land is buried the largest amount of energy".

Xinjiang sits in the midst of titanic plate collisions between Eurasia and Indo-Africa. The cataclysms have created some of the richest and most extensive mineral and petroleum deposits in the world. It is an exploration geologist's paradise.

KORLA

We stopped at Korla, dormitory town for the 50,000 oil workers who have invaded the Tarim Basin, 800 kilometres northwest of Lop Nor, the Chinese nuclear-weapons testing site. Exxon, Total, Agip and other foreign companies have entered into joint ventures called 'risk investments' that entitle them to explore and develop for five-year terms. Some of the drilling sites are within 50 kilometres of the ancient Silk Road city of Miran. Outside Korla, we saw production rigs set 100 metres apart, indicating the existence of a large and very productive reservoir.

Oil wealth at the crass level is beginning to seep into the Silk Road at Korla, where litter invades the streets and tacky hotels and restaurants of concrete and plastic are cropping up. No doubt it will spread its cultural monotony throughout the region over time. We felt fortunate to have travelled there while the place was still relatively unspoiled.

Traditional sensitivities survive, despite the salient that the modern world has driven into the old society. The elevating role played by songbirds, particularly the nightingale, a symbol of modest purity, is still a distinguishing element of Chinese culture there. The plain little bird with the heavenly song has always been revered in China, even entering the literature of the West, via Hans Christian Andersen. We saw six old men standing by a vendor of caged nightingales; they listened without speaking, rapt by the sound. Some shops keep the birds outside for ambience, not for sale. While we were there, a man walked down the street with 50 chicks in a wicker cage like a dim sum steamer suspended from a wooden pole.

Along with the traditional ambience, a water truck drove through the street, sluicing down the dust, with the sounds of *Frère Jacques* and *Happy Birthday* playing from its loudspeaker.

On the top floor of an unprepossessing concrete building with five storeys and no elevator is a little local museum. It seems that all Chinese museums are tucked away in inconvenient, inconspicuous spots, a functional reminder that today's masses in China are not interested in antiquity. This museum is remarkable, though, for not only does it display what is claimed by its director to be the oldest known piece of silk of the Tang dynasty, it also contains relics that, with others now in Urumchi, have forced a reappraisal of the identity of first Xinjiang inhabitants south of the Tian Shan mountains.

Carefully laid out in glass cases are desiccated corpses that the locals call mummies, 3000 years old, so well preserved by the dry climate that we could see personality in the faces. They were discovered in 1989 in the Loulan region not far from Lop Nor, their features and reddish-blond hair indicating them to be of Indo-European origin. Academics have been able to piece together, through evidence from old texts, material objects and, now, the mummies in Korla and Urumchi, a story of how people from the West, possibly Celts, migrated along the Silk Road in waves beginning as far back as the second millennium BC. They settled in the oases of the extreme eastern Taklamakan, in territory considered since time immemorial the land of the Turks and the Han.

Chinese records show that tall, blue-eyed people inhabited the region in sufficient numbers by the first millennium AD to have a tribal identity, with their own name: Tokharian. They even appear on the walls of some of the 1000 caves at Kyzyl. Through the Turkic inundations that flooded the land in the middle of the first millennium, the people were bred out as a separate race, but contributed their genes to the new society. If you see enough Uighurs, you will spot one with blue eyes.

We saw a mummified woman with a small child, probably six or seven years old, thought by the director to be members of a vanquished tribe and victims of human sacrifice. The next case held a man with his mouth open, apparently having suffocated. Body orifices were stopped up with strips of felt, and sometimes, coloured stones were placed over the eye sockets. Cakes, biscuits and wooden combs, 3000 years old, gave a sense of how these distant people lived. It was a simple life; their clothing, however, though made of wool, was twilled in a sophisticated pattern, with colour.

Seven kilometres north of Korla, on an excursion, we encountered the Iron Gate, which controlled the only ancient pass from north Xinjiang to the Tarim Basin through the formidable Tian Shan mountain range. It was also built to dominate the middle route of the Silk Road west to Kashgar. Destroyed during the rampages of the Cultural Revolution, it has been rebuilt as a replica, complete with a prominent swastika, showing that in the distant past, a Zoroastrian influence had reached this far east. It was called the Iron Gate because the narrow defile which it opens and closes is so difficult to penetrate, particularly for the Chinese in the days when it was in the hands of the Xiongnu, before the Han army defeated them, in 60 AD. Establishing themselves on both sides of the pass, the Xiongnu staged raids against the Chinese capital, Chang'an.

The pass, which is carved by a full and fast-flowing river, is a lush relief from the naked mountains. Safe now from marauders, one can walk in leisure through the leafy poplars and willows lining the cascading water's edge. And that is what many people who appreciate nature's alliance with history do. Unfortunately, the public in China has not the slightest concern about litter. Wherever people congregate, refuse reigns. A troupe of 20 or 30 Chinese farmers from 15 kilometres away came to the Iron Gate for a day off. They were friendly and relaxed, some them, full of smiles, asking us to take photos with their cameras. A child casually threw an empty soft-drink bottle on the ground as the crowd shuffled past us, even though there were rubbish bins around. Through Parida, we suggested to a guard standing nearby that he ask the mother to pick up the bottle. Overhearing this, she did, and threw it into the river.

We struck northeast from Korla in the direction of the Heavenly Mountains, by now far in the distance. The terrain was bleak and totally barren of vegetation, haphazardly uneven, like waste dumps after a mining operation before modern environmental management. We climbed steadily into the land swollen by the influence of the mountain range, but we were still not very high, about 1000 metres above sea level. Beige turned to green as we came upon an oasis and, suddenly, a lake emerged. On the side of the road, people were drying reeds for paper-making, an invention of the Chinese. We were at Lake Bosten, the largest in Xinjiang and one of 62 in this region. Local legend relates that the Earth goddess was in love with Bosten, but God intervened, for he desired to seduce her. When she refused his advances, he stopped the rain for 999 days. In defiance, Bosten rushed up to the mountaintop overlooking the lake and shot arrows at the almighty. Infuriated at the affront, God killed the valiant lover, plunging the Earth goddess into the despairing tears that created the lake.

At the lake, we had to pass through a tollgate, where the attendant tried to charge us double the rate because we were foreigners. Sharply, Parida asked the man, "Haven't you heard of the new policy published this year by the Central Committee to charge the same for all?". Not willing to show his ignorance, the attendant backed off. I doubt that there was a government policy one way or another.

We took a boat with a small Evinrude motor into the lake, passing along a clearing in the reeds that choked the edges of the shallow water. It seemed

Apricots, Korla

strange to be on a lake right in the middle of the desert. The distinction of Xinjiang is its contrast between vast stretches of desert and watered patches. In the distance, the mountains formed a wide, white-trimmed curtain. We went for a swim, but the water was so shallow that we had go 100 metres off shore before getting out of our depth.

It should have been an idyllic scene, but it wasn't. Human negligence destroyed it. The area is a relaxation spot for the local people, who have turned the swimming beach into a dump for all kinds of bottles, plastic bags, scrunched-up paper and half-eaten food. Litter was all over the place, choking the sand. People were treading on it, kicking it out of the way, barbecuing in the middle of it. There was so much, it stole the character from nature. A few metres from the beach, small restaurants like concrete bunkers crowded around a large entrance area that resembled a prison yard. Electricity wires and coal heaped on the ground added to the utilitarian atmosphere remorselessly pervading the resort. About 100 people were standing on an ugly bridge over a narrow section of the lake, fishing lines dangling 10 metres into the shallow water. The fish they sought, however, were no larger than minnows, so depleted is the stock.

TURPAN

We were happy to get back on the road, to return to the unspoiled expanse of the Taklamakan. From the high country, we descended through the Empty Valley pass (2000 metres) into a vast depression, at the bottom of which lies Turpan, famous for its grapes and raisins. The vine was brought there along the Silk Road from the West 2000 years ago, an exotic import, along with oenology. One hundred and fifty-four metres below sea level, it is the lowest place on Earth other than the Dead Sea. Its home, the Turpan Basin, is suffocated by mountains, which reflect the heat like the walls of an oven, creating convection currents that form vicious, dry winds screeching to force 12 at times and whipping up clouds of dust so dense that they eclipse the sun. Evaporation is 200 times the negligible annual rainfall. The heat in full summer – temperatures reach more than 50 degrees – would surprise even Australians inured to the Pilbara at Marble Bar. Ground temperatures can rage to a searing 82 degrees, inspiring its traditional name, 'land of fire'. It is said that one local official could muster enough energy for his job only if he conducted his office work while sitting in a tub of cooling water. The winter contrast is cruel: the

In the front of the
Tian Shan Mountains

thermometer dives to minus 15 degrees, where it sharpens the knife-like winds.

It was 43 degrees while we were there. Even the hotel was barely a relief, its oil-fired air-conditioner operating only for 20 minutes in the morning and afternoon, to conserve fuel. Looking at the oil rigs on the periphery of town – there were four – I wondered about the economics of the saving. Production from the Turpan Basin ranks along with that from the Tarim and the Junggar as the platform for Xinjiang's great petroleum leap forward. Outside, the heat was assuaged somewhat by a shade screen of grapevine arbours trellised over the main road, the Avenue of Grapes. As well as representing a cooling deliverance, it was a beautiful sight of cascading green mottled with patches of sunlight. Still, it was hot, so hot and dry that it sapped the energy, tempting one to rationalise that it wasn't really necessary to do anything or go anywhere. We carried bottles of water with us wherever we went and looked forward all day to the cold beer we would have in the evening.

Harsh though its climate is, the Tarim Basin is famous for the longevity of its inhabitants, many of whom claim to be over 100 years old. Local folk put it down to the health-giving fruit, of which they eat an average of 100 kilograms a year, and the dryness. The area's prolific orchards gush out apricots, fragrant pears, peaches, pomegranates, mulberries, figs, sand dates and watermelons. Hami melons are grown in numerous varieties, with droll names such as Black Eyebrow, Bag of Sugar and Golden Dragon. Over 10 species of grapes are cultivated. The raisins are the most delicious I have ever tasted, a sweet and sour flavour enhanced by a high citric acid and sugar content. All over town, we saw square brick structures not much smaller than houses, with holes left in the walls like latticework. They were raisin kilns, in which the grapes would be hung to dry in the hot winds that blew through.

The Tarim Basin's salubriousness has another property: its near-zero humidity has been known since ancient times to be a balm for rheumatism and arthritis. Sufferers come to Turpan from all over China to seek relief in a vast outdoor sanatorium. At the edge of the desert, on the barren dunes that spread out for miles like a choppy sea, they pitch rudimentary shelters for protection against the fierce sun. All day long, or for as much of it as they can endure, they sit with the diseased parts of their body covered in mounds of searing sand. A local Uighur medical centre supervises the fire-sand therapy, which is claimed to be highly effective in soothing all aches and pains.

We visited the secret of how this desolate place with virtually no rain could have borne life and become one of the important entrepôts of Silk Road trade. Parida took us to a wooded area near the outskirts of town and led us down a narrow, weed-choked gully to what seemed to be a small cave with a watercourse running along the bottom. It was an open channel in the Karez water-reticulation network, possibly the most remarkable hydrology system in the ancient world. It is still functioning today. Covering 5000 square kilometres, a series of connecting underground and open channels carry the glacial melt from the aquifers underneath the base of the distant Tian Shan mountains. Wells, usually 25 metres apart, are dug by hand in straight lines on top of the underground channels. The ones near Turpan are 20 metres deep. Mud from the digging is piled around the wells, forming circular mounds like small meteorite craters. They have to be neat and bevelled in order to prevent the earth from falling in. The system can be seen from the air, visible as pockmarked lines migrating symmetrically from the mountain range for miles across the desert.

The landform here curves down from the mountains as in the sides of a bowl, a feature that was a blessing to the ancient hydrologers. They sited the tunnels to slope less than the contours of the land so that they gradually came to the surface for easy access yet stayed lower than the source of the water, allowing gravity to do the carrying. The wells gave entry to the underground channels for the purpose of maintenance, a task that became not just a necessity but a moral imperative, as it was for the Dutch repairing their dykes. Cities of the Taklamakan which did not maintain their Karez at an acceptable standard would be condemned to die in the parched sand. Some did so anyway, for the Tian Shan glaciers have shrunk over time, so that, in places, the diminishing water supply fell below subsistence levels.

One man would be lowered by a rope into the well, where he would fill up buckets of the silt that clogged the channel like cholesterol. The bucket would be tied to a rope, and hoisted up by an animal supervised by a workmate. The wells are naturally climate-controlled: in summer, they offer a refuge from the heat, while in winter, warm vapour clusters around them like the steam that comes out of New York manholes in cold weather.

Knowledge has been lost as to where the technology originated. Some Chinese like to link it to their own inventive genius but the better opinion is that it moved along the Silk Road from Persia. Certainly, the irrigation system that kept ancient Mesopotamia fertile and which was destroyed by Hulugu in the Mongol invasions bears a telltale resemblance. It is further evidence that Indo-European settlement in these parts goes back a long way, certainly before the Han Chinese arrived to drive out the Xiongnu.

Gaochang

GAOCHANG

In the first century BC, Han military contingents established a walled garrison at an oasis 40 kilometres east of Turpan, calling it Gaochang ('high and prosperous walls'). It was our next stop. The fort grew to become a regional centre of power and Buddhist practice. Xuan Zang preached there, so successfully, it turned out, that the local king refused to allow him leave to continue his journey to India, despite increasingly urgent pleas. After several months of frustrated importunity, the determined monk went on a three-day hunger strike. His plight moved the monarch to allow him to leave.

Gaochang is a relic today, destroyed by the Mongols in their predatory swoop through the cities of the Silk Road in the 13th century. Sections of the walls remain, but the temples and palaces have declined to be irregular lumps of clay. Over centuries, local farmers have chipped off pieces of the fertile mud brick and rammed earth to use on their fields. The ferocious winds, too, have stripped shape from the once-proud buildings. Vestiges have survived into modern times, however, of the complex civilisation that used to exist there. Von Le Coq discovered a large mural in a seventh-century temple showing that the fugitive Manichaean religion, founded by Manes of Persia in 300 AD, flourished in the Silk Road city, at least for a while, until overshadowed by Buddhism and, later, Islam. The temple remains, its high crenellated walls of rammed earth surrounding a large square with devotional niches on the sides. Inside, a fire altar testifies to the Zoroastrian origin of the Manichaeans.

Persecuted in their home country, the Manichaeans, who believed in a reformed type of Zoroastrianism, fled east after Manes was crucified as a heretic. In the diaspora, some settled at Samarkand, while others migrated further, into China along the Silk Road. The ruins of a Buddhist temple

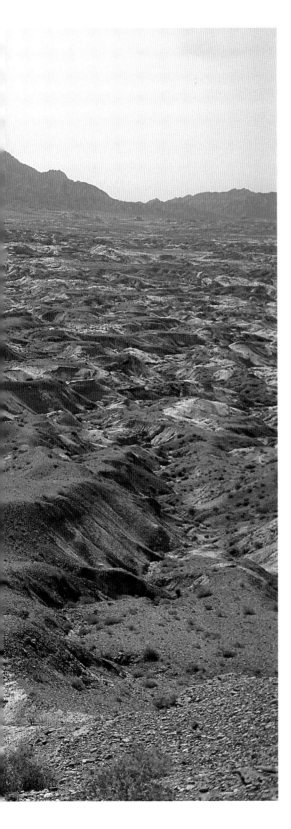

Left: Tian Shan Mountains, Korla

Below: Emin minaret, Turpan

destroyed in the Cultural Revolution display the ancient arch structure known, from its appearance, as the barrel vault. Builders in the region still employ the style. Inside, is a large image of Buddha, a solitary guardian of the past, when Gaochang was the last Taklamakan city to convert to Islam. Clouds of wasps now possess the fallen place of worship.

Opposite the slumped city looms an extraordinary, wrinkled rock structure, extending for 100 kilometres at the feet of the Tian Shan and separated from the mountains by a desiccated, flat plain. The rocks, ripped jagged with striations that seem to run up their face, leap out of the moving desert haze like a monstrous fire. Locals call them the Flaming Mountains. Deep crevasses engraved on the reddish Jurassic rock catch sunlight and make shape-creating shadows, inspiring the regional myth that the phenomenon was the result of a struggle between archetypal hero Karahoja and a fire-breathing dragon. Karahoja died with the dragon, his blood mixing with the monster's gall to form the mountains. From then on, the magical site brought prosperity to the region, and peace, until the Mongols came.

North of Gaochang, the vast Tang burial field of Astana, discovered in 1970, has yielded up more than 400 graves and 10,000 cultural relics. The dry climate is benign to bodies and artefacts. Silk fabrics of superb quality, as well as ancient documents, are well preserved. We visited the three graves that are open to the public, entering down a steep, narrow passage similar to the entrances of Egyptian tombs. Two contain wall paintings, the other well-preserved mummies of a man and wife. The museum director claimed that the mummies' hair and fingernails, which were very long, continued to grow for several years after death.

In one of the tombs, four murals depicted the virtues of Confucian philosophy. It was the first time we had seen evidence of the sage of China on the Silk Road, so dominant were Buddhism and Islam in Xinjiang. On the walls, Wooden Man, conscious of his vulnerability, does nothing in excess, Golden Man, with a piece of cloth tied around his mouth, is silent in public, Stone Man performs good deeds, while Jade Man seeks to get rid of earthly desires, jade being the Chinese symbol of purity. The English proverb "Silence is golden" is thought to stem from this Confucian dictate.

BEZEKLIK

High in the Flaming Mountains, on the side of a river-cut gorge, Buddhist monks who came here along the Silk Road chiselled their devotional caves out of the soft rock and created a mountain gallery of mural art. To get to the more interesting caves, we struggled up a steep, crooked path of friable earth hemmed in with wind-song poplars at the bottom, overlooking the hurtling stream. On the way up, we passed a sheer plane of pure, layered sandstone that rose sharply 200 metres from the river like a fortress wall. At the top of our climb, we could see the snow-cap of the highest mountain in the Tian Shan range, across the gorge over the wide desert plain. The usual dusty haze had disappeared as if washed off a window, revealing a crisp, crinkly line that separated the dark land from the sky's shining blue.

Von Le Coq reached the caves at the beginning of the 20th century, finding them filled with sand. He dug it out, revealing a wonder of Buddhist images on the walls in paint as bright as new. The figures were plump and fleshy, typical of the mature Tang period. He carefully excised most of the frescoes, shipping them west over the Silk Road by camel. They ended up in a Berlin museum, to suffer the depredations of the Second World War, though some did survive. As for the remainder, without their protective coating of sand, some fell victim to climate degradation and local Muslim-based disfiguration.

However it is still worth visiting the works left in situ, for some of the most facinating images remain. In one case, particularly, enough remains at the back of the cave to discern Sakyamuni preaching a sermon to princes from the 36 kingdoms of the Western Region. The faces disclose their ethnic origins: Persian, Turkic, Mongol, Han and Indian.

The flat, hard-packed loess rock 10 kilometres west of Turpan is split by two rivers that converge to form an island resembling a willow leaf. Millennia of water carving have set the rivers into deep gorges, their sides rising 30 metres to the island plane like mighty castle walls. On the unassailable plateau, the expanding Chinese forces built a frontier town called Jiaohe during the Han dynasty, safe from the troublesome Xiongnu cavalry, which had no hope of crossing the wide gap. From the second to the fifth centuries, Jiaohe served as the capital of Cheshi, one of the 36 kingdoms of the Western Region, but fell to destruction 1000 years later. The ruins are like a gigantic sculpture park built by ancient spirits. Mud-brick stupas, differentially weathered, stand like weird primaeval figures in gestural poses. As we walked in the silent, deserted streets, strange shapes and shadows loomed high in front of us, dark against the blue clarity of the sky. A noble solitude inhabited the place, brushed by a steady breeze. A cuckoo's voice resonated softly between the walls of the gorge. The only vegetation we saw on the desolate flats was a wild watermelon growing close to a stupa. Nearby, a beige-bellied brown snake, half a metre long and very poisonous, slowly slithered by, lethargic in the dry heat.

Again, we saw the confluence of the different religions that migrated along the Silk Road. A 10th-century royal temple of the Manichaean faith stood in recognisable form, a Nestorian church. Old Buddhist stupas were everywhere.

The early settlers dug down into the platform rock to make dwelling places and courtyards beneath the surface, connected by open streets. No windows or doors faced the sunken thoroughfares. Means of access was from the top. The strange system is easily visible today. Later, in the Tang period, the townsfolk built above ground. The local people, who live in the bottom of the fertile gorge now that defence is not an issue, carry on the tradition by means of subsurface basements, built to combat the heat and cold. In 1994, underground temples and tombs were discovered. The large, beaten-earth plain on the apparent edge of the town is thought to hide a lot more. No-one lives there any longer, and regional authorities lack the expertise or funds to look.

Once a city's inhabitants have gone, morbidity slowly creeps over, the agents of change chiselling and sandpapering the architecture, gradually wearing it down. But it does not die; life remains until the last stone falls and the last earth line blurs beyond recognition, and even, perhaps, forever, as long as it is remembered. Remembrance is the stuff of immortality. Gaochang is remembered.

TOYUK

The next day, we set out for the Flaming Mountains, to the little village of Toyuk, famous for its elongated green grapes, called 'mare's nipples'. It is near the site of what are thought to be the oldest Buddhist caves in Xinjiang, dating from the early third century. There are about 40 of them, but only the later ones have paintings. A long walk in their direction took us through a lush river-carved gorge lined with poplars. Steep cliffs scratched by deep erosion channels rose from the winding path. Rain began to fall, a soft warm scotch mist at first but then real rain. It was light but steady, refreshing in the heat and the exercise. Parida said it was the first time she had seen rain in the Turpan area.

Uighur Mosque, Toyuk

Flaming Mountains

The colours of the rocks in the gorge were vivid, like an abstract painting made by a colourist. Chalcopyrite bedding, as green as olive leaves and contorted under primaeval pressures, thrust up beneath discrete layers of beige loess. The loess was brushed with red haematite staining and twisted in random directions. Flat patches on the valley wall, left as surface sections, had sheered off, looking clean and smooth against the rough-textured weathering of the surrounding rock.

The air was misty with dust and moisture, rendering the mountainous landscape subdued and subtle, like a traditional Chinese painting. The parallel layering of the rock faces made them seem to move slightly in the haze. As we climbed, the dirt path narrowing into a defile, we heard the rushing sound of the stream far below, dashing along the mountain side. Parida had made special arrangements to engage a local guide, for these caves are not open to the public. The guide told us we were the only Westerners to have visited them since von Le Coq.

The path was getting very steep now, and quite hazardous in parts. We had to bend over and hold onto anything we could: large rocks, scrubby tree branches or roots. After a last-minute scramble, we reached a ledge cut along the side of the sheer cliff to connect the caves, which were carved in a line out of the rockface. We entered the four containing the best-preserved murals. Unfortunately, Islamic purists had defaced the images, though in most cases, they had scratched out only part of the faces. The artistic style was quite different from what we had seen in Kyzyl. It seemed more precise and formal, and consisted of human figures, not animals – lithe, graceful women standing in rectangular panels, hips slightly to the side, displaying a gentle curve of elegance. Bodhisattvas sat benignly in the lotus position, some dressed in red, some in black, others in white robes. Each panel was a complete picture in itself but, with the others on the wall, formed a complex harmony of form and colour. The small figures we saw on a ceiling in red, blue, white and black, set in a wheel with white spokes separating the panels, reminded me of the Persian miniatures we had seen in Iran, notwithstanding that the subjects were different. Certainly, Persian and Indian influences were at work.

We trekked down across the river and up the other side of the gorge to see the caves from a distance. Indentations appeared on the cliff where Buddhist statues, carved from rock, had been removed. The rain was subsiding now, and the sun was fighting the black clouds, looking like the baleful eye of a Buddhist guardian. The whole valley was shrouded in a haze that seemed to emphasise its remoteness. Wolves still live there, coming down from the hills to raid the farmers' livestock. Caves were everywhere, the mouths of many filled with sand. We uncovered a painting by pushing sand away with our hands. Our Uighur guide, who was in his mid-twenties, told us he used to play in the caves when he was a child. At that time, they didn't have doors, as no-one considered them significant.

After the visit to the caves, our guide invited us to have brunch with his family. We brought a melon and they provided tea, nan and raisins. The raisins were rock hard, but quickly became succulent in the mouth, slightly tart. They dry their own grapes. Our hosts had turned a bed into a dining table, which they placed outside, under a canopy of ripening vines. We all sat on it. The family had a private plot on the slope of the valley where they grew vegetables. The village is well known as a holy place, in memory of six Arabs who came to there to convert the local population. It is said that a pilgrimage to Toyuk is worth half a haj. But no-one had come there for three years, not even the cultural relics people to maintain the caves.

We offered the Uighur guide some money, since he had spent his entire morning showing us the caves and entertaining us, but he refused, pointing to the traditional hospitality of his tribe. We said goodbye to the friendly people, thanking them profusely, and went for a walk in the village. Parida took us into one of the mud-brick houses. Although the floor was unpaved, it was cleanly swept and watered, and the inside of the little house, in which seven people lived, was neat and tidy. Some houses are meticulously looked after; others kept in a slovenly condition. They can be side by side. I wondered how the people got along with each other in the face of such disparity. It seemed to be caused not by economic circumstances but by attitude.

If a Uighur family has done well in the eyes of the State, through obeying government policies – for example, paying taxes or adhering to the birth-control restrictions – it is presented with an award of stars. The awards start with one star. The house we visited proudly displayed a ten-star award (the highest) over the lintel. I wondered, somewhat unworthily, whether behind their friendly smiles, these people were insufferable sycophants. Parida said the Uighurs are a compliant people by nature, easygoing and simple, not given to rebelliousness. If that is the case, it would seem the provocations that have moved some of them to rebel from time to time against the Han Chinese must have been prodigious.

On the way out of Turpan, we stopped at the Emin minaret, built in the 18th century by the ruler of Turpan. In appreciation of his role in putting down a Mongol rebellion against Chinese rule, the Ching emperor in Beijing made him a prince. Chinese historians refer to what they characterise as his outstanding contribution to upholding the unification of China. The minaret is the tallest in Xinjiang, gracefully tapered as it climbs into the sky, and a beautiful example of Timurid mud-brick work in geometric and floral designs. The grand mosque attached to it, which has the capacity to hold 1000 worshippers, demonstrated how far Islam has reached into the northeast.

On the road to Urumchi, we passed a field of windmills generating electricity. There must have been several hundred acres sown with tall metallic towers like soldiers spawned from serpents' teeth. Silently, their propellers flailed the air in an eerie and mechanical sword dance. It made me think of a vast Biennale installation in the open air.

We completed our journey at Urumchi, which means 'beautiful pastures', a romantic hark-back to an earlier day before the concrete and asphalt had spread over the area to support an ugly modern industrial city of one and a half million people. While Urumchi has failed to use its standing as the capital of Xinjiang to create any charm, it does have a museum, which houses treasures of the Silk Road, and some secrets that, together with the discoveries at Korla, could cause a revision of history.

As well as silks from ancient Xinjiang, the museum displays woollen fabrics – twill woven into plaids and tartans belonging to the Tokharians. A case has been made that these remarkable garments indicate that the Tokharians might have originated from as far west as Europe, not necessarily, as previously believed, from Persia. Their language, apparently, is closer to the Celtic, Italic and Germanic branches of the Indo-European than is the Indo-Iranian.

Certainly, they were Caucasian people, a fact clearly shown by the 4000-year-old desiccated corpses discovered in the Lop Nor region and on display at the museum. With them are remains of a woman found in the sands of Loulan so well preserved that her features are lifelike and her brown hair still in place. She has become a famous fashion icon in Xinjiang, appearing on posters and other popular media as the "beauty of Loulan". The Chinese authorities are uncomfortable with the conclusions that seem inescapable from these revelations. However, they are not denying the scientific evidence that seems to point to the original inhabitants of the Taklamakan, long regarded as an integral part of China, being not Han nor even Turkic.

The story of the Silk Road carries the theme not only of ancient migrations lost to memory but also of the way ideas inevitably follow commerce. Besides concepts of religion, technology flowed along the venerable axis. The know-how to make gunpowder, the clock, the compass, printing and rag paper seeped into the West from China along the Silk Road, and much also ventured the other way. In China, glass was worth its weight in gold.

Today, we have new ways to convey ideas and, indeed, all forms of information. But, like the old Silk Road, they often involve a network of business dealings and are motivated by the desire to facilitate economic activity. We sensed part of that process, in its most romantic form, out there where the sand winds blow.

Toyuk

Epilogue

A colour-wheel of ethnic and racial diversity rolls across the vast swathe of land from Istanbul to Urumchi, and the history of its people smoulders with the cinders of war, yet a type of concordance is sweeping the region. As we travelled, we could not fail to observe that a movement of historic importance is taking place. Mullahs are active, their confidence regained; mosques are full, and more are rising on the skylines. The dominant social trend is a return to the Sharia — prayer requirements of the *Koran* are strictly observed, hejab-clad women appear without exception in Iran and more often than before in other countries.

As the West turns away from its mainstream religion and struggles to find another vector for morality, societies east of the Hellespont look more and more to the institution of Islam for a guide to appropriate behaviour. In a trend running counter to globalisation, Islamic peoples are concentrating on an identity unique to themselves and essentially hostile to outside culture. At the same time, they are attempting to build their economic and military capability. Their dilemma is that a rise to equality with the developed world in things material requires an importation of modern technology that has a Western provenance. Inside the technology lurks the culture of the provider. Once again the Trojan horse has been offered to the East.

Ironically, on a doctrinal level, Islam seems to have less trouble than does Christianity reconciling religion with science and its handmaiden, technology — they are perceived to be in harmony. The Muslim equivalent to the Galileo dispute did not produce the Western result of permanently alienating the intellectual class. While generally favouring a more liberal interpretation of the *Koran*, the intellectual elements in Islamic societies are nevertheless devout. Also, if modern technology had originated in Islamic countries and were clothed with Muslim culture, it is quite probable that the mullahs would be more supportive of it.

Throughout history, people have sought to define their identity by comparison with others, a subjective process that often leads to a sense of cultural superiority. Perceived differences promote denigration of others that, in turn, builds self-esteem. The ancient Greeks called foreigners by the pejorative term 'barbarian', which connoted lack of civilisation; today the peoples of Islam vilify the West as materialistic and morally decadent. A prominent sign we saw over the inside of the front door of our hotel in Shiraz proclaims: "Down with the USA". Perhaps with the recent thawing of relations between the United States and Iran, such overt expressions of animosity will recede, but it is doubtful that the adverse cultural comparison will disappear any time soon.

Detractors of the West cannot avoid acknowledging its superiority in the fields of modern science and technology. However, they take comfort in a comparison between their character-building commitment to the dictates of the *Koran* and what they see as a weakening of moral fibre in the West. To them, Western peoples are entering an age of decadence as they turn away from their traditional religion, favour rights over duties and slip into what appears to be lax personal behaviour. All this seems to be happening in the putrefying humidity of material affluence. Their perception, of course, ignores much that is good in Western societies.

East and West are the inheritors of such vastly separate traditions that they tend to perceive the same human characteristics from a distinguishingly different point of view. For example, the ancient Greeks placed emphasis on the individual, while the Eastern people stressed the community. When walking along a shoreline, the Greek would see the particular grains of sand; someone east of the Hellespont would see the beach. One led to a train over time of personal freedom, democracy and human rights, the other to a bending of the will to the needs of the State, rule by the powerful, and a sense of personal obligation. The Western view led to a spirit of competition, the Eastern to an emphasis on cooperation. These differences play themselves out in the way society is organised, how governments operate, and what is expected in personal behaviour. In addition, our civilisations are in dramatically different stages of development, particularly in relation to the role military activity plays in society and its behavioural norms.

Throughout the world, military prowess has played a pivotal role in nation-building. It is difficult to find a case where it has not. In the Eastern lands we visited, the Hittites under Muwatallis (the commander who fought the Egyptians to a standstill at the battle of Kadesh) dominated the Anatolian peninsula with their invincible armies, and military superiority allowed the Persians inspired by Cyrus the Great to form the largest empire of the time. The Turkish hegemony grew out of the dust of thundering cavalry. In the wake of the bellicosity, great nations arose that later distinguished themselves in the art of high civilisation.

In the West, the Greeks defeated their Persian invaders, Alexander spread Hellenism in a conquering drive to the East, the Romans built an empire upon their military discipline, the Teutons fought to inherit it, and the British created their own by force of arms. Again, the art of high civilisation followed. The United States is the inheritor of these European traditions.

A salient difference between contemporary East and West is that Western civilisation is closer in time to the peak of its military culture. It has been centuries since the societies we visited, or any Islamic nation, has produced a conquering army. This factor, I think, helps to explain why the emphasis in Islamic countries is on building strength, in the sense of what we have traditionally called virility, whereas in the West it is now on the softer virtues, strength being taken for granted. For this reason alone, it seems that misunderstanding of each other is our destiny. One of the great fears in the West is that military adventurism may follow the bellicose talk often heard in Islamic countries, particularly in Iran. While military capability there is limited by prevailing economic weakness, it is, clearly, the intention of Islamic countries to build their economies, notwithstanding the caution of some of the more extreme mullahs. That economic prowess is the sine qua non of the desired resurgence is widely accepted.

Over time, civilisations rise and decline, and some ascend again out of their ashes. The forces at the heart of the process remain a mystery, although it is possible to discern certain characteristics that probably need to be present in order to drive the cadence. In the lands east of the Hellespont, some of these can be observed, but at this time it would be foolhardy to make any predictions. It is far too early. For one thing, the peoples are completely different in background, even though their religion is a unifying force. Turkey is a mixture of Indo-European indigenous stock and later Turkic invaders. Iran is Aryan. Central Asia is Eurasian and Xinjiang Turkic.

These constitute the swathe of nations which were of particular interest to me. They have a complex relationship with the Arab peoples who are the custodians of Islam and, of course, also play a vital role in the revival of the religion. On the one hand, all Muslims are united in faith, despite underlying sectarian divisions, but on the other hand, their different ethnic backgrounds are not conducive to solidarity on a sociopolitical level — as witnessed in recent wars. On the socioreligious level, however, it seems that all Muslim countries are seeking a revival of Islamic principles.

While it would appear that the movement to the Sharia we saw in the countries visited could be described as reactionary in the sense that it seeks to turn back the clock to an earlier society perceived to be more characteristic of discipline, respect for authority, hierarchical structure and sense of duty, I think it would be wrong to do so. The revival of Islam is not a political movement per se, although at its fundamentalist level, particularly in Iran, it contains a strong element of politics. In any case, even its political side is not aimed at restoring an old regime. Essentially, it is a sociological force aimed at rebuilding the strength of the society. To do this, methods are being employed that have worked several times in the past. In the process, the younger generation seems to be fully engaged; young people are often more pious than their elders.

The process of rebuilding greatness after decline has occurred before in the lands we visited. In Iran, the Achaemenid dynasty, whose military glory and administrative genius had pushed the boundaries of the Persian Empire to encompass most of the ancient world, collapsed in what, at least among the conquering Greeks, was perceived to be the terminal pathology of decadence — lethargy brought about by luxury and licentiousness. For the Persians, centuries passed by in obscure societal mediocrity until

a burst of energy thrust Iran, still called Persia by the West, into celestial brilliance under the Sassanid dynasty and then again under the Safavids.

In the lands comprising Turkey, civilisation has also pulsed bright. The radiance of the Hittite civilisation dominated Anatolia and beyond, threatening the New Kingdom of Egypt and extending the frontier of science — the Hittites developed the technology of smelting iron, which curiously, like the Chinese inventors of gunpowder, they did not use for military purposes. After their decay, the Phrygians, led by their legendary king, Midas, rose to supremacy, followed by the Lydians under Croesus. The economies of these two mini-empires were so rich that stories about the wealth of their kings have passed through the ages as fairytales. On the backs of the hardy Anatolian farmers, the Byzantines reworked the traditions of the old Roman Empire into the dominant civilisation of the Mediterranean. Later, the Seljuks and Ottomans, bringing in fresh blood from the steppes, once again rebuilt the greatness of the region.

All these past glories are there for the visitor to see in the monuments, in the museums, and even in the artefacts made by the people of today. I wondered how much they operated at the inspirational level of consciousness. Certainly, political leaders have tried to harness them. The Shah of Iran staged an anniversary of the Achaemenid celebration of the Zoroastrian New Year, with thousands of costumed actors representing the endless procession of tributary monarchs coming with their gifts to pay homage to the King of Kings. The bas reliefs cut into the sides of the giant staircases at Persepolis offered pageant designers a precise guide.

It is impossible not to be impressed by the fact that, as in the Middle Ages, when Islam was at its height, the energy and skills of the Iranians are at the heart of Muslim society, arguably comprising the

Khomeini Shrine, Teheran

principal force that propels it forward. In its darker recesses lurks the engine room of terrorism, where the weapons of homicide aimed at perceived enemies of Islam are energised. There is little doubt that the Iranian State arms and pays extremist groups fighting for Islamic causes, such as Hezbollah in southern Lebanon. Iranian influence has been detected in several attempts to undermine support for Middle Eastern governments seen to be too secular. Leaders of Hamas recently visited Ayatollah Ali Khamenei to seek advice. Shortly afterwards Palestinian violence erupted to shatter the truce with Israel brokered by President Clinton of the USA.

Iranian mullahs have created the concept of an Islamic theocracy, albeit currently under a liberalising influence, to promote a strong Koranic society. The mullahs with whom we spoke fervently believe that an Islamic theocratic State along the Iranian model is the destiny of Muslim nations and that Iran has been chosen to lead the way. They touch a responsive chord with many Islamic people, even if their political message is too radical for most other societies to accept. It resonates with a visceral feeling, deeply held by all, that Muslims must regenerate their moral condition as a prelude to regaining their rightful place in the world, and following the true path of the *Koran* is the way to do it.

It seems that where a society has been in decline and determines to rebuild, harsh disciplinary methods, often of a puritanical nature, are required. There may be a parallel with defeated armies or sporting teams that have fallen from championship to cellar. Certain nations recently have tried the remedy. Mao Zedong forced the Chinese through the wind tunnel of puritanism, revivifying a society so decadent that, just before his time, almost 10 per cent of its people were opium addicts. In the process of regeneration, rights give way to obligation as the organising principle and self-denial is applauded. A personified evil in the form of a foreign society seen to be too luxurious is crafted in order to instil sufficient ardour. Ayatollah Khomeini put his people through such a purge, one that, while not as devastating, has some analogies to the Chinese experience. Like Mao, he introduced his society to hatred of the devil, against whom the virtue of his people could be compared. It was the same devil.

The clarion call of Allah's word in Iran and, to a diluted degree, elsewhere in the countries we visited seems to be a distant echo of the aspirations of the mediaeval Christian Church. Then, possibly for the last time in the West, religion was the unquestioned paradigm for ordering society and in individuals the arbiter of right and wrong. With the rebirth of the Greek heritage in the Renaissance, the West has inexorably moved in the direction of secular alternatives.

The retreat of the institutional Church in the West has opened up a gap in moral and spiritual guidance, small and slowly growing for a long time but recently wide enough to create a vacuum potentially destabilising to society. The void has drawn in an amalgam of the law, which handles the grosser aspects of human behaviour, and the media, who have appointed themselves the new priests of morality. Scientists have sought to substitute knowledge for spirituality. This process, essentially absent in the Islamic East, is occurring in Western societies, despite the undoubted strength of personal and institutional religious faith present in certain quarters. The dominant position on this sociological trend line is occupied by the overarching social theories of democracy and human rights, both outgrowths of the Greek celebration of the greatness of the human condition and the worth of the individual. The contrast between this orientation and the thoughts of Mohammed is epochal. Two of the scenes in which we saw it being played out most dramatically involved the different visions of the rights and duties of women and the nature of government.

That an advance of women towards equality is not considered by Islamic societies to be part of the process of returning to the true path needs no emphasis. Other imperatives rule. It is this difference

that perhaps instils the greatest chill among Western women contemplating a resurgence of Islamic power, at least among those who fear the risk of a roll-back in their gains. Clothing is the most visible symbol of the difference. The hejab, which we saw in ever-increasing use, in the East signifies piety and a public commitment to the Sharia but in the West is seen as a testimony to subservience.

In lands east of the Hellespont, the substance of government has always been perceived more from the perspective of outcomes than from that of process, and still is. The Greek belief in the superiority of democracy over other forms of governance, which informs Western political theory, does not seem to resonate profoundly in those countries. Practical application of common fairness and a demonstration of strength seem more important than the way a government comes about or what elements of society form it, except, of course, on the part of the individuals seeking power. Democracy as we know it fails to touch the hearts of most people. It would be wishful thinking to expect Western-style governments to be on the horizon. One reason is the perceived need for a strong central organisation.

Governments in the East face a daunting task in the rebuilding of their societies. Their economies are weak, overdependent on State intervention, and organised largely in small, cottage-style enterprises. Few big wealth-generators exist outside the State. Entrepreneurial activity on a large scale is not well understood. The minimal degree of commercial regulation together with uncertainty in business law inhibit the formation of large pools of capital. Consumer distribution is, essentially, still through local bazaars and small shops. The 'information age' has hardly dawned there. Great strides in education are required to bring the people forward, and communication of information throughout the society needs to be strengthened in order to reduce the scope for manipulation on the part of politicians.

There is no doubt that the dominant presence of the *Koran* ensures that the Eastern societies will move into the technological age in their own way, influenced perhaps by the West but determined, too, to keep the identity they have forged over centuries of self-development. As a visitor, one sees much to be admired in the form. The genuine empathy and cohesiveness of the family structure there are a way of life, features of which we are trying to reconstruct in the West, amidst distressing cases of breakdown and controversy.

Lifestyles in the East are simpler, graced with fewer creature comforts and less hygienic than those in the West, but the cultural traditions are impressively rich and people have time to allow the warmth of human nature to be expressed with largesse. Civility is practised in the streets. The 'hurry sickness' of the West has not yet infected their societies nor has anomie.

However, with the friendliness goes a pride born of the centuries and wounded by reduced status in the modern age. The pain of the wound can provoke touchiness and drive anger, even in some extreme cases to the killing point. And there are local causes of bitterness.

The vast swathe of beige land through which we travelled is bristling with tension at a level just beneath the surface. The history of past alliances, hatreds, massacres and cultural roots is never far from the animation of attitudes and events today. Old sectarian differences divide Sunnis from Shiites. In Turkey, the secularist descendants of Atatürk shudder at the gathering force of fundamentalists dreaming of Islamic theocracy. Iranian liberals, who recently won, under President Mohammed Khatami, a landslide parliamentary victory, are pushing the conservative forces of the theocracy for reform. Their concept of more liberty and political freedom, while modest by Western standards, clashes with the hard line taken by the religious establishment under the spiritual leadership of Ayatollah Ali Khamenei.

In Central Asia, ancient tribal rivalries, held down by Soviet hegemony, are bubbling to the surface now the cap has been removed. On the other side of the Pamir Mountains, their kin live in a prickly relationship with their Chinese overlords, mindful that too much self-expression could lead to a Tibetan-style put-down.

On another level, however, the lives of these diverse people are set in a harmony playing at the beginning of a crescendo that could grow to historic proportions. The resurgence of Islam is obvious to anyone who travels through these countries. Parents are teaching their children to be more pious than they were themselves and, in turn, are observing the Sharia to a greater extent than previously, perhaps in many cases more to set an example than out of real fervour. But the children are being guided to feel the ardour of faith. Complex though the effects of the widening role of religion are, and however discomfiting to the West, seen as the arch-Satan, no spiritual void exists in the Islamic countries we visited, nor any angst of the soul.

If the paradigm for future human conflicts is to be civilisational rather than national, which seems to be the case, it is likely that one of the most important trials of strength will be between a recrudescent Islam and the West, two of the major civilisations of the world. The fault line that defines them in aspiration, religion, social norms, philosophical tradition and history is so deep that if difference is the heart of conflict, we must have it here. Still, conflict can take many forms, some not at all malevolent. Which ones we experience will be driven largely by how people manage it. In that, hope lies in the greater opportunity for knowledge and communication the modern world provides.

Bibliography

GREECE

Homer
The Iliad
(translated by Robert Fagles)
Viking Penguin, 1990

J.B. Bury and R. Meiggs
A History of Greece
MacMillan Press, London 1975

Arnold Toynbee
A Study of History
Thames and Hudson, London 1995

R. R. Palmer
A History of the Modern World
Alfred A. Knopf, New York 1955

Michael Grant
The Classical Greeks
Weidenfeld and Nicholson, 1989

Edward Gibbon
*Decline and Fall of the Roman Empire,
1776–1788*

Manolis Andronicos
The Greek Museums
Ekdotike Athenon, 1974

Dyfri Williams
Greek Gold
British Museum Press, London 1994

Peter Green
Alexander the Great
Praeger Publishers, USA 1970

Peter Levi
Atlas of the Greek World
Phaidon Press, 1984

Michael Wood
In Search of the Trojan War
British Broadcasting Corporation, 1985

Iris Douskou
The Olympic Games in Ancient Greece
Ekdotike Athenon, Athens 1982

Iris Douskou
Athens, the City
Idotike Athenon, Athens 1994

G. Papathanassopoulis
Neolithic and Cycladic Civilization
Melissa Publishing House, Athens

Reynold Higgins
Minoan and Mycenaean Art
Thames and Hudson, London 1981

Gisella Richter
Greek Art
Phaidon Press, London 1974

George Mylonas
Mycenae
Ekdotike Athenon, Athens 1993

Richard Talbot
Atlas of Classical History
Routledge, London 1988

Pierre Amandry
Delphi and its History
Athens, 1984

T. H. Carpenter
Art and Myth in Ancient Greece
Thames and Hudson, London 1981

Herodotus
The Histories
(translated by Aubrey de Selincourt)
Thames and Hudson, London 1996

TURKEY

Robert Mantran
La Vie Quotidienne à Istanbul
Hachette, Paris 1989

Michael Maclagan
The City of Constantine
Thames and Hudson, London 1968

Cyril Mango
Byzantium
Phoenix, London 1980

H. W. Haussig
Byzantine Civilization
Thames and Hudson, London 1971

Steven Runciman
The Fall of Constantinople
Cambridge University Press, 1981

Halil Inalcik
The Ottoman Empire
Phoenix, London 1995

Noel Barber
The Lords of the Golden Horn
Macmillan, London 1973

Chris Hellier
Splendours of Istanbul
Abbeville Press, New York 1993

Ilhan Aksit
Turkey
Cem Ofset Sanat Ajans, Istanbul 1988

Ilhan Aksit
Treasures of Istanbul
Aksit Kultur, Istanbul 1997

John Freely
The Western Shores of Turkey
Butler and Tanner, London 1988

George Bean
Turkey Beyond the Meander
The Bath Press, Avon 1989

Claude Cahen
Pre-Ottoman Turkey
Sidgwick and Jackson, London 1968

Nurten Sevinc
Troia
A Turizm Yayinlari, Istanbul 1992

Anna Edmonds
Turkey's Religious Sites
Damko Publications, 1997

Fatih Cimok
Cappadocia
A Turizm Yayinlari, Istanbul 1987

Metin And
Turkish Miniature Painting
Dost Publications, Istanbul 1987

Yasin Hamid Safadi
Islamic Calligraphy
Thames and Hudson, 1978

Ugur Ayyildiz
Turkish Carpets
Net Turistik Yayinlari, 1995

Hans G. Egli
Sinan
Ege Yayinlari, Istanbul 1997

C. W. Ceram
The Secret of the Hittites
Alfred A. Knopf, New York 1955

J. G. Macqueen
The Hittites
Thames and Hudson, London 1986

Stephen Mitchell
Anatolia: Land, Men, and Gods in Asia Minor (volumes
I and II)
Clarendon Press, Oxford 1995

Mehlika Seval
Ephesus
Minyatur Publications, Istanbul

William Hallo and William Simpson
The Ancient Near East
Harcourt Brace Jovanovich College Publishers, Yale
1971

Osman Diracoglu
Corum
Unal Offset Matbaacilik, Istanbul

Turgut Ozal
Turkey in Europe and Europe in Turkey
K Rustem and Brother, Nicosia 1991

Nicole and Hugh Pope
Turkey Unveiled
The Overlook Press, New York 1997

Francis Robinson
Atlas of the Islamic World
Time-Life Books, Amsterdam 1991

Samuel Huntingdon
Clash of Civilizations and the Remaking of World Order

IRAN
Richard Frye
The Golden Age of Persia
Weidenfeld, London 1993

Sir John Chardin
Travels in Persia
Dover Publications, New York 1988

Donald Sinclair
Adventures in Persia
H. F. and G. Witherby, London 1998

John Simpson
Lifting the Veil
Hodder and Stoughton, London 1995

Bernard Lewis
Islam and the West
Oxford University Press, 1993

Bernard Lewis (editor)
The World of Islam
Thames and Hudson, London 1994

Edward W. Said
Covering Islam
Vintage Books, Random House, New York 1997

Edward W. Said
Orientalism
Penguin Books, London 1995

John Esposito
The Islamic Threat
Oxford University Press, 1995

Jacob Landau
The Politics of Pan-Islam
Clarendon Press, Oxford 1994

Raymond Tanter
Rogue Regimes
Macmillan, London 1998

Hossein Musavian
Imam Khomeini
Saffron Books, London

Rudolph Peters
Jihad in Classical and Modern Islam
Marcus Wiener Publishers, Princeton 1996

Moojan Momen
An Introduction to Shii Islam
Yale University Press, New Haven 1985

Desmond Stewart
Early Islam
Time-Life Books, 1975

The Essential Koran
Translated and Presented by Thomas Cleary
Castle Books, New York 1993

John Renard
Seven Doors to Islam
University of California Press, Los Angeles 1996

CENTRAL ASIA
K. A. Abdullaev
Culture and Art of Ancient Uzbekistan (vols I and II)
Moscow, 1991

Paul Ratchnevsky
Genghis Khan, His Life and Legacy
Blackwell Publishers, Cambridge, USA 1996

David Nicole
The Mongol Warlords
Firebird Books, Dorset 1990

S. A. M. Adshead
Central Asia in World History
Macmillan, London 1993

Edward Allworth
Central Asia
Duke University Press, Durham 1994

Robert Byron
The Road to Oxiana
Penguin Books, London 1992

Architectural Glories of Temur's Era
Sharq, Tashkent 1996

T. Pulatov
Bukhara: a Museum in the Open
Tashkent Art and Literature Publishers, Tashkent 1991

Khiva
Uzbekistan Publishing House, Tashkent 1994

Arthur Koestler
The Thirteenth Tribe
Picador, London 1983

Peter Hopkirk
The Great Game
Oxford University Press, 1990

Carl W. Ernst
Sufism
Shambhala, London 1997

James Fadiman (editor)
Essential Sufism
Castle Books, Edison, New Jersey 1997

Idries Shah
Sufi Thought and Action
The Octagon Press, London 1990

Idries Shah
Wisdom of the Idiots
The Octagon Press, London 1996

Idries Shah
Tales of the Dervishes
Penguin Books, New York 1993

Idries Shah
The Hundred Tales of Wisdom
The Octagon Press, London 1993

Idries Shah
The Subtleties of the Inimitable Mulla Nasrudin
The Octagon Press, London 1993

SILK ROAD

Gong Lizeng (editor)
Xian – Legacies of Ancient Chinese Civilization
Morning Glory Publishers, Beijing 1992

Bamber Gascoigne
The Treasures and Dynasties of China
Jonathan Cape, London 1973

Arthur Cotterell
The First Emperor of China
Macmillan, London 1981

Caroline Blunden
Cultural Atlas of China
Time-Life Books, 1991

A. Doak Barnett
China's Far West
Westview Press, Boulder 1993

C. P. Skrine
Chinese Central Asia
Methuen, London 1926

Sally Hovey Wiggins
Xuangzang
Westview Press, 1996

Duan Wenjie
Scenic Spots and Historical Sites on Silk Road
Xinjiang Peoples' Publishing

Mu Shunying
The Ancient Art in Xinjiang
Xinjiang Fine Arts and Photo Publishing House, Urumqi 1994

Zhang Shiying (editor)
Turpan – Xinjiang
Xinjiang Peoples' Publishing

Peter Hopkins
Foreign Devils on the Silk Road
Oxford University Press, 1980

Elizabeth Weyland Barber
The Mummies of Urumqi
Macmillan, 1999

Annabel Walker
Aurel Stein
John Murray, London 1995

The Travels of Marco Polo
(translated by Ronald Latham)
Penguin Books, London 1958

Heinz Bechert (editor)
The World of Buddhism
Thames and Hudson, London 1993

Index

Sydney MMI
Published by Halstead Press
19a Boundary Street
Rushcutters Bay, New South Wales, 2011
Australia

National Library cataloguing in publication entry:

Grey, Anthony, 1936-
East wind: from Greece to the Great Wall.

Bibliography.
Includes index.
ISBN 1 875684 52 2.

1. Muslims. 2. Islamic countries – History. 3. Islamic
    countries – Description and travel. 4. Islamic Coun-
    tries – Social life and customs. 5. Islamic countries –
    Civilization. I. Grey, Anna-Maryke. II. Title.

950

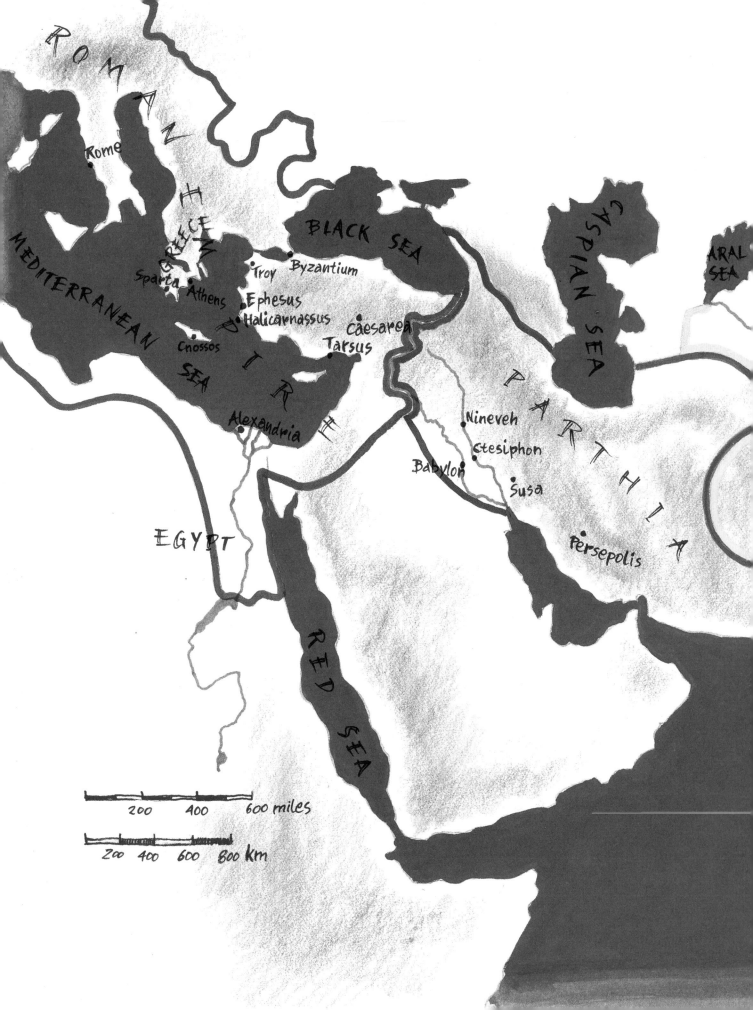